The Definitive Christian D. Larson Collection

6 Volumes
30 Titles

Compiled and Edited
by
David Allen

Volume 2 of 6

Copyright © 2014 by David Allen / Shanon Allen
All rights reserved. No part of this publication may be reproduced, distributed, or transmitted in any form or by any means, including photocopying, recording, or other electronic or mechanical methods, without the prior written permission of the publisher, except in the case of brief quotations embodied in critical reviews and certain other noncommercial uses permitted by copyright law.
Printed in the United States of America

Reprint

First Printing November 2014

ISBN: 978-0-9909643-1-5

Visit Us At **NevilleGoddardBooks.com** for a complete listing of all our books and **1000's of Free Books to Read online and download.**

Books include: The Power of I AM 1, 2, 3, The Neville Goddard Collection, Neville Goddard's Interpretation of Scripture, The Money Bible, The Creative Power of Thought, The Secrets, Mysteries & Powers of The Subconscious Mind, Your Inner Conversations are Creating Your World, The World is At Your Command - The Very Best of Neville Goddard, Imagining Creates Reality - 365 Mystical Daily Quotes, Imagination: The Redemptive Power in Man, Assumptions Harden Into Facts: The Book, David Allen - Your Faith Is Your Fortune, Your Unlimited Power

First Printing
Copyright © 2014

Foreword

The Definitive Christian D. Larson Collection is a 6 volume set of 30 titles from one of the most renowned and prolific new thought authors and lecturers of his day. No metaphysical, new thought, law of attraction collection would be complete without Christian D. Larson's books. Before Neville Goddard, before Ernest Holmes, before Joseph Murphy and Napoleon Hill and a host of many of the great authors and teachers of today, there was Christian D. Larson (1874 – 1954) who was credited by Horatio Dresser as being a founder in the New Thought movement.

Christian D. Larson books contain hidden secrets (hidden from the conscious minds of those not prepared to receive them) and treasures that you are unlikely to find anywhere else and if you do it is likely it originated from Christian D. Larson.

David Allen

All Christian D. Larson's books are in the public domain.

* Editors note: Some Christian D. Larson books were originally published without chapter titles. They were later added by other editors of Mr. Larson's works. To my knowledge none of them are copyrighted.

Christian D. Larson Titles
Volume - Original Year Published - Title

Vol. 1	1913	Brains and How to Get Them
Vol. 1	1912	Business Psychology
Vol. 1	1907	How Great Men Succeed
Vol. 1	1912	How the Mind Works
Vol. 2	**1920**	**Concentration**
Vol. 2	**1912**	**How to Stay Well**
Vol. 2	**1908**	**How to Stay Young**
Vol. 3	1908	The Great Within
Vol. 3	1912	The Mind Cure
Vol. 3	1912	What is Truth
Vol. 3	1912	Your Forces and How to Use Them
Vol. 4	1916	The Good Side of Christian Science
Vol. 4	1912	The Ideal Made Real
Vol. 4	1910	Mastery of Fate
Vol. 4	1907	Mastery of Self
Vol. 4	1916	My Ideal of Marriage
Vol. 4	1916	Nothing Succeeds Like Success
Vol. 4	1916	Steps in Human Progress
Vol. 5	1918	Healing Yourself
Vol. 5	1912	Just Be Glad
Vol. 5	1940	Leave it to God
Vol. 5	1908	On the Heights
Vol. 5	1910	Perfect Health
Vol. 5	1922	Practical Self-Help
Vol. 5	1912	Scientific Training of Children
Vol. 5	1912	Thinking for Results
Vol. 6	1912	The Hidden Secret
Vol. 6	1916	In Light of the Spirit
Vol. 6	1912	The Pathway of Roses
Vol. 6	1907	Poise and Power

Volume 2

Concentration	6
How to Stay Well	49
How to Stay Young	306

Concentration

Concentration

THE art of concentration is one of the simplest to learn, and one of the greatest when mastered; and these pages are written especially for those who wish to learn how to master this fine art in all of its aspects; who wish to develop the power to concentrate well at any time and for any purpose; who wish to make real concentration a permanent acquisition of the mind.

Whatever your work or your purpose may be, a good concentration is indispensable. It is necessary to apply, upon the object or subject at hand, the full power of thought and talent if you are to secure, with a certainty, the results you desire, or win the one thing you have in view. But the art of concentration is not only a leading factor in the fields of achievement and realization; it is also a leading factor in another field — a field of untold possibility.

The exceptional value of concentration is recognized universally; and still there are comparatively few that really know how to concentrate. Some of these have a natural aptitude for concentrated thought and action, while others have improved themselves remarkably in this direction, due to increased knowledge on the subject; but as yet the psychology of concentration is not understood generally; and that is why the majority have not developed this great art, although they are deeply desirous of doing so.

When we do not know how to proceed, we either hesitate or proceed in a bungling fashion; or, we may proceed under the guidance of a number of misleading beliefs. And in connection with concentration there are several ideas and beliefs that have interfered greatly with the development of this art. In fact, methods have been given out, and published broadcast, that are supposed to develop concentration, but that produce the very opposite effect. These things, however, clear up when we learn the psychology of the subject.

Among these misleading beliefs we find one of the most prevalent to be that we must, in order to concentrate well, become oblivious to everything but the one thing before attention now; but the fact is that when we become oblivious to our surroundings we do not concentrate at all; we have simply buried ourselves in abstraction, which is the reverse of concentration. The mind is highly active and thoroughly alive when we concentrate perfectly; and sufficiently alive and keen to be aware of everything in the mind and all about the mind, although giving first thought and attention to the work in hand.

Another belief is this, that we must use great force in the mind in order to concentrate well; that is, we must literally compel the mind to fix attention upon the object or subject before it; but here we must note that forced action, although seemingly effective for a while, is detrimental in the long run. This is true of the body as well as of the mind, so that we must find a better method. However, when we learn the real secret of concentration we find that no special effort is required; there is neither mental strain nor hard work connected with the process; the mind becomes well poised and serene; and, in that attitude, full power and capacity is applied where attention is directed.

The mind that concentrates well does not work in the commonplace sense of that term; wear and tear have been eliminated; there is no strenuous action; there is no desire to force or drive things through; and no tendency whatever towards the high strung or keyed up condition. On the contrary, all action is smooth, orderly, easy and harmonious; and work has become a keen pleasure. This we can fully appreciate when we learn that, in real concentration, the mind has gained that peculiar faculty through which it can at will open all the avenues of energy in such a way that all those energies flow into one stream; and that stream flows into the one place where work is going on now. Therefore, it is not a matter of main force, but a matter of knowledge; knowing how and where to open the gates of energy in the mental world.

When we study the psychology of concentration, we find that most of our previous beliefs on the subject will have to be discarded. They have only acted as obstacles; and as those obstacles have prevented the development of real concentration, another obstacle has arisen in nearly every mind — that of adverse suggestion — the most detrimental of all. Briefly, the majority, feeling the lack of concentration, continue to think and speak of this factor as weak.

They continue to suggest to themselves, ignorantly and unintentionally, that they are very poor in concentration; and therefore they hold this factor down in a perpetual state of weakness. No mental faculty or power can develop to any extent so long as we think or speak of that faculty as weak or inferior. Adverse suggestion acts as a blight, and must not be permitted under any circumstance. We should think as little as possible about our weak points. When we know that we have a certain weakness, we need not speak of it further. To dwell mentally upon weakness is to live mentally in weakness; and they who live mentally in weakness cannot develop strength. Therefore, we will not think or say, again and again, that we are unable to concentrate, or that we are weak or inferior in any respect whatever. We will eliminate all manner of adverse suggestion. We will think and say that we can. We will not complain that we concentrate poorly, but we will proceed to train ourselves to concentrate wonderfully.

Concentration

CONCENTRATION in general may be defined as an active state of mind wherein the whole of attention, with all available energy and talent, is being applied upon the one thing that we are doing now. We concentrate in the full meaning of the term when we give ourselves completely to the thought or the action of the present moment; and this is true whether we work with muscle, brain or mind, or express ourselves through thoughts, words or emotion.

The principle of concentration is to do one thing at a time, and to do that one thing with all the talent and power we possess. We literally turn on the full current of mental and personal energy — not only the full current of what we may feel on the surface of thought — but all that we can arouse in deeper consciousness, and bring forth from the greater self within. It is a leading purpose in concentration to lay hold upon deeper and greater possibility; for we are not giving our whole best self to the work in hand unless we apply all the life, energy and talent that we can through super-effort awaken and develop now.

How this may be accomplished we will understand clearly as we proceed with our analysis of the many phases of the subject; and we will discover that the power to concentrate well means vastly more and involves vastly more than most minds ever imagined. Although the general purpose of this art is to give undivided attention to the work in hand, the development of that purpose will presently lead us beyond this point, and we will enter a new field; we will discover in concentration a new power and a marvelous possibility.

There are many things that we may expect to accomplish through concentration; and in order that we may become familiar with this art from every aspect — which is necessary to its highest development — we will consider briefly the most important of these accomplishments. First of all we gain the power to hold attention upon any object or subject for a sufficient length of time to complete the work in hand, and the power to do this at any time and under any circumstances. This is vitally important as we all meet distractions at every turn, and must learn to give our work undivided attention whatever our surroundings may be.

When we concentrate well we may, at will, cause all the available energies of mind and personality to work together, with full capacity, upon the work in hand. This will increase remarkably the working capacity and the dependable endurance of both mind and body, and will mean a high degree of mental mastery. To be able to master the elements and energies of the mind sufficiently to bring them all together to work together anywhere any time — this is an advantage for which we would pay almost any price; but it comes as a natural emolument with the development of concentration.

We all appreciate the value of speed, and especially among the thinking processes of the mind. The mind that moves slowly is never brilliant; while the mind that can think and act with lightning rapidity is on the verge of attaining genius; and may reach the goal of genius in this way if depth and range are combined with the element of speed. It is not possible, however, to produce mental speed through forced action; it comes naturally through concentration; and it will mean more work and better work; more perfect plans and more brilliant ideas — a combination that will go very far towards the high goal we have in view.

You are equal to any occasion when the whole of your mind is called into action; and this very thing concentration has the power to do. More than that, the whole of the mind will be called to higher ground, thereby working itself out of

Concentration

mediocrity and restricted channels, and gradually developing itself into that wonder state where everything seems possible. Real concentration can lead the way; the whole mind will follow; and concentration invariably leads into worlds of greater results. When we concentrate well we exercise a peculiar influence over the whole mind; we create, in every part of the mind, an irresistible desire to go to work; and we inspire every element of the mind with a definite ambition to excel.

The act of concentration tends not only to apply effectively all available energy of mind and personality; but tends also to draw forth latent energies. The fact is that real concentration becomes in the mind a remarkable force of attraction — attracting to itself unused and latent energies from all sources in the mental world. That is one reason why the mind that concentrates well becomes so powerful, and why such a mind will invariably forge ahead, regardless of what the obstacles or difficulties may be. It is now a known fact that the subconscious supply of latent energy is enormous; and as concentration tends to attract latent energy from all sources, we perceive here possibilities that assume tremendous proportions.

Concentrated action will grow into greater action, and upon the principle that "much gathers more"; "nothing succeeds like success"; "make expert use of what you have and Nature will bountifully increase your supply." All things in life flow into the main stream — because the main stream is going somewhere — concentrating its movements upon a definite goal.

Concentrate the mind upon any problem, and if you concentrate wonderfully well, you will find the solution. The solution of any problem is locked up in that problem; and concentration is the key. The psychology of this involves a most fascinating study; but sufficient in this stage of our study to know that these things can be done. The same is true of any subject, situation or circumstance. You can, through concentration, find the main points or the inside facts of any subject or situation that you may consider. Real concentration has the power to break through the shell; to get beneath the surface; to get in behind the scenes; to enter into the very life of the thing, and thus get hold of bedrock information.

These things we may accomplish through concentration; and there is good reason therefore why it has always been looked upon as the master art; but there is one thing more, the greatest of them all. Mental action, when perfectly concentrated, tends to go farther and farther into the life, substance or principle that is acted upon at the time. Concentration develops a penetrating tendency — a tendency to lead the mind out of the usual and on into the unknown. Concentration forges ahead. It goes straight on. It does not tarry with known facts. It goes farther. It sets out upon a journey; and such a journey will invariably prove a journey of discovery. The mind will find and enter new fields of thought. New laws and principles will be discovered. A new region of possibility will open before the mind, and long sought secrets may come to light. Positively, we can, through a highly developed concentration, cause Nature to give up her secrets, and cause the mysteries of Life to be revealed.

Concentration

WHEN we realize what may be accomplished through concentration, we shall make every conceivable effort to develop this master art; and our persistence, determination and enthusiasm will know neither pause nor measure; we will purpose positively to learn how to concentrate, and therefore will want to know how to proceed — what principles to adopt and what methods to apply.

When we examine the psychology of concentration, we find that it is based upon mental actions that are deeply interested in a certain subject or object; that is, we concentrate naturally and without effort whenever or wherever we are vitally interested. This then is the first principle. Be really interested in that to which you are to address yourself, and you will give it your undivided attention.

The problem, however, is how to become really interested in subjects or objects that do not, on their own account, attract our attention; or that do not, on the surface, appeal to us in the least. This is the first and possibly the greatest obstacle we have to meet in the development of concentration; but the solution is very simple; and we proceed upon the fact that everything is interesting from a certain point of view — that everything can attract our attention if permitted to reveal its chief attraction.

To the superficial mind many things may seem useless or uninteresting; but not so to the mind that has learned to think. It is only on the surface, or from a commonplace viewpoint, that most things may seem unworthy of passing notice; and it is only when looked upon through the eyes of prejudice or ignorance that our associations may repel or produce indifference, or that life and its work may offer slight appeal. The situation changes entirely when we see things as they are; and especially when we seek for the deeper cause of

Concentration

every condition, and discover the greater possibilities that are awaiting back of the scenes everywhere.

The most commonplace object in existence, such as a simple rock or a turf, becomes a wonder-world when examined scientifically; and the ordinary duties of life, if examined from all points of view, will reveal opportunities and possibilities that will positively startle the mind. It is certainly true that everything is interesting from a certain point of view, and we may multiply illustrations indefinitely. The universe in all of its realities; life in all of its manifestations; and existence in all of its actions and changes — these things, when looked into, with eyes that see, will prove interesting to a wonderful degree, and frequently fascinating to an amazing degree.

Understanding this aspect of the subject, which is the all important aspect, we may make the following proposition: We concentrate naturally and perfectly when we are vitally interested. Everything is, in its chief attraction, extremely interesting. Therefore, we may, by seeking the chief attraction in everything, concentrate naturally and perfectly anywhere any time. This is simple and conclusive, provided we find the chief attraction; but here we meet another problem. We may grant that everything is interesting from a certain point of view, but is it possible to find that interesting viewpoint anywhere and on short notice?

It is true that we can, in due time, find elements of real interest anywhere — of sufficient interest to attract our undivided attention; but we may not always do so at the moment; therefore we have another problem to solve; and again, the solution is simple — within easy reach of anyone who will try. It is only necessary at first to proceed upon the conviction that everything is interesting from certain points of view; and to drill that fact into the mind with positive action and depth of thought. A situation will arise that can solve this other problem absolutely.

When you convince the mind that everything is interesting from a certain point of view, you establish, in the subconscious, a natural tendency to be on the alert for this interesting viewpoint. Your mind will, unconsciously and unfailingly, look for the interesting element in everything you meet in life, or that you may take up for consideration. And when the mind is on the alert, and keenly looking for the interesting element, the mind is really interested in that subject or object. Vital interest in the situation has sprung up subconsciously, without your making the least effort to become interested. So there you have the first and most vital essential for concentration.

The importance of this principle is so great, and the methods connected with it are so effective, that we should emphasize and reemphasize these things in our minds in every way conceivable. We should think on these things repeatedly; dwell upon this situation with the utmost of faith and confidence; and give special time and thought to the facts involved. There is a tendency in nearly every mind to take natural interest in a few things only; to work and act largely in grooves, and to think of things in the most general and superficial fashion. But real concentration is out of the question in such a state of mind; that is why special attention should be given to the facts under consideration, so that the tendency of indifference may be supplanted by one of wholehearted interest.

In practical life this is how the plan will work. You are called upon to give attention to something you do not understand, or something that does not appeal to you in the least. You are not interested, and therefore you cannot, at the moment, concentrate properly, or give the matter

Concentration

undivided attention. But you remember the great fact noted in this study, that everything is interesting from a certain point of view. Instantly you become curious to know what the interesting element in the matter in hand might be. You have made your own mind curious; and a curious mind is on the verge of becoming an interested mind.

If this be your first attempt in the application of this method, nothing more than a mild interest may arise; and even that might aid you decidedly at the time; but suppose you make use of this method many times every day for weeks and months. Suppose you make it a part of your daily work to impress upon your mind, again and again, the fact that everything is interesting from a certain point of view. The subconscious will soon receive these impressions and make that fact its very own. Then suppose you are called upon to consider a subject towards which you have been wholly indifferent. But the subconscious has been advised that there are elements of interest everywhere, and the subconscious never forgets what it has once really learned. Accordingly, the mind will be prompted, by powerful impulses from within, to seek the interesting elements in the subject before you; and, before you are hardly aware of the fact, this subject has become interesting and attractive. Suddenly, a keen desire has come over you to look into this subject thoroughly. You want to know. You are vitally interested. You are giving the matter undivided attention. You are concentrating perfectly in that direction.

When it becomes a part of your mind to know and feel that there are interesting elements in everything, and that everything, when looked upon with eyes that see, becomes a wonder-world, you develop a permanent faculty for looking into the vital elements in all things. You are interested, deeply and permanently, in the workings and possibilities of all aspects of life; you are wonderfully attracted to the real

Concentration

and the true everywhere; and therefore you will instantly, and without effort, give your whole attention to anything that you may meet, or that you are called upon to consider. Wherever you think and act, you do so with your whole mind; you concentrate perfectly, not because you are trying to do so, but because you have developed that something in yourself that produces perfect concentration.

Concentration

TO develop this idea farther, and secure all possible results, we should make it one of the permanent rules of life to meet everything with the desire to discover its real worth and chief points of interest; and whether the element of interest be found or not, the act of looking for that element will create interest in the mind, thereby producing a certain degree of concentration.

Whether we meet the commonplace or the exceptional, this rule should be rigidly observed; and whenever we have moments to spare we should apply the rule definitely to any subject or object at hand, so that the mind may develop a permanent and a powerful tendency in that direction. To illustrate, we may take an ordinary looking rock and ask ourselves what there is about this rock in which we may become interested. We would ask what this rock is composed of, how many elements it may contain, how they combine, how they are attracted to each other and how they happen to hold together. We might proceed asking questions, and we would find that we could ask anywhere from fifty to one hundred very interesting and most scientific questions about this very ordinary looking rock; and everyone of those questions would arouse the deepest interest in the mind because they would be questions that would involve some of the greatest principles in science.

The same method may be applied in connection with any object or any subject we may wish to consider; and in every instance we shall be surprised to find how many points of interest will come forth to attract and even amaze the mind. The truth is, that if we are wide awake to the meaning and purpose of everything in existence, we shall not find anything to be commonplace or uninteresting. What appears to be uninteresting appears so simply because we have not taken the time to make an intelligent examination. The moment, however, that we really examine the thing itself, and look into its elements, its nature, its qualities, its powers, its possibilities and its very soul, we shall find so much that is interesting that we might occupy the mind for days, weeks and months in a deeper and further examination.

We shall find nothing to be of greater value as a daily practice than to take up objects or subjects, actually interested, and direct the mind to look for interesting viewpoints, elements or factors in connection with those objects or subjects. We shall be richly rewarded, because we will not only find much that is interesting, but we will, through this practice, train the mind to look naturally for that which is of interest everywhere; and we know that there is nothing that adds so much to our fund of knowledge as the happy faculty of being able to look for facts, or for the truth everywhere; and the same faculty tends to develop, not only intellect, but all the finer mental faculties as well.

This practice will produce a permanent tendency in the mind to look for the interesting in connection with everything that we may see, or hear, or think about; and this tendency will expand and develop the mind, and place us in a position to secure direct or firsthand information from every experience and from every object or subject that we meet on the way. More than this, the same tendency will develop in the mind the faculty of searching for the chief essentials, or the real thing, that invariably exists in the actual life or soul of that with which we come in contact; and it is hardly possible to overestimate the value of such a faculty, knowing as we do that the average mind skims over the surface continually, and seldom, if ever, discovers the real, vital principle involved anywhere. When we develop the faculty of finding the real thing, the real truth, the real principle, the real power, the real factors that exist in everything we meet in life, we have gained immensely.

Concentration

Whenever we meet what does not seem interesting, we should proceed at once to examine that particular thing with a view of finding something of interest; and we will find it. And when we have work that does not seem interesting — work upon which we must concentrate in order to do it well — we should take up such work in the same attitude; that is, we should inquire deeply and scientifically as to what there is about such work that is in reality interesting. This question coming up, will cause the mind to become interested; and at once concentration will begin. And as we continue this practice, the tendency to look for the interesting everywhere will become second nature; that is, concentration will have become a permanent power in the mind, and will act thoroughly and effectively of itself, wherever the mind may proceed to act. The rule is simple:

Look for the interesting, and the mind becomes interested; and wherever the mind is interested, there you concentrate naturally and effectively; provided, of course, that you subconsciously feel that there are interesting elements in everything; and, provided further, that your mind is keenly alive with the desire to know, to achieve, to excel.

Concentration

A MOST important essential in the development of concentration is to learn to control the actions of the mind — all the leading actions, both objective and subjective; and although this may seem to be a difficult undertaking, it is really quite simple, for in fact we exercise this power almost hourly to some degree. We all have experienced moments when the forces of the mind seemed to be under perfect control — when it seemed as if we could move those forces, in any mode or manner desired, just as we move our hands or feet. And when we analyze our states of mind during such moments, we find that we are in deeper or closer touch with the finer forces of mind and personality — that is the secret. To acquire the art of entering into this closer touch therefore must be our purpose; and to begin, it is deeper feeling that prepares the way for that desired state of mind.

Whenever we proceed to concentrate, we should try and deepen the feeling of all thought and all mental action; in fact, we should try and feel so deeply about everything that we think or do that the mind actually enters into the very spirit of the process; that is, into the undercurrents of mental life, those finer currents that determine results in everything that is being done. We may, when concentrating in a superficial manner, secure some slight results temporarily, but it is those deeper, finer, more penetrating currents that produce real results, and that alone have the capacity to produce extraordinary results. Besides, it is the consciousness of those finer currents that gives the mind the power to exercise complete control over all the actions and forces of the mental world — an attainment that is most important in the development of concentration.

You may find it a problem at times to enter into this state of deeper feeling; but you can, by giving special attention to the principle, master this situation absolutely; and the secret will be found in comparing the two ways of listening to music. When you listen to music and remain in a superficial state, you are simply aware of pleasing sound, but nothing more. However, if you are in a deeper state of mind at the time, wherein you can appreciate the very soul of music, you will not simply hear pleasing sound, but infinitely more. Every tone of that music will actually thrill the atoms of your being, and arouse feelings in mind and soul that are so deep, so lofty and so beautiful that you could not possibly describe them. Briefly stated, your entire being would be alive with the deepest and finest and most sacred emotions, and the experience would be such that its effect would remain with you for weeks, months and possibly years.

This illustrates what happens when we meet experiences, or anything in life, in the attitude of deeper and finer states of mind. At such times we do not simply discern the surface of things, or come in mental contact merely with the outer meaning; we actually discern the very life of things, and come in mental contact with the very kingdom of the soul. We find that we invariably enter into this deeper feeling when we try to live every act, thought or experience that may appear in our world; and the reason why is found in the fact that whenever we try to live anything, we enter into the very life of that particular thing.

To develop the tendency to enter the deeper states of the mind, we should work in harmony with a leading law in the mental world; that is, the peculiar proneness of the mind to produce within itself any state, condition or tendency that we continue to desire with persistence and sincerity. It is the truth that your mind will do anything for you if you really want it done.

When we make it our purpose to enter into deeper states of feeling in connection with every thought and action, the mind will soon develop a tendency that will invariably take all mental action into deeper states of feeling. To encourage the mind in this connection, we shall find it a most excellent practice, whenever we hear good music, to look for the soul of music, to try and feel the finer touch of the real life of music, and to try to appreciate the most delicate harmonies that exist in the very spirit of music itself.

We shall find it an excellent practice to apply the same principle in connection with anything that is beautiful, or anything that may appeal to the mind as being worthy of our deepest and highest attention; and in fact, whatever we may be thinking about, we should try and enter into the very soul of the thought or the theme. In this manner, we will develop a natural desire to seek for the real, to enter into the depths of life, thought and feeling; and gradually consciousness will deepen all of its activities until we find we can feel more deeply in every thought or experience; and we shall also find that the conscious domain has been increased remarkably.

We shall find it profitable to apply the same principle to every aspect of physical sensation, and to every experience of the sense life. If we make it our aim, not to be satisfied with the grosser side of physical sensation, but try to discern and feel the finer elements that are invariably expressed through all forms of sensation, we shall not only find every sensation more delightful than before, but also that it has been lifted to a higher plane — that grossness and crudeness have disappeared, and that the physical body, as a whole, has become more refined in every form and manner.

These exercises and experiences will tend directly to prepare the way for the development of those states of mind that we must possess in order to enter into this closer and finer touch with the higher and finer forces of the mind — a most important essential in the art of controlling all the actions of the mind; for we know that when we have gained perfect control over all the actions of the mind, then we shall be able to concentrate all the energy we possess upon any object or subject we may have in view.

The purpose must be to live beneath the surface; to make the great within our chief realm of life and concern. We may act upon and with the external aspects of life; but we must make the deeper fields of thought our real place of business. For surely if we would master the deeper forces of life, we must live and think where those forces arise and develop. This, therefore, is a matter of imperative importance.

Concentration

AN indispensable element is that of a good strong will; and the use of the will in connection with concentration may be illustrated variously; but we will first examine the effect of will power, correctly applied, in the process of thought creation. To illustrate, we will suppose that you have several facts concerning a proposed invention, but have not as yet succeeded in bringing those facts together in the combination required for the perfecting of that invention. If you understand the use of the will, you will apply will power upon that group of facts, knowing that you thereby increase mental activity in that particular part of the mind; and wherever mental activity is increased, there the creative process is intensified and expressed to a higher and more perfect degree. The fact is this, that whenever an idea may seem indistinct, although you know you have all the elements required, the reason is that the mind is not sufficiently active in connection with the creative process that is working to perfect that idea. The use of the will, however, will not only increase activity throughout this creative process, but will also make concentration more perfect, because the power of will, when applied in connection with concentration, increases invariably both the power and the capacity of the force of concentration.

You will find it possible to perfect almost any idea you have in mind, if you can bring to bear upon that idea all the available energy existing in your mind; and this may be accomplished through concentration, provided concentration is deeply expressed, and in a positive manner — results we may secure through the full action of the will. For when we fully apply the will, we increase power and activity. We intensify the process involved; and there is nothing that tends more directly to increase the power of concentration than the act of increasing the rapidity of action wherever concentration may be taking place.

Concentration

We all appreciate the value of brilliant ideas; and most minds are in a position to create brilliant ideas at frequent intervals, but as a rule they merely come up to the point of creating a brilliant idea; they do not quite reach the point itself. The reason is that they have not the power to bring together all the elements required for this new idea; and this power is lacking because the will is weak and concentration undeveloped. The same is true regarding the perfecting of plans or methods. We may have the essentials, or all the factors required, but we may not always have the power to bring them together to a focus, where the required combination can be brought about so as to evolve the idea or plan we desire. The use of the will, however, in this connection will produce remarkable results. The will always intensifies any mental process, and thereby tends to bring to a climax any creative process that may be going on in the mind. The creation of rich and valuable thought may be furthered in the same manner, because such thought is almost invariably the result of the bringing together, in the proper combination, of the best impressions that may have come into the mind through our own study or experience.

Regarding the psychological use of the power of thought, we shall find the same principle of exceptional value, because whenever we use the power of thought, whether for the overcoming of physical ailments, for the elimination of adverse mental states, or for the building up of character or mental faculties — wherever we may apply the power of thought — a perfect concentration is indispensable; and the use of the will in connection with concentration invariably tends to increase both the force and the capacity of the process. In fact, we never can concentrate with all that we are unless we express through concentration, the full power of the will. To express the full power of the will, however, every action of the will must be positive, and the will must act subjectively; that is, it must act through the undercurrents, or through the attitude of finer feeling — the importance of which we have previously considered. We understand therefore that if we would learn to concentrate well we must also acquire a thorough knowledge of the will, and develop the will to the highest possible degree.

Concentration

THE power of Persistent desire is invaluable wherever increased results are wanted; and therefore the full force of desire must invariably combine with concentration. When we desire persistently the object in view, we become deeply interested in that object and we cause the whole mind to work for its realization. Besides, the element of desire will instill a something into concentration that is really alive. It will eliminate the tendency to make mental or personal actions mechanical or forced, and will give to every action that vital spark that means so much. The force of desire will also deepen and expand every mental process involved — a situation that may, at times, become the opening way to remarkable results.

To concentrate successfully we must direct and focalize all the creative energies of the mind upon the object of concentration; but these energies must first be aroused; and here is where real desire becomes invaluable. Wherever we turn on the full current of persistent desire, every energy and force in the mind becomes alive, and may be enlisted for good work in any place where the power of concentration has been directed. We find therefore that the force of desire becomes a direct and powerful aid to concentration fn two distinct particulars';' first, by creating wide-awake interest all through the mind — by causing the mind to become vitally interested in the goal in view; and second, by arousing, or making alive, the latent or dormant energies of the mind, thereby providing the process of concentration with a vast amount of additional power.

All of this we understand perfectly; and the more we investigate the psychology of the process, the more reasons we find why we always get what we want when we want it "real bad." The secret then is to want what you want with all the life and power that is in you. We can reach any goal, or realize any ideal when we concentrate perfectly, and with the full force of a perfect concentration; and persistent desire proceeds to give concentration more and more of the two chief essentials; that is, deeper mental interest and greater mental power.

In this connection inquiry may arise as to the best methods for creating this deeper and more persistent desire, especially where we may not be personally interested in the final results; but here we should remember that we always gain personally from anything that is done right. If we develop greater mental power through the use of any psychological law, we gain to that extent, even though the greater portion of the tangible results may, in this instance, go elsewhere. The future is long; every form of gain will come to each one of us in due time — in a very short time if we take advantage of every opportunity to increase our own capacity and power. We should therefore be interested, personally, in the best and most thorough use of every psychological law we may have the privilege to employ.

Realizing this fact, we will want to desire success, the greatest possible success, for every enterprise with which we may be connected. Such a desire will improve remarkably, not only our own concentration, but also all other powers and talents we may possess. Our own gain therefore will be strictly personal, and most direct; and although tangible gain may not come at once, it positively will come in the near future. The future is both larger and richer for those who improve themselves in the present; and greater opportunities are waiting everywhere for greater minds; but improvements must be genuine, not merely superficial.

To increase the power of desire we should deepen and intensify all such desire in every form and manner, realizing the fact that the more the mind acts in a certain direction the greater becomes its power to act still more in the same direction. The force of desire therefore may through this simple rule become immense. And the more we increase the force of desire the more we increase results in every field of thought or action. Furthermore, we may cause the forces of concentration and desire to act and react upon each other to great advantage; that is, the more we concentrate for the increase of desire — worthwhile desire — the more powerful and persistent will such desire become; and the more deeply we desire the power to concentrate well — wonderfully well — the more life, energy and action we express in the building of real concentration

Concentration

THE greatest faculty of all is that of imagination; but it is the least understood, due principally to the fact that most minds have remained in grooves of thought, and therefore have not given extensive attention to their own creative possibilities, the richest and most numerous of which exist in the fields of imagination. In the development of any power or talent, however, these creative possibilities must receive direct and scientific attention; and this is especially true with regard to the power of concentration. Besides, some of the functions of concentration are so closely related to those of imagination as to seem almost identical.

When you employ the faculty of imagination, one of your chief objects is to bring together ideas or mental images with a view of creating some new or greater idea; and in concentration this "bringing together" tendency — this uniting the many in one, is the leading object in view. It is clearly evident therefore that a better training of imagination will largely increase the power of concentration.

When you employ the faculty of imagination, you also tend to bring together the many creative energies of the mind, combining those energies in the one process to which you are giving attention at the time. A highly developed faculty of imagination therefore naturally becomes an invaluable aid to the power of concentration; and when we understand how concentration can, by working with imagination, bring together. into one powerful line of mental action, all the best ideas of the mind and all available creative energy, we know why we usually find an excellent imagination wherever we find a remarkable concentration.

Analyzing the subject farther, we find that a vivid, well trained imagination tends to "light up" the entire mental world; or, in other words, to make everything in the mind more clear. The result is, that the idea or object upon which

Concentration

we concentrate becomes more distinct; and accordingly, we not only concentrate better, but the entire mind becomes interested in this idea on account of its vividness and distinctiveness. Thus we call into action the many aspects of mental attention, an action that increases directly and instantaneously the power of concentration. We all know through experience how much better we can think when the ideas with which we are dealing are vivid, or stand out clearly in the mind; and also how much better we can concentrate when we have a distinct mental picture of the object in view. And imagination, if well trained and scientifically applied, will invariably turn the light upon any idea that we may call up for examination or further development.

When imagination is vivid, every mental process will be literally filled and surrounded with light; and we all can appreciate what an immense advantage this will be in the practical application of concentration. To illustrate, we will call imagination into action wherever we wish to concentrate, and immediately that place or process in the mind will become so vivid, and stand out so clearly, that all our faculties will become interested. The entire mind will turn its attention towards the point of concentration; and in a moment the entire mind will concentrate. And when we have the whole mind working for the object in view, the results desired will positively be realized.

As a practical suggestion we should, whenever we begin to concentrate, proceed to imagine all the forces of the mind coming to a focus at the point of concentration. This simple rule will not only produce some startling results in the process of concentration itself, but will also train imagination for definite and practical work. Herewith, let us note that imagination does have the power to take the lead in the mental world; and therefore whenever we imagine that a certain thing is being done in the mind, we lead a majority of the energies of the mind to go and do that very thing; provided of course that imagination be vivid and highly positive in its actions. Here then we have within easy reach a most remarkable possibility.

Concentration

TO concentrate well is not sufficient; we must also concentrate with the greatest possible capacity; and therefore, we should train ourselves to concentrate with the whole mind; or to express more and more of life and power in every thought and action. But the average mind makes actual use of only a small fraction of what is possible in ability and power; and that is one reason why the concentrated efforts of such a mind are so weak or utterly futile.

Where concentration is weak and imperfect, we always find most of the mind in a dormant state; and vice versa, where concentration is exceptional, we find marked activity all through the mental world. The problem then is to awaken more of the mind, and express more of the power of the mind in everything we do — a problem that would largely solve itself if we would abandon completely all halfhearted modes of thought and action.

We should make it a practice to express the whole self in everything we do, think or say; and the increase in mental capacity would be remarkable. We should eliminate indifference absolutely. Whether we turn to the left or to the right, we should turn with all we have in feeling, purpose and will. Wherever we act, we should be a power, and aim to make all action constructive — conducive to greater capacity for action tomorrow. There is no gain in saving up power for another day. If we use it all now, we will have still more when the other day arrives. The power that is generated in the system today should be used today — not scattered — but used — used in constructive expression. And the law is, that the more power we use today, the more we shall have tomorrow.

When we think, we should not simply think with the brain, but think with every force and element in the entire

Concentration

personality. There is nothing that will increase mental capacity so quickly and so effectively as the training of the mind to use the whole personality in every thought and expression. And when the mind can, in concentration, draw upon the entire personality for power, conscious and subconscious, we can imagine what the force of such concentration will be. Our principal object, therefore, should be in this connection to awaken the vast regions of dormant energy all through the mental world, and express more and more of this new energy in everything we do. Thus we provide concentration with an ever-increasing measure of power.

A most excellent practice, in order to express more of the mind in every thought and action, is to lay hold upon all the energy of the mind with deep feeling and will, and actually take up that energy as we would take up a book with the hand, and place it where we want it now. This can readily be done; and with practice we will find that we can control our mental energies just as effectively as we control the movements of hands or feet. When this control is gained we shall be able, at any time, to increase the expression of the power of mind, thereby increasing directly the power of concentration; and when we realize that even exceptional minds use less than five per cent of their latent energies, we gain some idea of the vastness of our own possibilities.

To further this increase in mental capacity, we should give definite and frequent directions to the subconscious for this particular purpose. In fact, there is nothing that will avail so much for such a purpose, which fact we can readily appreciate when we note what the subconscious is, and what it can do. We should make it a daily practice therefore to direct the subconscious to awaken the whole mind, and to express, in constructive action, the full power and capacity of the mind. Remarkable increase will be realized, as the weeks pass, both in working capacity and in thinking power.

Concentration

Then we should proceed farther and direct the subconscious to develop and perfect concentration itself; and we shall be amazed at what can be done in this regard. We know that the subconscious can do anything within the range of human possibility, if properly directed; therefore the creative power of the great within can build for us all the most effective and the most perfect concentration conceivable. This marvelous power is latent in every mind — waiting to be used with intelligence, super effort and real faith.

Concentration

IN the science and art of concentration, it is the deeper forces and the finer energies of mind and personality with which we deal directly; and therefore we increase the power of concentration as we acquire the ability to take up or control those forces at will, and according to our purpose or desire. To accomplish this, we must gain interior hold of those forces, because they do not respond to any action of mind or will that is merely superficial. And here we find another reason why it is only the few who really can concentrate; it is only the few who think deeply and who cause the actions of the mind to work among the powerful undercurrents of life, thought and mentality; but anyone can acquire this power; and the first step towards that end is to gain this interior hold of the finer energies of the mind.

When we can take hold of the forces of the mental world, and direct or sway those forces in any way desired, just as we sway or extend the arm in any mode or direction desired — when we can do this, then we are beginning to acquire the power of real concentration. This inner mastery of the forces and energies of the mind, is a purely subjective process, and is developed only as we learn to act consciously and positively what we may Term the Inner field of thought, consciousness and mind action. And although there are many who can and do act, to some extent, in this inner field, the majority can acquire this power only through extensive practice.

The value of this power, even aside from that of concentration, is very great, especially in connection with the creation of effective and brilliant ideas; for the fact is, that it is only in this inner field of mind and thought that brilliant ideas are created; and besides, every mental creative process of genuine worth depends directly upon the action of these finer energies. If we would develop the real power of concentration, therefore, and also master the art of creating

Concentration

brilliant ideas, we must think and act in the consciousness of the "inner field" of mentality, and gain, more and more, this interior hold upon the forces of mind and personality.

To advance in this direction, we should endeavor frequently to take up and apply the deeper forces of the mental system; that is, to take positive hold of those forces with mind and will, directing them first upon one sphere in the mental world, then upon some other sphere; to move those forces to and fro as we may desire; to cause them to move in circles one moment and in straight lines, either towards the depths or the heights of the mental world, the next moment; to gather them in large groups or in small groups according to desire; to focalize them all upon any subject or idea we have in mind, and to see how long we can continue such focalization without losing interest in the subject or becoming oblivious to our surroundings. And here we should remember that the moment we lose interest in the subject before us, that moment we cease to concentrate; and also, that the moment we become oblivious to our surroundings, that moment we cease to concentrate.

Concentration involves, on the one hand, undivided attention to the subject or object before us; and, on the other hand, complete wide-awakeness to everything going on among our surroundings. The moment we become oblivious to our surroundings, the real power of concentration is lost for the time being; it is very important therefore that we continue to be wide-awake, both to the objective and to the subjective; in fact, in as wide and deep and large a sphere as possible.

To gain this interior hold upon the deeper forces of the mind, it is continuous practice that will give the power desired; and every imaginable method should be employed, because the more ways through which we can handle, sway or manipulate those forces, the greater will become our conscious hold upon those forces; and when this conscious hold becomes remarkable, then we can apply those forces anywhere at any time, and with full capacity and power. In other words, we shall be able to concentrate perfectly, and turn on the full current of all the talent, energy and power we possess.

An excellent practice is to turn attention frequently upon the great within, concentrating the deeper forces of the mind upon the vast and marvelous possibilities that exist in the fathomless depths of the mental world. This practice will not only aid the mind remarkably in gaining this interior hold upon the finer energies, but will also awaken latent forces and new talents; and will invariably arouse increased capacity and power in every faculty and talent we may be using now.

When we find that the faculties and talents we employ do not possess sufficient force and capacity to make that work a success, it is most important that we take up the above practice and do so with determination and enthusiasm. We will soon experience most marked improvement; the mental engine will have more "steam" and we shall be able to speed on with twice and thrice the usual cargo of plans, propositions and achievements. Furthermore, this practice will enlarge immensely the field for concentration; and here it is important to remember that the greater the scope and range of the mental world, of which we are actively conscious, the greater becomes the power of concentration. Every faculty or power in the mind gains exceptional advantages when given more and more to work with; and the practice of concentrating frequently upon the great within will give every faculty more to work with, besides giving the mind, as a whole, an ever-increasing world for attainment and achievement.

Concentration

THE possibilities of concentration are many; but there is one possibility in particular that we all should seek to understand most thoroughly, and develop to the highest degree conceivable. The results will be amazing; and every step in advance will open new worlds to conquer.

The principle is this, that we can through concentration clear the way for almost any achievement, attainment or discovery within the range of human life and power; and this range is a thousand times greater than we have supposed; in fact, no limits or restrictions can be found.

This principle can be applied to almost anything that we may wish to find or accomplish; and for practical illustration we will consider first the problems we meet in daily life. It is the usual custom, when we have difficult problems to solve, to waste a vast amount of time and energy worrying about how we are to find the solution; and as we know this is an easy way to failure and defeat.

The new way is to concentrate; to concentrate upon the problem with all the energy and intellect we possess; and this is what will happen: The full light of the mind will be focused upon that problem; that problem will be placed under the penetrating gaze of a powerful mental search light; and, accordingly, the mind will be able to look into and look through the entire situation. Thus the solution will be found; for the fact is, that situations or problems seem difficult or perplexing only when viewed in the dark or in subdued light. When we can look through the thing, then we know what to do.

Turn on sufficient light and all mystery disappears. Problems cease to be problems when viewed in the clear light; and we can, through a highly developed concentration, turn the full light of the mind upon any subject,

Concentration

circumstance or situation. Therefore, we should concentrate upon those things; concentrate with all the energy and intellect we possess; concentrate for days or weeks, if necessary, and with unflinching faith and determination. We will soon penetrate the mystery and find what is wanted. We will see through it all, and see clearly what to do.

The same principle will apply if you are working on some invention. Do not give up at any stage; concentrate upon the thing you wish to develop or perfect; and concentrate with more and more persistence until the thing is done. Nothing is impossible. Nature will give up her secrets to those who really want them, or to those who will come into her greater realms and get them; and concentration has the penetrating power to go on in anywhere.

It is a well known fact that most inventions have come through persistent concentration; or through mental processes that involved lightning speed creative power; and such processes are always due to previous moments of exceptional concentration. Furthermore, the possibilities of the mind become simply marvelous when the full light and the full creative power of the mind are concentrated upon the goal in view. We realize therefore that greater inventions than the world has ever dreamed of may be expected when a much larger number learn to master the wonder working art of concentration.

Inventive genius involves, among other things, the power to create new ideas; and we can realize that the more intellect and energy we apply in any creative process the greater and more brilliant will that idea become. We also realize that when we apply all our faculties and forces upon the creation of an idea or the perfecting of an invention, the results will be far greater than if we applied only a fraction of those faculties and forces. And it is the function of concentration to apply, upon the work in hand, the full power of the mind and the highest and most effective actions of that power.

Rich things grow where producing power is abundant; and the producing power of the mind at any point will be abundant in profusion when we concentrate the best that we have and the best that we are upon that point. And to emphasize this fact, let us note again that the power of concentration when persistent and highly developed, will not only cause all the talents and forces of the mind to work together at the point of action, but will also awaken latent energies in mind and personality — sometimes an enormous amount of new energy — until you feel as if you were a living dynamo.

When you are in need of a new plan in your business, or in your field of endeavor, do not consult all the people you know, the majority of whom may not be really interested. That is the old way, and it leads to confusion. The new way is to concentrate upon the plan you want, and with the highest and greatest actions of the mind. Thus you cause the highest and greatest in your mind to go to work and evolve the plan you desire. They can do it; and if you concentrate exceptionally well, you will cause those actions to make a super effort — the result of which will go far beyond your every expectation.

Here you should note well the fact that your own mind has the power, active or latent, to work out any plan you may require for your best welfare and continued progress. Nothing is more true than this, that your own mind is fully able to take the very best care of you. This is a statement that should be shouted from the house tops, and drilled so thoroughly into every human brain that it becomes a positive and ever conscious realization. Your own mind can solve your problems and work out the plans that you need for advancement in your life and your work. And your own mind will do these things if you concentrate persistently upon that which you want, and concentrate wonderfully well.

A large and valued field for the application of the same principle, is the field of ideals. And in this connection we should consider well the great fact that whenever the mind gains the insight to perceive an ideal it also gains the power to make that ideal real. But it is only through a well developed concentration that this power can be applied effectively. The majority, however, among those who entertain high ideals, do not give sufficient thought to concentration. They dream and dream, hoping the dream will come true; or, when they do try to concentrate, they journey off into abstractions and transcendental speculations — a process that does not call into action the power that is able to make those dreams come true.

The same is true of young minds who are ambitious. Most of them merely hope and hope that their ambitions will be realized somehow; but they do not concentrate persistently and continually upon the great goal they have in view. They do not call into concerted and organized action the sum total of their forces and faculties; and, in consequence, their ambitions never materialize. The fact is that where one ambitious mind scales the heights of achievement, fifty give up their early ambitions after a few years and decide to resume an average existence; and the chief reason is, that these fifty do not concentrate; or, if they do concentrate, it is only for a time and in a weak, uncertain fashion. The successful one, however, turns on the full current of concentration, and persists, with undaunted faith and determination, until the goal in view is realized.

Concentration

This should be the rule: Whatever you want, concentrate; concentrate upon the purpose you have in mind; concentrate upon those greater forces and possibilities within you that can get you what you want — that can see you through successfully. For it is positively true that your own mind can get you anything within reason; provided of course that your whole mind is working for you; and your whole mind will work for you — will work for you with the highest degree of effectiveness — if you concentrate wonderfully well.

The possibilities of concentration are not confined, however, to the usual fields of achievement, or to those mental domains with which most of us are familiar. There are other and greater worlds that we may discover and take possession of through the use of this master art. To illustrate, if we wish to evolve or develop something that is entirely new, or decidedly different, the principle is to concentrate in that direction. Thus we shall make a super effort in that direction; that is, if we concentrate with full capacity and marvelous skill; and we will, with absolute certainty, develop something that is beyond all previous effort — something that is distinctive, that stands out in a class by itself, that reveals clearly the master touch of genius.

The elements of genius are latent in every mind; and any mind may, through the super efforts of a marvelous concentration, call those elements together into positive, creative action. Thus something new or startling may be developed. It may be a new and most brilliant idea; or, a new and superior plan for the realization of certain highly desired changes in life; or, an entirely new way of doing things — ways and methods, which when applied, might revolutionize everything in that sphere of human thought or endeavor.

Concentration

The most wonderful possibility of all is this, that concentration can lead the mind on and on, out of present restrictions and beyond present states of knowledge and consciousness, into new realms, richer kingdoms and greater worlds. We know that concentration does have the tendency to go farther; and that it has real penetrating power, so that it may delve into anything in the vast domains of Life, Mind or Nature. It is possible therefore to cause the power of concentration to go so far into any state of reality that new and marvelous domains will open before the mind. Thus we might find long sought secrets in the natural world, or make discoveries in any field or region that would prove amazing to the mind and invaluable to human progress.

It is the positive truth that a highly developed concentration can carry the mind farther and deeper in any direction. This is something that the great minds of every age have demonstrated repeatedly. And if we go deeper or farther into Life, into Mind, into Nature, we are going to make discoveries.

We are going to find secrets that no mind has known before. We are going to meet forces, laws and principles, the knowledge of which may reduce to simplicity a thousand so-called impossibilities. We are going to discern the inner workings of things in many fields and regions, and thus secure information that wise men have sought all through the ages.

These things are not exaggerations nor the mere picturing of a highly stimulated imagination; for when we accept the fact that concentration can lead the mind farther and deeper in any direction — which fact we all accept absolutely — we realize that we may, through this use of concentration, discover or accomplish almost anything; that is, if we carry on the process far enough. It is a matter therefore of deciding to concentrate until we find or secure what we want. The outcome will be as expected; for in due time we shall meet the great and the wonderful; we shall learn how this remarkable power can open to the mind regions beyond regions of untold possibility.

Here then is food for thought whatever our work may be, or whatever our fields of study may be. Here we have promises rich and rare for those who aspire to excel; for those who are looking for new worlds to conquer; for those who are in search of the deeper secrets of life everywhere. And as we give thoughtful attention to these things, we perceive most keenly that we are ever on the brink of wonders and marvels — with the power to go on into those fabulous regions and take possession.

To the practical mind it is clearly evident that if we train the mind thoroughly along all essential lines, and learn to concentrate wonderfully well, we are going to move forward steadily and surely, gaining capacity, power and speed as we proceed. And if we continue in this manner, we will not only accomplish what we have in view, but we may at any time strike a new trail leading directly and quickly to the highest pinnacle of achievement.

To the mind of ideals, and to all who have faith in greater possibilities, it is equally evident that a well trained mind can, through a highly developed concentration, take a charmed journey into Nature's wonder world — with the positive assurance that something of untold value will be found. For when we realize that the mind holds marvels and possibilities far beyond what we ever dreamed; and when we know that these mental marvels can be gathered and trained for super effort — for creative work on any scale — or for going out upon expeditions of discovery, even entering into the secrets of life and the heart of things — when we note these things we stand amazed at what might be done. But the mind of faith and courage will stand amazed only for a moment. Such a mind will resolve to master this wonder art at once — for in it there is a power that never knew failure nor defeat — a power that is fully able to cast the mountains of impossibility into the sea of oblivion.

How to Stay Well

How to Stay Well

Table of Contents

Chapter 1 - The New Way to Perfect Health — 51
Chapter 2 - The Metaphysical Process of Cure — 69
Chapter 3 - The Curative Power of Thought — 78
Chapter 4 - The Inner Force of Thought — 86
Chapter 5 - Renew Your Mind and Be Well — 94
Chapter 6 - How the Mind Can Produce Health — 103
Chapter 7 - How to Maintain Perfect Health — 112
Chapter 8 - The Real Man Is Always Well — 120
Chapter 9 - Realizing The Perfect Health Within — 132
Chapter 10 - Purity of Mind and Body — 142
Chapter 11 - The Happiness Cure — 151
Chapter 12 - How to Rest and Recuperate — 158
Chapter 13 - Letting Go of Your Ailments — 166
Chapter 14 - How the Subconscious Creates Health — 173
Chapter 15 - The Power of Mind Over Body — 191
Chapter 16 - The Relation of Mind and Matter — 198
Chapter 17 - The Greater Powers in Man — 217
Chapter 18 - The Higher Curative Forces — 223
Chapter 19 - The Use of Spiritual Power — 232
Chapter 20 - How to Enter the Silence — 246
Chapter 21 - The Use of Positive Affirmations — 258
Chapter 22 - Statements of Truth & Selected Affirmations — 268
Chapter 23 - Chief Essentials in Prevention and Cure — 274
Chapter 24 - Practical Helps to Good Health — 295

How to Stay Well

Chapter I

The New Way to Perfect Health

Introduction — There are many systems of healing, and their number is growing steadily, but there is no single system in existence as yet that is based on all the laws of life.

Disease comes from the violation of one or more of the laws of life, therefore, it can be cured only by bringing mind and body back again into harmony with those laws that have been violated; but if the system of healing employed ignores certain laws it is unable to bring mind and body back into harmony when those certain laws are violated.

Here we find the real cause of failure in all systems. A system that is only physical can produce cures when certain physical laws are violated, but it is powerless when the malady comes from the violation of moral or mental laws. A system that ignores all laws except a few mental laws may produce cures when it is those few mental laws that have been violated, but when the trouble comes from the violation of other laws such a system can do nothing.

It is, therefore, simple to understand that a complete system of healing must not only recognize all the laws of life, but must embody exact scientific methods for correcting all the possible violations of those laws. Such a system must be both physical and metaphysical and must have the understanding of all the laws of life as its foundation. That such a system could cure everything is a foregone conclusion, and that it is possible to formulate such a system every thinker must admit. There is so much knowledge in the world today on the subject of health that no one ought to be sick any more, but the fact that most people you meet are ailing in some way, proves that this knowledge is not bringing practical results. The cause is lack of system. Therefore, if we can formulate all of this knowledge into a complete working system, and we can, we shall have the privilege of rendering a great service indeed. We all agree that it is everybody's privilege to have perfect health, and when we study the subject carefully we must admit that it is possible for everybody to secure perfect health.

There are no incurable diseases. When we encounter ailments that do not respond to the cures we employ, the cause is simply this, that the methods we employ do not reach the laws that have been violated. But there are methods that can reach those laws. For every ill there is a remedy, because every negative has its own positive, and there is no wrong that cannot be made right. If we have the power to violate a certain law, we have also the power to correct that violation; but we cannot correct the matter unless we understand the law that has been misapplied. Therefore, if our system of healing is to be complete it must be based upon the understanding of every law in human nature, metaphysical as well as physical.

To establish such a system one of the first essentials is to remove every form of prejudice and narrow-mindedness. That truth can come from all kinds of sources and through all grades of mentalities is a fact that we all ought to be familiar with in this age; and when we recognize this fact we will not confine our research to the limits of anyone of the regular schools.

Millions of people have been sent to their graves because prejudice has refused to try something else; and thousands are still going the same way every year for the same reason; but there are many ways of doing things, and, since it is everybody's privilege to live a long life and enjoy health as long as he lives, no person should be left to suffer and die until every possible method of relief has been tried. Those who are engaged in the healing of the sick are not dealing justly with the public unless they are prepared to employ and recommend everything that is known to have healing power; and they are not competent to decide as to what does not possess healing power unless they have made a personal test, or personally witnessed such a test.

We daily hear intelligent and well educated people declare that there is nothing in this or that particular system of thought; but upon what do they base their conclusions? Prejudice, or the habit of accepting mere public opinion as truth is usually the cause of such narrow views and in the meantime millions suffer and thousands die on account of those views. The fact is that the more we learn, the more convinced we become that there is something in everything, that every system has its virtues, and every belief its latent truth. To find this virtue in every system, and bring forth the hidden truth in every belief, and then arrange them all into a working system for everyday, practical use this must be our purpose.

Life is too important to be cut short on account of prejudice, ignorance or narrow-mindedness; and the joy of living a large and full life is so great that no one should for a moment be deprived of its pleasure. The new age demands completeness, the best of everything for everybody, the removing of all barriers, that all truth from all sources may minister to all minds. And when all minds will come together and work in such a spirit, the full emancipation of the race will be at hand, and the coming of a fairer day will no longer be a dream. But it is all possible, and what is possible will surely come to pass.

With this spirit in mind we shall proceed to outline what we consider to be a complete system of prevention and cure a system that can bring health to everybody.

The Value of Health — To do one's best in life, to fully enjoy life, to get everything of worth from life that life has to give, to fulfill the purpose of life and realize in the fullest measure any aim, ambition or ideal that one may have in view in life, perfect health is necessary.

Perfect health should be sought by everybody and sought with unceasing persistency, but it should not be sought simply because it insures the comfort and the wellbeing of the individual; it should be sought principally because it is an absolute necessity to the full use and right use of everything that has worth in human existence; and we are here to make the largest and best use of all that is in us.

To fail in health is to fail, in a measure, in everything; to continue in poor health is to continue in a condition where no faculty or power can give itself justice. To add to one's health is to make it possible to add to one's power, one's worth, one's usefulness and one's efficiency; and to gain perfect health is to gain possession of one of the most important factors in the making of human life all that nature demands it should be.

It is in perfect health alone that man can be true to himself, that he can be true to his work, that he can be true to the race. Perfect health, therefore, is not a mere matter of personal comfort, though that in itself is a great deal. We all have the right to personal comfort to the very highest degree; but perfect health is more, vastly more; it is a necessary element in all the workings of nature; it is an indispensable factor in the great universal plan.

The New View of Health — We have recently discovered that it is natural to be well; that it is possible for everybody to be perfectly well, and that perfect health can be secured by all through methods that are not beyond the understanding or ability of anyone. In the past we looked upon sickness as inevitable; now we look upon every form of ailment as positively wrong. We do not criticize or condemn the man who is sick; we give him sympathy and practical help instead, as we have no right to condemn anybody; nevertheless we insist that he should know better, and we are making it our personal business to see that he does know better.

The new view demands that no one should be sick at all, that no one should be incapacitated for a moment that no one should ever be compelled to suspend physical or mental activity on account of ill health; and even more than that, it demands that no one has a right to be sick. And the new view is not irrational; on the contrary, it is based upon the most substantial facts in modern science. It is not possible to become sick unless one violates the laws of life, which include the physical, the mental, the moral, and the spiritual. But no one need violate any of these laws at the present time nor henceforth, as the key to the understanding of the right use of all natural law is now within the reach of everybody. The new view, therefore, demands perfect health of all; and demands it with the same right as it demands manhood, womanhood, morality, justice, liberty, truth.

The Purpose of This Study — The chief purpose of this course of study is to present a complete and practical system of life, through which the new view of health may be realized; that is, a system that will enable anyone to get well and stay well no matter what his physical or mental condition may be at the present time. This study will aim to present all the facts known in the science and art of attaining health; it will give due attention to all efficient methods of cure, with special attention to those that have proved themselves to be the best; and will aim to give instructions with regard to the use of those methods that all can readily and successfully apply. It will explain in the clearest and simplest manner possible the real cause of disease, and how every ailment known to man may be prevented as well as cured. And it will aim to carry out this broad and far-reaching purpose by turning the light of exact science upon the whole nature of man his spiritual and mental nature as well as his physical nature. In brief, this course of study will aim to present sound, thorough and practical information concerning those principles, laws and methods that will, by whomsoever applied, lead to the very highest degree of health, strength and wholesomeness.

The Cause of Disease — It is natural to be well; therefore, the presence of disease indicates that the human system is not in harmony with nature; and as it is not possible to get out of harmony with nature without violating one or more of nature's laws, we conclude that all disease must come from the violation of natural law; but to refrain from such violation and thereby avoid disease, it is necessary to know, first, what constitutes natural law, and second, what to do to continue in harmony with natural law. Complete information, however, on these important subjects has not been given in the past. A few of the physical laws of nature have been studied and carefully observed, but little or no attention has been paid to such other laws as might operate in conjunction with human activity. For this reason vast numbers have become sick without being able to arrive at the cause. Living in the belief that they are caring for themselves properly, they could see no reason why they should not remain well, but in caring for themselves they observed certain laws only, while others equally important were ignorantly and completely ignored.

To enable everybody to avoid all disease by living in harmony with all the laws of nature, we must understand the sphere of the natural, so as to include all activity that may transpire anywhere in the world in which we may act, think and live. In brief, we must study and observe mental and moral laws as well as physical laws, because they are all natural laws; laws that are so closely connected with the actions of man that he will either use them or misuse them, as the case may be, nearly every hour of his existence.

The following outline and division of the subject will therefore prove valuable in connection with this part of the study:

(1) Violation of Physical Laws — We have heard much about physical exercise, but the truth is, that not one person in a thousand exercises his body properly. The majority pay no attention to the subject, and therefore most of their muscles do not receive sufficient exercise, and a large percentage of those who do give the matter attention, overdo it, so that in either case the proper exercise is barely secured. The same is true of breathing. Natural law demands a certain kind of breathing, but there are very few that comply with that demand. With regard to nourishment, we are face to face with the same condition. Foods that should not be taken are taken by the majority nearly every day, and there are very few people who do not eat too much. The other physical laws are misused more or less in the same way. It is readily seen, therefore, that causes of disease are produced in abundance almost daily in the physical life of the average person; but all those causes can be prevented both easily and completely.

(2) Violation of Moral Laws — The lack of vital energy is one of the chief causes of the ills of man, and all immoral thoughts or actions tend to deplete the vital energy of the system. We have frequently been told that certain things are wrong, but we have not been told why. Therefore, we have doubted the sinfulness of those particular actions. When we find, however, that such actions almost invariably drain the system of vital energy, thereby placing the system in a condition where all kinds of disease may get a foothold, we understand why they are wrong. Whenever we do anything that will decrease or lower the natural amount of vital energy, we violate some of the most important laws of nature, and at the same time we originate those causes that are responsible for more than one-third of the ills of the race.

(3) Violation of Mental Laws — To be in harmony with nature, the mind should always be in a state of harmony with itself, and should always be wholesome in its actions and tendencies. To permit mental disorder in any form is therefore a violation of natural law, and it is a well-known fact that mental disorder is nearly always followed by physical disorder. The consequent physical disorder may in many instances be too slight to produce actual illness in the body, but it will in every case interfere more or less with the normal functions of the body. And if that particular disorder is continued, as it usually is, physical diseases will be the final result. To permit such mental states as worry, fear, anger, hatred, envy, gloom, depression, discouragement, dread, anxiety, grief, antagonism, revenge, excitability, and all other mental states of a similar nature, is to violate natural law; and such violation always leads to physical and mental weakness, and frequently to actual disease. To fear disease, to think of disease, to expect disease or to suggest the possibility of disease to oneself or others, is likewise a violation of natural law; and such violation leads to ailment of some kind in the majority of cases. How the misuse of the mind and the entertaining of wrong states of mind may cause disease, is therefore simply understood, and it has been estimated by close observation, that most of the ills of the human race come originally from this cause; but, as is true of all other adverse causes, it can be prevented or removed completely.

Prevention and Cure — Since all ills come from the violation of natural law, all that is necessary to remove an ailment is to restore the human system to perfect harmony with natural law; and for the same reason all that is necessary to prevent disease is to maintain the human system in continual harmony with natural law; but it is not possible to live in complete harmony with the laws of nature unless we understand them all. To be in harmony with physical law is not sufficient, neither is it sufficient to be in harmony with the mental or moral laws. To continue in perfect health we must be in harmony with all the natural laws, and to restore health we must restore harmony in that particular part of the human system where disorder is found.

If the ailment comes from the violation of mental law, we may employ all the hygiene in the world and the best medical treatment to be secured without securing any results whatever. It is only when we restore harmony and order in the field of that particular mental law that results will be secured in that case. In every case we must know what law has been violated before we can effect a cure, and we must adopt that method that can restore the system to perfect harmony with the law that has been violated. This, however, necessitates a complete study of all those laws of nature that act in the life of man; that is, the moral and the mental as well as the physical.

To prevent disease we must know all those laws so that we may live in harmony with them all. To cure disease we must know all those laws so that we can find the law that is violated and restore order in the very place where order is required. But this need not mean an extensive or complicated study. Nature is simple. Anyone can understand nature. It is only necessary to study the whole of nature instead of fragments only, as we have done in the past; and we shall find that the whole of nature is far more interesting than the fragments, and much easier to understand. Important Principles.

To secure the best results from the application of the many methods presented herewith, the following principles should be observed:

(1) Live a Natural Life — The laws of nature, physical and mental, should be observed with the greatest of care in all things and under all circumstances. Gain as clear an understanding as possible of what it means to be natural; then make it a point to be as natural as present conditions will permit. Become fully familiar with those laws of nature that operate in body and in mind; then live, think and act at all times in harmony with those laws. Violate no natural law, neither in action nor in thought, but aim to apply more and more of the laws of nature in everything you think or do, and you are on the way to the living of a natural life.

(2) Think Wholesome Thoughts — Train the mind to think and entertain only such thoughts as are conducive to health, harmony and wellbeing. Think of the good, the true and the perfect; think of the larger, the greater, and the better; think of the worthy, the strong and the superior; think of the pure, the beautiful and the ideal. Give attention to those things that build, that elevate, that make for a richer state of existence, and create only such thoughts as have a rising, growing and expanding tendency. Give health and wholeness to every thought, by thinking health into every thought. Use the power of thought to produce health and direct every mental action to add to the quality and the measure of health.

(3) Believe Yourself Well — If you are perfectly well, continue to believe with all your mind and heart and soul that you always will be well. If you are not perfectly well, believe with the same absolute certainty that you are getting well; believe that the conditions you desire are being produced for you now; believe in the possibilities of your own power to produce any condition that you may desire, and make that belief as strong as the limitless strength of your own soul.

(4) Feel Yourself Well — Aim to live and think constantly in the consciousness of health, and enter as far as possible into the deepest feeling of health; try to feel well at all times, and try to impress that feeling upon your deepest feelings. Permit every feeling of health to sink into a deeper feeling of health until you consciously realize that perfect health that forever abides in the purity, the wholeness, the strength and the divinity of your own soul. Know that perfect health is always within you, always existing in the depths of your real being; then try to feel this perfect health by training yourself to feel health at all times, and by permitting that feeling to enter at once those depths of life and consciousness where perpetual health may always be found. What we feel we express, and what we become conscious of in our deeper life we gain possession of in our external life.

(5) Imagine Yourself Well — The imaging faculty should constantly picture before the mind the perfect health that is desired. What we imagine we think, and as we think we become. See yourself well in your own imagination and claim the actual possession of what you have thus seen. Know that when you imagine yourself being in perfect health you cause all the powers of your system to produce perfect health. What you imagine becomes the pattern, and the mental workmen always build in the likeness of that pattern that stands out most clearly and most distinctly. Therefore, picture yourself well in your imagination and make that picture strong, positive, clear and distinct.

(6) Be Morally Clean — Live a clean life both in thought and in action. A clean life means a strong life, and a strong life means health, vigor, endurance and power. Entertain only such states of mind as are clean, wholesome, and uplifting, and encourage only such actions of mind and body as are directly conducive to higher attainments and greater achievements. Be true to the best that you know, the best that you are and the highest that you aim to realize. Train your ambitions to seek that richer life which is found by acting in harmony with purity, and that greater greatness that he alone can reach who has mastered those finer elements that exist in the world of virtue.

(7) Maintain The Masterful Attitude — In all things and at all times be your own master, think your own thoughts, feel the way you want to feel and act the way you know you should act. Permit no condition in yourself or in your environment to influence your mind or determine your conduct. Know that you can control your own life your own body and your own mind; and be determined to exercise that control for the complete emancipation of every atom in your being. Master yourself for the attainment of better health, greater strength and a higher state of physical, mental and spiritual wellbeing. Know that you can then proceed with all the life and power that is in you, to do what you know you can do.

(8) Have Faith in All Things — To have faith is to enter into conscious touch with the best that exists in that in which we have faith. We can have faith only in that which is worthy of faith; therefore, to have faith in all things is to live in mental contact with the worthy in all things; and when the mind comes in contact with greater work it invariably ascends, and to ascend is to gain freedom. We always become free from the lesser, or that which we do not want, when we rise into the realization of the greater, or that which we do want. Have faith in your own power to produce and maintain perfect health and you place your mind in possession of that very power. That power is already within you. To have faith in that power is to enter into its very life and action and thereby gain, personally, the possession of it for actual use. Have faith in the perfect health that is in you, and have faith in faith; thus you enter into that health, and accordingly all will be well.

(9) Depend Upon Higher Power — Recognize at all times the presence of higher power; know that you are surrounded with higher power; that you are filled with higher power, and that this power will work with you in everything you may wish to do. Whatever the condition of your mind or body, know that this higher power can restore all things. Depend upon that power, have faith in that power, enter into the spirit of that power, permit every atom in your being to become alive with the active presence of that power, and complete emancipation will be realized instantly.

(10) Live On The Heights — All is well on the heights. Go up and live in the perpetual sunshine of truth, in that smile of God which has the power to change everything. Transcend the world of things and dwell constantly upon the mountain tops of supreme spiritual existence. Learn to work with things and to master things, but live always above things. Ascend to the heights and you take mind and body out of weakness and limitations up into the freedom of greater strength and perfect health. You also refine the entire personality, thus making the personal man a more perfect instrument for the expression of the richer life and the greater powers of mind and soul. Live above conditions. Live in the real, the perfect, the true, the sublime. Live with the

Infinite, in conscious unity with the Supreme and feel at all times that you are living, walking and working with God. There is immense power in such a realization a power that can never fail whatever it may be that we wish to have done.

Important Facts — Before entering upon the study of this vast subject it will be well to note certain important facts connected with this particular field facts that clearly indicate the nature and possibilities of the new way to health, and that are admitted by all, even the most exact among scientists, in every line of research, who have given this unique subject their consideration. A few of these facts are as follows:

(1) A complete change of mind tends to produce a similar change among the vital conditions of the body, so that when the mental change is uplifting and wholesome, all unhealthful conditions of the body will tend to disappear.

(2) All unhealthful states of mind nearly always produce physical disturbances, which, when deeply felt and prolonged, frequently result in actual ailments both functional and organic.

(3) The restoration of healthy states of mind tends to produce physical equilibrium and improved health, with added strength and vitality.

(4) The functions of the body are aided remarkably by a full and continued state of mental harmony. Most stomachs could digest almost anything if the mind was always in harmony, and the other organs of the body would greatly increase their strength and endurance in the same way.

(5) The fear of a certain disease has frequently produced it; even contagious diseases have been produced through the fear of contagion when that contagion did not exist in the vicinity.

(6) People who are absolutely fearless and who are absolutely certain that they will not catch it, may go where there is contagion and not get it, provided there is a full supply of vital energy in their systems at the time.

(7) The more faith you have in a medicine, in a physician or in a certain form of treatment, the better the results; while if the patient has no faith or confidence in a treatment, or in the one who administers it, it is almost impossible to get satisfactory results.

(8) Emotions that are deep, strong and exhilarating tend to increase the activity and the energy of the vital organs, thereby promoting the functions of the system. Depressed emotions tend to decrease activity and energy, thereby preventing those organs from doing their work properly, and such a condition is frequently the beginning of disease.

(9) Depressing memories tend to decrease functional activity and physical energy, while pleasing memories and exalting or inspiring ideas have the opposite effect.

(10) The attitude of expectancy, if deep, strong and continued, tends to produce the very conditions expected. Those conditions are nearly always produced in the mind, and in most instances in the body, frequently to the fullest degree.

(11) A nervous, anxious, agitated state of mind will prevent digestion, while states of mental sunshine, good cheer, lightheartedness and pleasing anticipation will promote digestion.

(12) Mental states with deep feelings will affect the flow of the juices of the physical system. The flow of any juice, such as saliva, gastric juice, etc., can be increased or decreased at will by entertaining certain deeply felt states of mind.

(13) A strong, continued desire for health and life will stimulate all the energies of the system, and usually to a sufficient degree to increase permanently the health and the vigor of the body.

(14) When a patient deeply and vitally believes that a certain agent has remedial powers, benefit will be derived from applying that agent, even though it may have no remedial virtue whatever.

(15) When a patient absolutely forgets, through some startling event or other cause, that he is ill, the ailment nearly always disappears for a time, and in many instances disappears permanently.

(16) When the mind lives in the exhilarating atmosphere of an inspiring ideal there is a decided increase in the quantity of mental energy and a marked improvement in the quality. And in nearly every instance, a similar increase and improvement in the physical energies follows.

(17) A new and uplifting mental atmosphere can take the body so completely out of old or diseased conditions as to cause those conditions to disappear completely. The entire physical system is thus taken up out of its usual state into a state that is new and wholesome, and all the elements of the body change to correspond.

(18) To secure something new and something most desirable to live for will renew the life of the body, increase vital energy, stimulate the circulation, bring color to the face, health and charm to the personality and restored activity to the mind.

(19) When the mind enters a deep and perfect calm where it feels the interior serenity and fullness of life, and continues thus for several hours, disturbances of mind or body as well as threatening ailments will disappear.

(20) When you believe that a certain thing is harmful, you will be harmed by it mentally in every instance, and in many instances you will be harmed physically, especially in the nervous system.

(21) The action of the mind for or against any mode of treatment will assist or retard that treatment as the case may be.

(22) When a man works with a definite aim in view, his energy and working capacity will be maintained indefinitely, and hours of actual weariness will be few; but if he works with no aim in view, weariness and exhaustion will come frequently and his working capacity will be decreased from twenty-five to fifty per cent.

(23) A courageous and hopeful state of mind aids remarkably in the overcoming of disease, no matter what the treatment may be.

(24) In functional and nervous diseases, thoughts and ideas can be made direct remedies in every case. And in organic diseases those same agencies can so assist nature as to insure complete recovery; that is, when nature is given a fair chance in all other respects as well.

(25) Nature is constantly at work to keep the well man perfectly well and to make the sick perfectly well. To give nature a fair chance to do this work right is frequently all that is necessary to restore health, but there is nothing in human life that can assist or interfere so much with nature in this respect as the attitude of the mind.

(26) Medicine, or any material substance can produce certain definite effects upon the chemical life of the body; therefore, those substances do have the power to change physical conditions, and accordingly promote cures, when those particular changes are needed for the welfare of the system; but that power is limited, and the change the medicine will produce will depend largely upon the state of the patient's mind at the time.

(27) The attitude of the patient's mind at the time the medicine is taken will modify the usual effect of that medicine. That attitude can and frequently does neutralize the expected effect of the medicine; and in many instances the effect desired by the medicine is produced wholly by the mind through expectation and faith.

(28) Certain kinds of music, stimulated emotions, promise of reward, a new purpose in life, an agreeable change of work, new opportunities, the appearance of greater possibilities all of these, and scores of similar factors or experiences, invariably increase the activity of the mind and the vital energies of the body.

(29) Through the direct and intelligent use of the mind any physical ailment may be prevented or permanently cured.

Chapter 2

The Metaphysical Process of Cure

There is a belief among many that mental and spiritual healing is produced by some extraordinary or mysterious power, a power that is very difficult to obtain if one does not naturally possess it; but when we understand the power that heals, or the process of cure, we shall find that it is like all other great things, very simple.

All healing is the result of mental change, and the various systems of cure that are being employed are simply different methods for producing the same thing mental change. The mental change, however, must be towards higher and finer states of thought, or the cure will not follow. And here we find the reason why spiritual and metaphysical systems of thought are usually very successful whenever they attempt the art of healing. The same is true of the various systems of optimistic suggestion. Any suggestion that can produce an elevating change of mind will produce a cure whenever such a change is made, and this is true even though the system of suggestion employed may not be exactly scientific nor possess a complete understanding of the truth.

The beneficial results that come from going away for your health are produced through the same law mental change. New scenes, new associations, new experiences, etc., produce new impressions upon the mind, and these, if deeply enjoyed, will change the mind. When one expects to regain his health by going away, the results are usually better, because the change of mind produced will have health in view, and whatever the mind has in view it always tends to produce.

How to Stay Well

Our thoughts are created in the likeness of those ideas that are uppermost in consciousness; therefore, if health is the predominating purpose, the conditions of health will naturally be instilled into every thought. In some instances, however, a change of scenes does not produce a change of mind, the reason being that the person either lacks impressibility or the new scenes lack impressiveness.

The physician who sends his patients away for their health is simply giving them metaphysical treatment without the name. The real object is to get the patient away from his present state of mind, and anything that will accomplish this can produce a cure; but it is possible to get away from your present state of mind without taking a journey to some other country, and it is usually more convenient. Until recently people have depended upon a change of environment to produce a change of mind, but we are now learning to change our minds in any way that we like, regardless of the environments in which we may be placed. We are beginning to become masters over ourselves, and we are learning to so live that external conditions will not control us anymore. We have discovered that we can change our own minds whenever we like, and in any way that we like; also that mental changes produce physical changes, and that we may be completely transformed through the renewal of our minds.

The secret of all healing and all changes in body, mind or personality is thus revealed, and instead of being a mysterious power, is simplicity itself. It is not something far beyond our reach, but a power that we are using more or less daily simply the power to change the mind.

Since any change in the human system can be produced through the proper mental change, our leading purpose in this connection will consequently be to find the best methods for producing such changes, and we shall not have to search far nor wide to find the methods desired. The first principle to learn is that every mental change must be subconscious; that is, the change must be a change of the heart or no change in life will follow. The thought of the heart is the thought created in the subconscious, and as the subconscious thought is the only thought that produces effects in the system, we understand readily why the change must be subconscious.

Every idea or belief that is impressed upon the mind in deep feeling will enter the subconscious. Therefore, every effort to change the mind should be made in deep feeling. The fact that feeling plays such an important part in this respect, proves why impressionable minds respond the most readily to those systems of healing that are based on mental change. It also explains why emotional and religious systems are so very successful in healing whenever they attempt this fine art. Emotional methods, however, do not always produce permanent results, while those results that come from deep metaphysical systems are nearly always permanent.

The best system of healing would consequently be a system wherein feeling and intellect were combined, where the emotional was employed to give speedy mental change, and the metaphysical employed to establish those changes permanently.

To produce mental change, three different factors may be employed; first, new impressions from without; second, new ideas formed through the usual intellectual process; and third, new states of consciousness. Those impressions that come from without will at times produce decided changes in the subconscious mind, though as a rule they simply divert attention so that you will not think about your ills. This is important, however, because so long as you think deeply about your ailments you impress them more deeply upon the system and make matters worse. But when you stop thinking about the trouble, nature will have a chance to restore harmony and health without being interfered with.

When attempting to produce new ideas through your own independent thinking, it is well to remember that the most wholesome ideas are always those gained from thinking about the real, the absolute and the perfect; in other words, metaphysical thinking is the most wholesome, provided it is truly metaphysical and not speculative; and all metaphysical thinking will be true and wholesome that is based upon man's highest understanding of the ideal. To produce a change in consciousness, various methods may be employed.

Anything that touches the inner life, such as good music, words of inspiration, higher mental experiences, growth and ascension in soul life and similar mental attitudes, will produce new states of consciousness. If the attention of the mind is centered upon health, while the change of consciousness is taking place, the mental change that follows will always have a tendency to produce better health. A change in consciousness is always the most decided change and should therefore be sought in preference to any of the others. And the reason is because such a change affects directly the real life and action of the mental forces; and these in turn affect the chemical life of the physical system.

A chemical change in the system is always required before health can be restored, and it is upon this principle that medicines aim to work; but it has been thoroughly demonstrated that the subconscious forces of the mind can produce; chemical changes in the body with far greater rapidity and certainty than any drug taken into the system. And what is important, subconscious changes will be correct changes, while too often medicines produce the wrong chemical change, thus making matters worse. In many instances medicines produce no chemical change in the system whatever, and there is no cure unless the patient has sufficient faith in the medicine; in that case the change is produced by faith, and it is well to remember in this connection that faith can produce any change in the system that is possible under natural law.

Of all states of the mind, that state usually described as faith is the deepest, the largest, the most penetrating and the most powerful. Since mental change is the real secret of healing, and since this change must be towards the higher, the finer and the interior nature of life, the greatest results in healing would naturally come from that mental process that always moves towards the ideal; and that is faith. Faith is that state of mind that always goes up into the higher and more perfect; in fact, it is not faith unless there is mental ascension into or towards the absolute.

Faith is a normal, upward mental change, and there is no upward mental change possible without faith, because every mental process that will have the power to produce an upward change must be inspired by faith. For this reason faith can never fail, because faith is an upward mental change, and every upward mental change will unfailingly produce a change for the better in the body. When we have faith in anything we elevate the mind. No matter what it is we have faith in, the mere matter of having faith will elevate the mind. The elevating of the mind causes the renewal of the mind, and when we renew our minds we always change things for the better.

Every subconscious action of the mind is a cause; and when the mind is taken up into a new and more perfect state, all these causes will become better and more powerful because they will accordingly produce greater and better effects. When the mind is taken up the entire system is taken up and is taken out into the freedom of the more perfect. The same process tends to produce right mental states, and such mental states are always conducive to good health. All wholesome impressions formed upon the subconscious will produce wholesome effects upon the system. And all ascending, enlarging and perfecting states of mind, if deeply felt, produce wholesome impressions upon the subconscious. This proves that faith can never fail, because faith is always ascending, always enlarging, always perfecting, and is always deeply felt. "As your faith is, so shall it be unto you," is a strong statement, but we know it to be absolutely true when we discover what faith really is, and what it has the power to do.

Faith invariably awakens the powers of the inner life, and those powers are higher and stronger than the ones that act in the external personality. Those powers, therefore, can accomplish more, and, what is well to remember, they can accomplish anything because they are unlimited. Failure, however, becomes impossible when unlimited powers are at hand, so, therefore, we realize again that faith can never fail.

It has been stated that the ascending change of mind is the secret of all healing, regardless of what the treatment might be, and as there are many ways to bring about such mental changes, our object must naturally be to find the best way; and we find the best way in faith. How to secure faith and how to employ faith will, therefore, become great questions in this study.

Faith comes from having faith in all things and at all times. There is nothing that develops so rapidly with use as faith, and the reason is because the attitude of faith is towards the larger, the higher and the superior at all times. To have faith and to exercise faith is to press on directly to greater things. It is therefore self-accumulative and self-developing, and demonstrates most positively the truth of the statement that to him that hath shall be given.

"I have faith," and "I have faith in faith," are statements that should be employed constantly, and the meaning of those statements should always be deeply felt. Whenever you think of faith or try to exercise faith turn your mind upon the great within, the boundless, and try to feel your consciousness entering into the seeming void with the assurance that it is all solid rock. If your faith has become well developed you will know through your own interior perceptions that whatever realm your consciousness may penetrate, it is only the real and the substantial that will be found. You then realize that you can go out anywhere in the vast mental world and always be on solid ground.

In the application of the laws of mental and spiritual healing the value of such a realization is simply unbounded, because those systems of healing depend very largely upon realizing the reality of the real. When disease is present the system is in confusion; therefore, if the mind can change into harmony by entering into the understanding of that which is ever real, right, perfect and absolutely good, the regaining of health must positively follow.

While in the consciousness of absolute harmony we can know neither confusion nor disturbance of any kind, and we cannot be in a condition of ill health while we are in a state where all is well. The great secret of healing, therefore, is to change the mind from a state of confusion, disorder and false action into a state where the absolutely good is realized to be real, omnipresent and eternal. It is leaving the storm tossed billows of perverted life and landing safely upon the solid rock of absolute truth. And here we should remember that it matters not where you may be upon this angry sea, faith will guide you safely, surely and speedily to the harbor of perfect peace.

To depend absolutely upon faith is of the highest importance, because faith cannot fail. We may fail, but faith never; and the reason why we fail is because we do not take advantage of the highest wisdom, the superior insight and those mightier powers that may be given to us through faith. In this connection we should fully realize that faith is not blind belief; belief may be blind, but faith sees everything.

Faith is constantly ascending into more and more light, because faith is the mind growing into the light. When you say that you take things on faith, you really mean that a superior insight has informed you that those things should be taken, and that it will be very profitable in some way for you to do so. When you are trying to help yourself or others, this taking of things on faith will prove to be the one perfect path to remarkable results.

Faith declares that all things are possible, and after making this statement faith proceeds to awaken those greater powers in your larger and higher life through which the mind may gain the capacity to do the very things that faith declared could be done. Faith knows that in the great within there is health in abundance; that the real man is always well and that there is sufficient power at hand to bring this perfect health into positive and tangible evidence in every part of the physical system. Faith not only knows this, but acts according to its convictions.

The result is, that what we took on faith we received through faith, and we found it to be very substantial, profoundly real and absolutely good. What we receive through faith is always good, because faith is the continuous ascension of the mind into the absolutely good. Faith may also be defined as the mind's ascension into absolute truth; therefore, the more faith we have the more of truth we shall understand; and it is the understanding of truth that brings complete emancipation.

Chapter 3

The Curative Power of Thought

To make practical application of these principles in the cure of human ills, it is the metaphysical process that must be employed, and the reason why will be evident when we consider the true meaning of metaphysics.

When the term metaphysics is employed, however, in connection with modern thought or any feature of this study, we do not refer to those vague speculations about mind that class the elements of mind as parts of the unknowable; nor do we refer solely to certain mental forces or qualities that have no direct connection with practical, everyday life. Modern metaphysics, in its largest sense, includes the entire field of mind and consciousness, and deals with the scientific study and practical application of all the forces, elements, powers, states, qualities and attributes that may exist in the great mental domain.

The metaphysical world, broadly speaking, includes the mental world, the moral world, the spiritual world, and all the worlds of consciousness; and metaphysics, as applied in this connection, constitutes the art of applying any force or element embraced in the metaphysical world for the purpose of preventing or removing human ills, be they mental, physical or moral. Metaphysics in its modern interpretation signifies the scientific use of the highest powers of the mind to the needs of practical life, and among these higher powers, the power of thought occupies the most prominent position.

The principle that underlies the power of thought, which is the psychological principle, becomes therefore the fundamental principle in the science and art of healing; and although a number of mental, moral and spiritual forces may be called into action in this mode of healing, still all those forces must express themselves through the power of thought.

The great central action in the metaphysical world is mind in action. How the mind acts determines how other metaphysical forces are to act; and the manner in which the mind is harmonized with those functions, determines how powerful and efficient the action of the mind is to be. The secret, therefore, of the metaphysical process of cure is, first, to place in action such powers of thought as naturally produce health; and second, to increase those powers by combining all other metaphysical forces and elements with the healing power of thought.

Any method of healing that does not give first place to the power of thought is not based upon the fundamental principle of metaphysics, nor is such a method in perfect harmony with the laws of nature, because nature has given the greatest power in human life to the power of thought. On the other hand, any system of cure that depends directly on the power of thought, but does not combine with that power every other force and element in the human domain, is likewise incomplete and out of harmony with natural law. To formulate a perfect system of prevention and cure, a system that would apply harmoniously, conjunctively and effectively, all the health producing elements in human life, the power of thought should be made the direct channel of application.

Everything from the metaphysical side that could increase the power of thought should be employed in conjunction with that power, and everything from the physical side that would make the body more responsive to the curative power of the finer elements of mind and soul should be employed in perfect harmony with the metaphysical process. Such a system, therefore, would not only invite but demand hygienic living, wholesome diet, pure air, reasonable physical exercise, temperate habits, natural remedies, good nursing, and even nonpoisonous medicines and common sense surgery, when these would tend to place the body in the most receptive state possible for the curative power of thought.

These external methods, however, should not be looked upon as the powers that heal. The power of thought should occupy that position, not only in the mind of the patient and the physician, but also in the minds of all those who are in any way interested in the case. We should always think of the power of thought as the one principal healing power. We should always give this power the best possible conditions, both physical and metaphysical, through which to work. The power of thought is mighty, but that is no reason why we should place physical obstacles in its way in the form of unhygienic living, impure air, unwholesome food, intemperate habits and the like; nor is there any reason why we should not remove physical obstructions with physical means when this can be done safely and effectively.

To depend wholly on external means, however, is to decrease the power of thought, and in consequence to lessen the power of nature to restore normal conditions; but so long as the power of thought is given the first place in every stage of the curative process, it will increase its efficiency, even though many external methods be employed at the same time.

The principle is to depend upon the power of thought, and make that power as strong and effective as possible; but while this power is being applied, any external method that can make the body more responsive to thought, or that can assist the natural healing process, is not only permissible but demanded. There is no warfare between the physical and the metaphysical. The two are not antagonistic. On the contrary, they are necessary to each other, but the physical is the servant and the metaphysical the master. Therefore, in a complete therapeutic system the metaphysical should be looked upon as the physician, while the physical should be expected to assist in every manner possible.

To place the metaphysical first is to act in perfect harmony with nature, because every action in the body originates in the mind, and every function in the body is governed by the mind. The voluntary actions of the body are produced by the conscious side of the mind, and the involuntary actions are produced by the subconscious. Even what is called the efforts of nature to restore normal conditions, is a process that is governed completely by the subconscious side of the mind. It is the subconscious that directs the vital force of the system in healing the wound or in replacing healthy tissue where disease has been conquered. It is the subconscious that restores flesh to the emaciated body when the fever has been removed, and it is the subconscious that gradually restores energy, strength and vigor during the period of convalescence.

It is the subconscious that governs all those processes in the human system that we speak of as nature, and as the subconscious can be assisted, modified, changed or "governed by the power of conscious thought", we realize what a power there is in the power of thought when intelligently employed. Every dormant force found in the body responds to the subconscious mind; and the subconscious mind responds to the power of thought. Therefore, the power of thought is necessarily the great central power, both in the physical and the metaphysical domains of man; and for this reason it becomes the most important factor in that system of healing that aims to be true to nature, true to the laws of life and true to the entire being of man.

To exercise the power of thought in the cure of any disease, physical, mental or moral, the first essential is to train the entire system to depend absolutely upon the power of thought for health, wholeness and strength. This step will not only increase the health producing powers of thought, but will also make every part of the body more responsive to the curative forces of mind and soul.

When the body responds readily to those finer forces, any threatening ill can be nipped in the bud almost instantaneously by simply using the power of thought according to the laws of applied metaphysics. To train the physical system to depend upon higher power for perfect health and respond to that power whenever there is a desire to produce health or increase the life of health, constant attention should be given to that interior or higher relationship that exists between the physical and the metaphysical.

We should think a great deal about how the mind affects the body and how mental action both originates and governs physical action. We should realize the fact that mental states have a tendency to work themselves out into physical conditions, and that any positive mental state can remove a corresponding opposite physical condition. We should also realize that all the vital forces of the human system, even the chemical forces, not only can be affected, but constantly are being affected, modified and changed by the force of thought, mind and soul.

The first step in the regaining of health through the metaphysical process is not to learn how to exercise some new mental power, but to learn how to make common, everyday thinking wholesome. In fact, so closely is the mind related to the body that if everyday thinking was wholesome, and always wholesome, the body would enjoy perfect health all through life.

The power of thought may be employed either for or against the welfare of the human system, and which it is to be, depends upon whether the thinking is wholesome or not. To discriminate between thinking that is wholesome and that which is not, a clear understanding of general metaphysics becomes necessary, though the line that separates the two modes of thought may be readily found by anyone. Wholesome thinking is the result of any mental action that is constructive in its tendency, and that has the ideal in view, while any mental action that is not naturally constructive and that moves away from the ideal is always unwholesome and detrimental.

When the actions of the mind move towards the ideal, everything in the human system has a tendency to move out of present conditions, and the natural way to freedom is out of the lesser and the adverse out into the larger, the better and the ideal. To train the action of the mind to move towards the ideal, the first essential is to impress the ideal upon every mental state and every element of consciousness. The ideal of anything is that something that contains the very thing that is wanted. Therefore, to move towards the ideal is to enter into that which is wanted. To move towards the ideal is to make real the ideal; to move towards the light is to gain more and more light, and the mind does move towards, and into, that which is constantly being impressed upon thought and consciousness.

To impress the ideal upon the mind the existence of the ideal should be constantly in the mind; that is, think and affirm that you have in the ideal what you want in the real.

How to Stay Well

You thus incorporate the ideal in every form. You make all your thinking ideal; and ideal thinking is wholesome thinking. Such thinking will produce perfect mental health, and when the mind is perfectly well the body will also be perfectly well.

Think with depth and feeling that you are well, and you give your thought the power to make you well. Every thought you think has an interior power. This interior power is exactly like the thought itself as to nature and quality, and it will express that nature and quality in the body. This is one of the supreme facts in metaphysics. What you give to your thought you give to your body, and what you think into your thought you work into your body. When you always think that you are well, you think health into every thought, and the interior power of every thought will express health in the body. There can, therefore, be no disease in your body while all your thinking is giving health to your body, because the entire system will be so thoroughly filled with the life and the power of health that no adverse condition can possibly gain a foothold.

The average mind, however, is not in the habit of thinking health, and a large portion of the thought produced in the average mind is not wholesome, the reason being that no systematic effort has been made to apply the mind directly in promoting the welfare of the human system; but through the affirmation of the ideal, wholesome thinking will become a habit, and the power of every thought will promote the realization of the ideal.

The statement "I AM well" should be used constantly in the deepest and most sincere attitude of realization in order to secure a basis for healthful thinking. To this statement should be added as many constructive statements as may be necessary to express the true, the perfect and the ideal in every part of human life. The principle is, to think constantly that you are well and never permit yourself to think anything to the contrary. You will thus give the power of thought the power to produce health, and such thought will permeate every part of your body with the very life of health. By giving expression to the idea of health in every mental state, and in every action of consciousness and feeling, you add health producing power to the power of thought.

Your wholesome thinking is strengthened from every source, and everything you do will tend to make your system more and more wholesome. To add health producing power to the power of thought, such mental states as anger, worry, depression and doubt, should be removed, and such states as faith, love, peace, joy and harmony established in their places. Eliminate all negative thinking; that is, never think of that which is adverse, or that which you do not wish to become a part of your life. Think of only those greater and better things that you want, and continue in the positive faith that you will get them. Live on the sunny side; count everything joy; believe most thoroughly that all things are working for greater and greater good for you, and be determined to prove it in greater and greater measure.

Chapter 4

The Inner Force of Thought

There are certain forms of mental action that exercise a direct power upon the human personality, while there are other forms of mental action that do not exercise that power. How to tell the difference between the two is a great problem, and a most important problem, because to find the solution is to find the real secret of practical results in the metaphysical field. Those who have tried to secure results through the application of right thinking have found that at times results came almost instantaneously, while at other times it seemed almost impossible to accomplish anything, even though the same methods were employed to the letter. Then there are many who never secure any results whatever, though they apply the same principle, as those who are exceptionally successful, and the reason why seems a mystery.

The mystery disappears, however, when we learn that thought does not become power unless the inner force of thought is brought into action. Two persons may with the same enthusiasm and perseverance affirm "I AM well"; one finds no change, while the other begins to mend at once, and is soon restored to perfect health. The same idea and the same method was employed in each case, but only in the one did thought become power. In like manner two persons of equal intelligence may live according to the same system of metaphysics or idealism. The one gains ground every day, while the other finds conditions no better than he did while employing his previous helter-skelter modes of thought. It is evident, therefore, that it is not the thought itself that produces results, but some power that is back of or within thought.

There is no inner force in all mental action. This force is hidden, so to speak, in every thought, but it is not aroused in every thought. When it is aroused the thought becomes alive with power and produces results according to its nature. When you think of health, and arouse the inner force of every thought, you will give every thought the power to produce health. In consequence those thoughts will produce health in your system just as surely as fire produces warmth. When you think of peace and feel the action of this same inner force, the very thought you think will become a power for peace. You can in this manner restore perfect peace and harmony to your system in a few seconds, no matter how agitated or disturbed you may be.

The inner force of the thought, when awakened, will express and produce the exact nature of the thought; and therefore, whatever you may wish your thought to produce, if you think the right thought and think living thought, the results will come as expected. To think the right thought is simple; all that is necessary for general purposes is to affirm that you are what you wish to realize and express through body, mind and personality, and to form in the mind as clear a mental picture as possible of those conditions you desire to produce in yourself. If you wish to produce health affirm mentally, "I AM well", "I AM strong", "I AM strong and well", "I AM perfectly whole and sound through and through", "Absolute health fills and thrills every atom in my being", and statements of a similar nature. Think these thoughts over and over again with deep conviction until your mind is actually full of them; and at the same time picture mentally the condition of health in every part of your system.

The other essential is to think living thought; and here is the problem, the chief stumbling block of those who have failed to secure the desired results through the metaphysical process. No matter how much you may affirm this statement or that, or how well you may picture certain conditions in your mind, you will have no results unless your thought is alive. Your thought will have no power to produce the desired effect in your body unless you awaken the inner force of that thought.

There are some minds that are naturally conscious of this inner force, or what may be called the finer force, the spirit or the soul of thought, and, therefore, they take naturally to metaphysics and idealism, securing good results from the beginning. Others, however, have to acquire this finer consciousness before there is any power in their thought; but this is not difficult. Those who have secured results may think that their understanding of the principles of right thought is so much better than that of those who fail, but this is not necessarily true. Many of those who succeed in metaphysics have very little understanding of the principles involved, while not a few of those who understand metaphysics as perfectly as they do mathematics, secure no results, the reason being that the former naturally express this inner force through every thought, while the latter do not.

The understanding of the metaphysical principle is necessary to the best results. No one can accomplish very much without this understanding, but the awakening of the inner force of thought is just as important. Therefore, every person, no matter how well he has succeeded thus far, should learn more fully how to awaken and direct that inner force that is latent in all human thought. We may depend upon natural endowments up to a certain point, but to go further we must take conscious control of our powers, and develop them as required for the greater purpose in view. What we use consciously, intelligently, and according to known law, always produces far greater results than what we use naturally while in ignorance of the law. Those who depend upon their own determined efforts instead of upon the gifts of nature always climb the highest in the scale. The same is true in the field of practical metaphysics.

To awaken the inner force of thought, give spirit to all your thought; that is, give depth of life and feeling to your thought, and give what may be termed the action of soul to every mental action. This force is not forceful and is not purely mental, but contains an element that is much finer and stronger than the usual energies of mind. In fact, this inner force has tremendous power when deeply realized and properly concentrated. When fully awakened there is no disease in the body that this force cannot remove, and there is no adverse condition anywhere in the human system that it cannot make right.

When failures occur through the use of the metaphysical process the cause may be found in the fact that this inner force is not alive in the thoughts we think; and without the living action of this inner force the mind has practically no power over the body; but when this inner force is alive in every mental action, the power of the mind over the body becomes extraordinary.

This force is entirely distinct from intellectual action or ordinary feeling or will. It is a force by itself and fills every thought, as we would say the soul fills the body. To awaken this force, or rather place it in action in every thought, deep conscious feeling is necessary; and a deep, strong, positive will is required to direct it. But both feeling and will must be trained to sound the depths of the human system, as mere superficial action, however earnest or determined, will not avail. The object must be to train consciousness to actually grasp this finer element in thought, and as consciousness goes deeper and deeper into the interior world of thought, this finer force comes forth with more and more power until every thought you think is a power. Then use wisdom in your thinking and the results that you will henceforth secure will be remarkable indeed. When every thought you think has the power to produce a definite effect upon your body, your character or your mentality, you can afford to think only thoughts that are wholesome and true, and accordingly will find it necessary to adopt a complete system of scientific and constructive thinking for everyday use.

Aim to live, not on the surface of your mind, but in the very spirit of your mind. Do not think mechanically, but with feeling, spirit and soul; and whenever you proceed to use the power of thought in producing definite results in your system, such as health, life, harmony, peace and purity, enter into the finer, deeper, stronger life of your thought. Try to feel the inner force of thought when you think. You will soon succeed in doing this almost at any time; and when you do your thought will become actual power.

When this inner force is given action and made alive in every thought, the complete mastery of every physical condition becomes possible. You can then remove any adverse conditions from your system at once because you have liberated that force of thought that is so deep that it undermines everything that is not in harmony with the true order of natural law. This finer force, when placed in action in your system, will remove the wrong, consume it as with fire, and will give life and power to every function and faculty you may possess.

When your thinking is right, the inner force of your thought will give you the power to do whatever you think of doing. Therefore, when you adopt a complete system of scientific and constructive thinking and awaken the inner force of your thought, your life will be in your own hands and you will have the power to produce and build up any desirable condition of body, mind or personality that you may desire.

Special Rules — To apply the principles and methods of this work, in the most successful manner, to the attainment of health, the following rules should be observed as closely as possible.

1. Continue in a calm, harmonious, well-poised frame of mind at all times and under all circumstances, and know that such a frame of mind will cause your system to increase its vital energy, and to retain all that energy.

2. Be determined to secure and maintain perfect health. Concentrate your whole attention upon the realization of perfect health, and firmly believe that you will gain ground steadily.

3. Train yourself to feel that there is life, health and wholeness in abundance in every atom of your system, and make this feeling so deep and so realistic that you can actually feel that life and health coming forth into every part of your body.

4. Learn to think health. Give every thought the idea of health, and impress your most perfect conception of health upon every thought or mental state that you entertain. Think of yourself constantly as perfectly well. Think of yourself as strong, and think of yourself as gaining in health and strength constantly.

5. See yourself well in your own imagination. Whenever you think of yourself, see yourself with the mind's eye as being perfectly well and strong. Make that ideal picture of yourself as plain and distinct as you can, and dwell upon it with expectant joy many times every day.

6. Whenever you are reminded of pain, illness or disorder, turn your attention positively upon the highest and best thought of health, life and harmony that you can form in your mind. Give deep and sincere feeling to this effort, and know that the moment you produce a change for the better in your mind you will realize a change for the better in your body.

7. Continue in a happy frame of mind. Be always cheerful, and feel it with your whole heart. Live on the sunny side of your life. Think of the bright side of everything. Look for the bright side of everything, and expect to find more and more of this brighter side every day. Train your heart to sing and your soul to rejoice at all times, and know that the more real happiness you feel the more health and vigor you will have in mind, body and personality.

8. Live in the upper story of the mind. Realize that you are above mind and body, that you have full control of mind and body, and that you express your whole life and power through every part of mind and body. Think of yourself as living in an upper, finer atmosphere of thought and life, where freedom is complete, where power is unbounded, and where all is always well.

9. Look for health, life and strength in everybody. When you see illness anywhere, think the more deeply of the perfect health that is in the real life of everybody, and expect that perfect health to express itself in an ever-increasing measure. Make it a practice to take note of and to emphasize the good and the wholesome that you find in everybody you meet, and do not hesitate to speak of these better things at every available opportunity.

10. Live mentally in a wholesome atmosphere. Keep your mind in peace and order, absolutely free from strife or discord of any kind. Fill your mind completely with thoughts of the good, the true, the strong, the perfect, the beautiful and the ideal; and take great delight in dwelling upon those thoughts as frequently as you can find the time.

11. Believe thoroughly in the methods you employ to get health and strength. Know within yourself that those methods can produce the results you desire. Have unbounded faith in yourself, in the thoughts of health you think, and in everything that you can do to produce health. Have unbounded faith in the good that is in you, and all about you, and in that higher power in which you live, and move, and have your being.

12. When things do not seem to change for the better as you should wish, know that the wrong shall surely pass away, while the good shall increase perpetually. Then set your will to your purpose. Know that you can turn the tide in your favor. Be strong and persistent. Proceed to apply everything of worth that you know. Make the best use of everything of worth that is in you. Think, act and work in that sublime realization that makes you feel that you are filled and surrounded with the unbounded power of the Infinite; and proceed in the consciousness of the great truth that all things are possible to him who lives and works in such a power.

Chapter 5

Renew Your Mind and Be Well

That the mind exercises great power over the body, that every mental state is a cause, producing its corresponding effect upon the moral, the mental and the physical conditions of the individual, and that every thought is a force that can change, transform, or at least modify almost anything in the human system these are facts that are no longer disputed. The metaphysical side of man is now receiving its due share of attention, and the facts just stated are therefore being firmly established among all who discern them. Knowing the fact, therefore, that mind and thought have such great power over the human system, and that the whole of life depends for its qualities and conditions upon the nature of one's thought, we find ourselves face to face with a principle of stupendous proportions; and we cannot proceed very far in our study of this principle before we discover that a change of thought means a change of practically everything, and therefore we realize that to make the proper change of thought is so important that nothing in life could be more important.

Metaphysical students in general understand that the renewal of mind means a renewal of everything in life; but to change the thought at will, and to bring about those mental changes that we desire, is an art that the majority have not mastered, the reason being that it is much easier to believe than to act; though it is a fact that we should remember well in this connection that every possibility can be worked out and made actual in the life of anyone. When we consider the subject of mental change and the renewal of mind, we find that there are two ways through which this may be brought about. We may change our thought through impressions received from without, or through perceptions developed from within. We may renew the mind by living among new scenes and environments, or we may bring about the same result by directing our mind to live in a new field of consciousness; though we shall find that where thousands change their thoughts by the former plan, only a few do so by the latter.

That we can change and renew mind without changing external environments is a fact that is well known, but it has never been looked upon as of real importance. We shall soon learn, however, that it is of the greatest importance; and we shall also find that no one can attain complete emancipation, or realize steady growth of mind and soul until he can change his thought from within according to his desires. Physicians send their patients away because they know a change will do them good; but what does the change consist of, and why does it prove beneficial? Simply this: that different people are met, strange houses and landscapes constantly appear, and what is heard or seen differs more or less from what was experienced in the former locality. The new place has no magical power of healing; it does not give the system any new elements, and has no special virtue along any line. With a few exceptions, one place is usually as good as another. We find in each place the same earth, the same atmosphere, and the same natural forces. A few slight modifications may exist, but where there are some conditions superior in the new place, there are other conditions that are inferior.

When we go to some new place to secure a change, we find many of the people in that new place planning to go elsewhere, that they may have a change; consequently it is not the place that is beneficial, but the change; and the change is beneficial because you get new impressions upon your mind. You get something different to think about, and your thought is more or less renewed. A change of thought, according to well-known metaphysical laws, produces a change in the system. Old and burdensome conditions pass away through the coming of the new, and you feel a relief. That is why the change is beneficial.

To go away for your health is to take a course of metaphysical treatment from the visible forms of nature, and the results will depend very much upon how favorable an impression those forms make upon your mind. What you see, hear or experience is different, and produces different impressions upon your mind. From these different impressions come different thoughts, different emotions, and different mental states. There is a change of mind and thought, which is invariably followed by a change in the physical system.

We all know that new thought produces new life, and that new impressions upon mind produce new thought. These new impressions may not all be wholesome, but they are always different, and the old is thereby modified to some extent. Should you go away and not be well impressed with the new scenes, you will receive no benefit whatever. You do not respond to the new impressions, consequently there is no change of thought. As a man thinketh, so is he; therefore, so long as you think the way you did, you will feel the way you did. You are the same as before, physically and mentally; you are no different, and in consequence no better.

We can easily establish the fact without multiplying arguments or illustrations, that the benefit received from a change of scenes or places comes because there is a change of thought; and we must naturally conclude, therefore, that if you can change your thought without going away, you can have just as good results by staying at home. This, however, is an art that few have mastered, but it is an art that all must master if perfect health is to be enjoyed all through life.

The majority cannot change their own minds. They require new impressions from without to accomplish this feat; they are dependent upon the five senses and what comes through the five senses, and think, not as they wish to think, but according to the impressions they receive from without, coming into mind through the sense channels.

It is not to be inferred, however, that it is wrong to receive new impressions from without, or that it is detrimental to our best welfare to absorb the life and the impressions from new scenes; but it is a fact we should well remember that no man can be master of himself who cannot change his thought without first being placed in a change of scenes. We cannot obtain emancipation or realize our highest ideals so long as we are dependent upon things for a change of thought. We must, therefore, proceed to make this change ourselves, independently, regardless of surrounding circumstances or the world in which we live.

If you are compelled to go away to secure a change of mind or feeling, you have practically no control over your own thinking. You think according to what you see or hear, or according to the sensations you receive from physical or mental experiences. The thought of thousands is governed to a great extent by what enters the stomach. What you take into the system produces a certain sensation. This sensation produces an impression upon the mind, as all sensations do; and this impression originates ideas, thoughts and mental states as all impressions do. If these ideas and thoughts are helpful, harmonious and constructive in their nature, you have been benefited. Otherwise, what was taken into the system will prove detrimental. It is a well-known fact that thousands of failures have been traced directly to mental disturbances produced by food that was indigestible; and it is also a well-known fact that thousands of misdeeds, even some of the most serious can be traced to food that was not properly prepared. The culinary art, therefore, is not to be ignored. It holds a position, even in connection with metaphysical and psychological studies, that is among the first. The thought of other thousands is governed by what they read in the daily press, most of which is a detailed account of deeds of darkness. Others form their ideas from their surroundings, what they see or hear at their work, or what they receive from the influence of home and companionship. Still others think what they are told to think by religious authority, and never change until told to do so by that same authority. Illustrations and details could be multiplied indefinitely, but the fact we wish to emphasize is simply this, that the average person does not change his own thought by exercising his own power of independent and original thought. He thinks according to impressions that act upon his mind, and those impressions come from what he sees or hears or conies in contact with in the external world. He is therefore in bondage to things because he is compelled to think according to the impressions that things make upon his mind. A change among the things that surround him produces a change in his thought, and he feels differently. If the change is wholesome, he feels better, and may even be cured of serious ills in this way alone; but if the new scenes do not produce good impressions upon his mind he may, and often does, become sick both in mind and body.

We realize, therefore, the enormous importance of the subject, and no further details are required to prove that it is entitled to one of the first places in this great study. That there can be no improvement in body, mind, intellect, ability or character until there is a certain change of thought is now a well-established fact; and since every new impression that conies upon the mind will, to a degree, change the thought, the art of forming only those impressions upon the mind that are favorable becomes one of the greatest of arts. The mastery of this art means absolute control of one's own thinking, which involves the power to produce any impression desired upon mind, regardless of scenes, sounds or environments, and also the power to prevent anything from the without, coming through the senses, from producing any impression upon our minds if we do not desire such impressions. The object we have in view is the change of thought and the renewal of mind, not through a change in outer things, but through a change of interior perception.

It is well to receive all kinds of good impressions from without, and everybody should mingle as much as possible among different people and environments that are wholesome; but no one should be dependent upon new scenes for a change of thought, or permit any change of thought from any cause whatever, unless that change is individually desired.

If we wish to change our thought along right lines, and improve our thought constantly along all lines, we must be able to form upon mind new impressions and the desired impressions whenever we wish, regardless of where we may be at the time. Every person should be able to entirely renew all lines of thought or sensation without being compelled to change locality or association. He should be able to change his thought, not by going to a different place in the without, but by going to a different field of consciousness in the within. When he can do this, he can think his own thought, and change his own thought just as he likes, whenever he likes. He will be mentally free; and no other freedom can come until we have secured mental freedom. And here we should remember that no one is mentally free until he can think at will whatever he wants to think, regardless of what he may read, hear, see or experience.

There are scores of conditions of bondage in the world at present, and thousands are at work seeking the way of emancipation from each particular condition; but there is no real, permanent freedom from anything until we attain mental freedom. When mental freedom comes, all kinds of bondage will disappear as if they never existed; and the first step to mental freedom is to be able to think your own thought, change your own thought, renew your mind, and form your own ideas, regardless of circumstances, persons or things. Not that we are to become oblivious to the objective, or become utterly indifferent to the world about us. On the contrary, when we attain mental freedom we shall so much the better see all things, hear all things, and be aware of all things; but we will form our own conclusions. We will change when we like, and remain unchanged when we like.

This great attainment is possible to all; and the art is acquired by training the mind to form new impressions through new experiences gained in consciousness. In other words, employ your interior perception in trying to discern the nature of new and inner states. Instead of looking for new places and new scenes in the without, whenever you feel the need of a change, look for new sensations and experiences in your own consciousness. What exists in the within is just as real as that which exists in the without, and it is of more importance to understand. Therefore, by training the mind to take journeys into the beautiful worlds within, you are not only acquiring the art of forming new mental impressions within; you are also enlarging mind and consciousness. You are gaining valuable information about many things that material man knows nothing of; and you are preparing the way for real freedom and much higher development.

The real purpose, however, of these journeys to the within, should be the change of thought, and for that reason should be taken whenever the need of mental change is felt. To begin, realize that the larger life within is the fullness of life, and cannot in any way lack the real essentials of life. Realize that the worlds within are ideal worlds, and are therefore not imperfect in any way. Realize that the new inner states of consciousness that you may discern, contain the unlimited possibilities of absolute existence, and are therefore neither incomplete nor imperfect in any way whatever. Then realize that those inner places are not separated from you, but are necessary parts of your whole being, and also that the I AM, the real you, is at the very center of this whole being; and lastly, realize that whenever you turn your attention upon the potential, the within, the ideal, you are looking upon something that contains within itself all the elements of absolute perfection. To illustrate: When you feel discord, you know that you can obtain peace just as soon as you change your thought to a state of harmony. You know that the very moment an impression of perfect harmony establishes itself in mind, harmony will begin to express itself through your whole system; but how is this impression of harmony to be secured from within? You can secure it from without by listening to soft and gentle music, or by having someone you love minister to your heart and soul; but these good angels are not always at hand. We are usually dependent upon our own efforts, therefore if thought can be changed from a state of confusion to a state of perfect peace, through mental impressions gained from the silent within, we have discovered a great secret. To bring this about, we look to the silent within instead of the help of persons and things; and by looking upon the silent within with the eye of the mind, we are impressed with the thought of peace.

When you look upon a quiet scene in nature through physical sight and become absorbed in that scene, you soon become perfectly still in mind and body. The reason why has been explained above. In like manner, when you look upon the silent within through the mental eye, you soon become perfectly still, in the same way exercising the same law. Likewise, when you look upon any ideal and become deeply impressed with it, an image of that ideal will form upon the mind, and you will begin to think thoughts just like that ideal or perfect image.

It is therefore an easy matter to create thought at will that can give peace, life, joy, health, strength in brief, almost anything you see in the within will impress itself upon your mind, and you will think thoughts that correspond exactly with that impression, thereby producing mental states to be followed by physical conditions that are similar in every respect to the nature of that which you originally saw in the within. But the power to change your own thought by impressions received from the ideal, or the within, is, aside from this, of exceptional value other ways. It is this power that gives us the secret of original thought; and it is original thought that makes man great in mind, character and soul. It is the original thinker who becomes the mental and spiritual giant, and it is from original thought that everything proceeds that has value and worth in the promotion of human growth and welfare. The power to change your own thought in this manner also produces mental freedom, and with mental freedom comes all the necessary states and avenues of consciousness through which we may gain whatever the heart may wish for. When we are mentally free then it is that we can fully employ the wonderful powers that are within us, but until we attain that freedom we are more or less hampered; therefore, to be able to change your own thought, and to renew your own mind at any time through impressions gained from the ideal within, means far more than tongue can ever tell.

Chapter 6

How the Mind Can Produce Health

Every force and element in mind has a tendency to act in a certain way, to move in a certain direction, and to produce certain results. Therefore, when we learn to control the tendencies of the mind we may determine what actions and results are to be. We may also determine whether we are to go forward or backward, towards health or disease, towards weakness or strength, towards bondage or emancipation, towards inferiority or superiority.

When we begin to move in a certain direction, it is not always an easy matter to stop that action; therefore we should direct our movements in the right direction before we begin; and to determine in what direction we desire to move, we must train the mind to produce such tendencies as will tend to cause all actions to move in the direction we desire to go.

When any mental tendency is fully established, the actions of the mind will move naturally and unconsciously in that direction, and will carry out those desires that may be realized through that particular movement. The creative forces of mind obey and follow those tendencies, and always go with those tendencies that have the greatest intensity and the most perfect concentration. Therefore when the tendencies you desire are made strong, and are properly concentrated upon the object you have in view, all the forces of your system will work with those tendencies, thereby making it almost certain that the object in view will be realized.

Whenever you begin to think that you should desire a certain thing, you proceed to form a tendency to create, not

How to Stay Well

only a strong desire in that direction, but also a movement of the mind that will tend to produce the thing desired. At first, this desire can be controlled, but if the tendency continues, the desire may become so strong that it cannot be controlled. We realize, therefore, how important it is to place in action only such desires as we may want, because when a desire gets beyond our control we may be compelled to follow that desire and do many things that we did not in the first place intend.

All mental tendencies are born of desires; and it is possible to create any line of desire that we may wish to develop and realize. This being true, we can form any mental tendency that we may think favorable to the purpose we have in view. Every impression that is formed in the mind has a tendency to multiply itself, because every impression is energy centralized, and creative desire always appears with such centralizations. When the tendency of the impression to reproduce itself is permitted, that impression, however tiny or insignificant at first, may eventually become a powerful mental state so strong that all other states of mind must obey; and as this state of mind is, so will be the man himself. Some people are exact externalizations of a single predominating mental state, while others have formed their personalities and characteristics from a group of mental states; but since every mental state originated in some tiny impression, and every impression may be multiplied and developed by desire, we understand what may become of us when we permit every impression to increase and follow its inherent tendency.

Every large object, physical or metaphysical, has a tendency to draw all smaller objects into its own path, and also to make all things in its atmosphere like itself. This, however, may be more or less modified by counteracting tendencies, which are usually at hand in considerable numbers. In the metaphysical world, the understanding of this law is very important, both in the building of character and in the development of talents. If you have a good character, it means that the strongest tendencies of mind are wholesome, elevating and righteous in nature; while if your character is weak, it means that you have no one elevating tendency strong enough to predominate in the world of conduct. A perverted character is always the result of the ascending tendencies either being absent or too insignificant to exercise any influence; and ascending tendencies are always the results of thoughts, ideas or impressions that are wholesome and constructive; while descending tendencies come from opposite causes.

The weakest as well as the most perverted character may at times perform some noble act, and the finest character may at times do something that is beneath his true worth; but the explanation is simple. In the first case, the weak ascending tendencies were permitted to act without being interfered with by the predominating descending tendencies; while in the second case, the predominating ascending tendencies were suspended for the time being, and descending tendencies were temporarily created, due possibly to impressions formed upon the mind through some strong or overpowering temptation. Such temptations, however, can never exercise their power over the conduct of any individual who naturally has a strong character, provided the ascending tendencies of his mind are always in positive action. The strongest tendencies, however, may at times become negative, and it is at such times that the good man falls and the weak man responds favorably to wholesome influences from without.

In this connection we realize the great importance of having such full control over mind and thought that we can always desire what we want to desire, and always cause our wholesome and ascending tendencies to continue in a constant and positive action. When you think more of the external things of life than of that which is within, you create in consciousness a tendency to dwell on the surface. The result is, you become more or less superficial, and may finally become inferior to what you were in all respects. On the other hand, by thinking a great deal of those things that are lofty and profound, you create in consciousness a tendency to penetrate the deep things of life. The result is that you become conscious of a larger world of thought. You increase your mental capacity, improve decidedly the quality of your mind, and may at times make valuable discoveries. When questionable pictures and suggestions are placed before minds that are not well established in purity, a strong tendency to produce uncontrollable desires may be created in those minds; and if those tendencies are continued and nourished, such desires may become too strong to be controlled; the victims may thus be carried away by them, even at the risk of name and reputation, or life. The mind that thinks a great deal about spotless virtue, and keeps the idea of virtue constantly before it, will soon create such a strong tendency to virtue that all desires and feelings will actually become virtuous. For such a person it will be simplicity itself to continue in virtue and in perfect self-control. When all the elements of your being are actually producing purity, virtue and self-control, you do not have to produce those things, and you do not have to resist or fight desires that may lead in opposite directions, because all your desires have begun to act in harmony with that tendency that is producing spotless virtue in your system. Your energies, therefore, do not create abnormal desires any more, but have instead been trained to create physical force, vital force, energy, personal power and mental brilliancy. When the tendency of the mind is towards real virtue, all the creative energies of the system will become constructive, and will accordingly build up mind, body and personality.

How to Stay Well

The man who is ambitious is daily training all the tendencies of his mind to act upon those faculties that are required to carry out his plans; and as it is the nature of the building forces of the mind to follow the strongest tendencies, those faculties will naturally be developed and perfected to a degree where they can readily carry out the desired ambition. Whenever you positively resolve to accomplish certain things, you will succeed in proportion to your ability, a fact which is easily understood when we know how the tendencies of the mind always act in this connection; but a positive resolution is not a mere spurt. A resolve, to be genuine, must be constant and strong, and must never waver in the strength of its power. The reason why such a resolve must always win, is found in the fact that such a resolve leads to a powerful mental tendency; and a tendency of this kind will draw all the powers and talents of the mind into the line of its action, so that everything that is in use will work for the one thing we are resolved to accomplish or achieve.

When we think a great deal about the refined side of life, we create tendencies that will cause all the forces within us to recreate everything in our systems according to a more refined pattern. Accordingly, it will soon be second nature for us to become more refined, and all those things that have been crude or undeveloped in our nature will gradually disappear.

In the average mind we find the belief that the body naturally decays and grows old, and as this belief is subconscious in nearly everybody, there is in such minds a tendency to produce that very condition of decay. For this reason, that tendency is actually producing decay and old age contrary to the laws of nature, where there would be no such conditions of decay were that tendency absent. Nature renews the physical body every few months, and there is no natural process of decay in the system of anybody. If the physical system decays, that process of decay has been created through the violation of mental or physical laws, and therefore can be removed when that violation is corrected. If there is a process in your system that is making you look older every year, that process is a false one. It was not placed there by nature. You have produced it yourself by perpetuating that tendency towards old age that we have inherited from mistaken race belief. The tendency to become weaker in body and mind as the years go by is also a false one which we have inherited and perpetuated through our own belief in the reality of such inheritance; but it is just as easy to create a tendency to become stronger and more intelligent the longer we live. We are therefore not in bondage to what we have inherited, because we can change everything and bring everything in ourselves into harmony with natural law.

We can also create the tendency to improve personal appearance and personality the longer we remain upon earth, because the tendency to lose the elements and vigor of youth is unnatural; it is a false tendency with which we have been born, and to which we have added life and power. We are born with all these false tendencies, and then we make them stronger through our own tendency to follow the grooves in which we have been placed by unnatural heredity; but, as previously stated, every undesirable inheritance can be removed. Every impression formed in the mind is a seed that will produce some tendency; therefore we should not only remove those impressions that we do not wish to cultivate, but should also prevent inferior and undesired impressions from forming in the mind in the first place.

When we see people growing old or, rather, making themselves older every year, we are impressed by the aging process. We think that process is natural, and therefore permit it to be impressed upon our minds. That impression contains the tendency to produce the same process in us, and as it usually receives our permission to have its way, we also begin to grow older every year, regardless of the fact that nature gives us a new body every few months. In this manner we cause the aging process to become stronger and stronger in us the more we see it in others, until we soon discover that we also are creating for ourselves older bodies. The new bodies that nature gives us this year we change through this false process, so that those bodies look a year older than the bodies we received from nature a year ago.

Thus the habit continues, and we consider the whole thing natural, when it is nothing else but the most ignorant violation of natural law. We think certain things natural and inevitable because we see them everywhere about us, but when we understand nature we discover that we make all the undesirable things in life ourselves, simply because we do not understand the real purpose and the greater possibilities of nature. To change all these things, we must begin to transform all the tendencies of the mind so that every tendency will move the way we want it to move, and produce those conditions in mind and body that we desire.

In the attainment of health and strength, this same law can be applied with decided success. When we think a great deal about health, desire persistently to realize perfect health, and positively expect to gain and maintain perfect health, we create strong mental tendencies that have the power to produce such health; and as all the forces of the system always work with the strongest tendencies, we shall thereby cause all the forces within us, physical and mental, to produce better health, and to build up every part of mind, body and personality. By creating strong mental tendencies towards health, and by increasing the force and determination of those tendencies every day, you train the

How to Stay Well

mind to produce health, and you cause the health-producing tendencies in your system to become so strong that they will completely govern the condition of your system; that is, they have the power to maintain healthful and wholesome conditions under all sorts of circumstances, and accordingly your physical system will become practically immune from all disease. You can in the same way increase your physical strength and endurance so that whatever you may wish to overcome, develop or increase further, you may do so by creating the necessary tendencies in those directions. In the training of the mind to produce the tendencies we desire, the first thing to do is to find in what direction we are moving mentally; and to discover this we must not simply examine our objective aims or intentions, but try to find where the real self is going; is it moving towards sin, sickness and decay, or towards character, health, youth, freedom and power; is it moving towards weakness and inferiority, or towards strength, wisdom, attainment, and abundance? Look at yourself closely and examine every mental tendency so that you may find in what direction the majority of them, and the strongest of them, are moving. Thus you will realize your present position, and may proceed intelligently to change your life and yourself according to your highest ideals.

When we discover the tendencies of our minds, we shall know what our future is to be, provided those tendencies are permitted to continue their present lines of action. We shall at the same time realize that our present physical conditions, our present strength, our present ability, our present character, our present attainment and our present achievements, are all the results of the way our mental tendencies have been moving up to the present moment. The way we have lived, thought and acted during the past, we shall find, has been determined by those same tendencies; and when we know these things, we shall know with a certainty how we may gain freedom and reach the goal we have in view. When we understand exactly the law that has produced everything in us thus far, we can, by using that law more intelligently proceed to create better and greater things for the future. What we are creating, what we are building, what we are developing these things depend upon how the tendencies of the mind are directed; and if we wish to create our own destiny, we must take positive hold of all those tendencies and cause them to move in a manner that will result in these better conditions that we have in view. The first thing to do is to determine where you wish to go, mentally speaking, and what you wish to accomplish and realize. Know what you want, and what you want to be. Then examine the tendencies of your mind with a view of finding how many of those tendencies are at present moving in the right direction. Those that are not moving towards the goal you have in view must be changed; and those that are already moving towards that goal should be given added power. Then proceed to carry out your new purpose under the full control of your own consciousness of self-mastery. Do not waver for a moment; never look back; let nothing disturb your plans; and keep your aspirations too Sacred to be mentioned. You will find that you will steadily and surely move directly where you wish to go. You will achieve more and more what you have planned, and your destiny will gradually take shape and form as you have desired.

Chapter 7

How To Maintain Perfect Health

There is intelligence in every atom in your body; every organ in your physical system is governed by a mind of its own, and this mind has the power to produce any change in its own organ, within the sphere of natural law that you may direct. To place yourself in such close connection with the intelligence in your body that you can readily direct it as you may desire, train yourself to think of every organ, every muscle, every nerve, every cell in your body, as possessing intelligence. Then speak the truth to this intelligence. When you are giving a metaphysical treatment to any organ, do not think of the physical organ, but address yourself to the intelligence that is in that organ. Tell this intelligence that it has the power to keep its own organ well, and that you expect it to do so. The response will be immediate, and the results you desire will, in nearly every instance, be secured instantaneously.

Do not think of your body as dead matter, but as living substance, and mentally speak to every atom in your system accordingly. When you think of your body as mere matter, you separate, to a degree, the life of your mind from the life of your body; in consequence, your mind and body do not work in harmony; the body fails to respond to the direction of the mind, and you frequently feel as if the body were a burden instead of a perfectly tuned instrument, as it is intended to be. But when you think of every atom in your system as possessing intelligence, you place mind and body in perfect harmony; and as your conscious realization of this intelligence in every atom develops, your body will respond perfectly to almost anything your mind may direct.

How to Stay Well

When there is something wrong in any organ in your body, begin at once to give instructions to the intelligence that is in that organ. Speak the truth to that intelligence; give it good, strong, positive suggestions, and proceed in the faith that this intelligence can carry out your suggestions. It is perfectly in accord with exact science to speak to this intelligence as you would to any conscious mind. Science has positively demonstrated that there IS intelligence in every atom; also, that this intelligence will respond to the directions of the human mind, and carry out any instructions that may be given by that mind. You are therefore acting upon sound principles when you proceed to educate the intelligence in every organ in your body as you would educate your own children.

To speak the truth to the intelligence of any organ is not to call its attention to the presence of sickness, weakness or inharmony, but to tell this intelligence what it has the power to do. Use words to this effect: "You know that you have the power to keep your own organ well; you can so govern your organ that it will perform its function perfectly; you know that you can do this; I expect you to do it, and I know that you will carry out my wishes to the letter; you are a part of universal intelligence; you are a perfect expression of infinite intelligence; and infinite intelligence is always well; therefore you are, in yourself, always well; you know perfect health; you have within yourself the power of perfect health; accordingly, you can produce perfect health; you can produce perfect health in your own organ now; and I know that you will; I have perfect faith in you; I know what you can do, and I know that you want to do everything that you can do; this means that you will produce perfect health in your own organ at once; I leave the rest to you, knowing that you will be perfectly true to your trust."

How to Stay Well

Whenever you think of any organ in your body, think of the intelligence within that organ, and always give it the best instructions you can think of. You thus not only arouse the mind of every atom to greater effort, but you also train this mind to work in harmony with your purpose. The minds of all the atoms in your body will thus become a well-drilled army an army of workers, working with you for better health, for more harmony, for greater strength, for higher attainments in brief, for everything that you wish to realize to make your dreams of the ideal come true.

To retain perfect health, one of the great essentials is to cause all the organs of your system to perform their functions perfectly, and this the intelligence of these organs can readily do if so directed. Think of your stomach as an organ of intelligence, and say to this intelligent organ that you expect a perfect digestion at all times. Speak firmly, but in love, as you would to a trusted servant, and speak in the tone you would employ when you fully expect your wishes to be carried out. Eliminate all doubt from those instructions and give a deep ring of supreme faith to the silent tone of your mental speech. Encourage your stomach to do its best, as you would encourage a horse or a child or some other intelligent being that is under your direction. Intelligent encouragement, to whomsoever given, always increases results, and especially so when your words have a positive ring of confidence, trust and faith.

Speak to your eyes as if they were intelligent beings, and tell them that they can see perfectly; speak to your ears as if they were intelligent beings, and tell them that they can hear perfectly; speak to your heart as if it were an intelligent being, and tell it that it can perform its function calmly, harmoniously and perfectly, and that it can give a full circulation to every cell in your body without any exertion whatever. Speak to your nerves as if they were intelligent beings, and tell them that they have the power to be always serene, well poised, in perfect harmony, and in the highest state of efficiency. Speak to all the organs in your body as if they were intelligent beings, and tell them that they can do their work right; encourage them all to do their best; tell them that you expect to get the best from them all and that you know that you will get it. Look upon all the organs in your body as constituting one great family, all working together in perfect harmony; take them into your confidence; tell them what you wish to accomplish; tell them that you need their help their very best help in all your undertakings, and that you know they will respond as one man. Speak to all the organs in your body as if they were intelligent beings, and know that they all are intelligent beings.

Every atom is intelligent, and every organ is a being of intelligence; it should therefore be treated as such and spoken to as such. Do not think of the organs in your body as so many physical organs, but as so many minds, because that is what they really are. The idealist is right, though he does not always make himself clear. Reduce anything to its last analysis, and you will find it to be MIND. Even iron, when reduced to its last analysis, becomes a MENTAL FORCE in nature; and many scientists believe if they could reduce still further they would find it to be absolute spirit. What we speak of as matter is simply mind vibrating in the scale of tangibility. Matter does exist, but it does not exist apart from mind. Matter is mind in tangible expression. It is therefore strictly scientific to think of the body as visible mind, and to think of all the organs in the body as being centers of intelligence. And we shall find that when we take this view of the body, the physical system will no longer be a chunk of clay, but will become a more and more highly organized instrument, responding perfectly to every desire of the ruling mind the conscious mind, the "I AM" in man.

How to Stay Well

When the body responds perfectly to the mind, the body will be perfectly well as long as thinking is wholesome; and the stronger the mind becomes the stronger will the body become. To keep the mind wholesome at all times, however, is not difficult; nor is it difficult to perpetually increase the strength of the mind. These are things anyone can do; therefore, anyone can stay well, and continue to grow into more and more life and power for an indefinite period. Know that there is no dead matter to deal with in your body; know that every cell in your body is living intelligence, and that this intelligence will readily comply with your desires for better health, greater strength and higher efficiency. It is only necessary to think of this intelligence as actually being intelligence, and then to give your instructions in the faith that everyone of them will be carried out to the letter.

Have faith in your body. Expect your body to be well at all times, and make the power of this expectation so deep and so strong that it enters into the very life of every atom in your system. What you constantly expect your body to become, you give it the power to become; in brief, by constantly expecting certain results you awaken and develop the power that can produce those results. There is nothing that will help you so much to prevent all sickness as to constantly and subconsciously expect your body to be well at all times. Dwell on this expectation as much as possible, and make it a permanent part of your conscious existence.

Expect every organ in your body to perform its function perfectly; do not expect anything to the contrary, nor even think for a moment that anything to the contrary could happen. Impress this expectation upon the intelligence of every organ in your body, and expect that intelligence to carry out your wishes. Expect your physical strength to hold out under every circumstance; never expect to feel weak or tired at any time; expect your strength to increase

How to Stay Well

perpetually, and make that expectation a living power in every thought you think. Expect your body to stay well, to stay strong, to stay young, and to continue in health, youth and vigor as long as you live. Expect your eyes to have perfect sight as long as you live; never expect to have to wear glasses; do not think of such a thing for a moment. What you always expect, you get; therefore expect only what you want. Expect your ears to hear perfectly as long as you live; expect your lungs to be sound as long as you live; expect your liver to be thoroughly alive as long as you live. Expect your stomach to digest anything. (But give your stomach nothing but that which is wholesome.) Eat moderately; eat anything you like, so it is wholesome, nourishing and properly prepared. Then expect to digest anything. You will never know that you have a stomach, so perfect and thorough will your digestion become.

Expect your physical endurance to be equal to any occasion, and expect to stand anything. Never say that you can't stand "this" or "that"; say that you can stand anything, and expect your system to "make good." But in all things use moderation. Be ready for anything; expect to be equal to any extreme that may be met, and do not hesitate to comply with any demand that emergency may call forth; however, in the ruling of your own life, let moderation be your keynote in all things. Whatever you may do or partake of, aim to secure or bring forth the best, and just enough of the best; no more and no less than enough; and let your idea of "enough" correspond with actual need properly harmonized with actual capacity. In the actual, all increase should be gradual, but in your thought, expect everything now.

Think well of your body, no matter what its present conditions may be. Speak well of your body and compliment your body at every opportunity. Never say that your stomach is "no account." One of these days it will make your evil words come true. Thousands of people die every year because they have condemned, vilified and slandered their body this beautiful temple of the soul. But it is just as easy, to speak well of the body, and there is nothing that pays better. Praise your body and every organ in your body, and you will add many, many years to your personal life, while your days of sickness will be reduced to almost nothing.

Say that your stomach is all right; not only once, but any number of times, and mean it; your stomach will appreciate the compliment by making a special effort to be all right. Speak of every organ in the body in the same way, and they will do their very best to "make good." Say that you have the best eyes in the world, the best lungs in the world, the best digestive system in the world. Say it to yourself and mean it; say it to others when you are approached as to your good health. If people think you are only "talking," never mind; continue to praise your body and it will positively prove worthy of more and more praise; continue to stand by all the organs in your system, and they will continue to stand by you.

Never say that your lungs are weak, that your heart is bad, that your nerves are all shattered, or that your system is not much good any more. Refuse to use such talk and refuse to listen to such talk; it is better to lose a friend than to lose your respect for your whole physical system. Friends that are worth keeping will think far more of you if you positively and uncompromisingly stand up for everything that is wholesome in thought and speech.

We are now in a new age; it is no longer good form to find fault with anything. To look for the best in everything, and to emphasize the virtues of that "best" in all thought and speech is becoming the "correct thing" among a rapidly increasing number; you may therefore adopt the new method without any danger of isolation, no matter where you may go in the world.

Do not underrate any organ or faculty in your possession; believe thoroughly in every fiber in your being; to underrate is to weaken, and weakness leads to disease. To think of an organ as inferior or unimportant is to decrease the life and the working capacity of that organ; and to continue to expect an organ to fail, or fall short of its functions, is to depress the life of that organ so that it actually becomes crippled in everything that it may be called upon to do. On the other hand, to continue perpetually to expect an organ to do its best, and to believe that it can do better, is to awaken more and more life in that organ. Accordingly, there will be a continual increase of strength; and more strength leads to better health invariably. To habitually underrate your body is to decrease your strength and shorten your years; but to praise your body, encourage your body, and expect more and more of your body, is to increase your strength and lengthen your years. Think of your entire system as being fully competent to comply with every requirement that you may meet in life; think so well of your body that you expect it to be more than equal to every demand; then make that thought a living power during every moment of your existence; in consequence, your body will serve you better and better; it will develop in health, strength and vigor, and will daily come up, nearer and nearer, to your highest expectations.

Chapter 8

The Real Man is Always Well

The real man is the soul or the' individuality the "I AM"; and that part of man is always perfectly well; in fact, cannot possibly be otherwise than well, a statement that can be demonstrated to the scientifically exact. To know that this is true, and to know that you yourself are the real man that something in human nature that is always perfectly well, is to know the truth the truth that makes man free.

To the beginner in metaphysics and psychology the statement that the real man is well may appear to be without foundation, but it is a statement that can be readily demonstrated in a number of ways. It can be demonstrated by pure reason, psychological research, finer personal experience, the evidence of higher states of consciousness, and several other effective methods. Besides, it is a truth that has been proclaimed in every age by the highest and best minds that the race has produced.

The recognized foundation of this idea is found in the great truth that the real man, the spiritual man, the soul, the individuality, the "I AM," is created in the likeness of the Infinite; and as the Infinite of necessity always is well, the real man, created in the Divine Likeness, must also be well. Those, however, who do not accept the statement that man is created in the image of God, and who claim that we have no scientific evidence for the belief that the human individuality is always well, are requested to examine carefully that something in man that we speak of as the conscious "I AM." If the conscious "I AM" were ever sick the very principle of human individuality would cease to be a principle, and, therefore, could not continue to maintain individuality. In other words, if that principle were sick, it would be out of harmony with natural law, and, therefore, would necessarily cease to be that factor that governs, controls and maintains conscious existence in man. Accordingly the human entity would literally go to pieces and all the elements and the forces of the human system would be in chaos. The fact, however, that individuality persists in sickness as well as in health proves that the individuality itself is always well, must necessarily be always well.

We can take man as we find him in the ordinary, visible, tangible sense, and, by examining him carefully according to the ordinary recognized scientific method, demonstrate conclusively that the foundation of his being, the soul, the real man, the conscious "I AM," is and must be always well. In the first place, we will examine a person who enjoys perfect health and try to find why he enjoys perfect health. We shall find that he enjoys perfect health because all the faculties of his being are performing their functions properly; but why do they perform their functions properly under the circumstances? Evidently because they are acting according to natural law. But what is a law, and where do laws come from? Laws are inherent in man, and the power to properly obey and comply with those laws is also inherent in man. Man is created with all the laws necessary to his welfare and growth. These laws are at the foundation of his being and constitute in themselves a state of absolute order; and what is health but a state of absolute order? We understand, therefore, that the cause of health is inherent in man, and, therefore, that something in man which contains the cause of health must necessarily always have perfect health.

We will now examine a person who is not enjoying perfect health and try to discover why he is not well. We shall find that he is not physically well because certain parts of his system are not performing their functions in harmony with natural law; but when we bring his system back into harmony with those laws, order is restored and perfect health regained.

We conclude, therefore, that there are two states of being in man. The one is produced by virtue of natural law being inherent in man, and by virtue of the fact that that state itself must necessarily continue in perpetual harmony with natural law. The other state is produced whenever any of the laws of nature are violated. The first we call a state of perfect health, and it must of necessity be permanent, because a state that is produced by changeless law cannot come and go; it must always continue and always be what it naturally is. There is, therefore, within man a permanent state of health, and it is readily seen that that state pertains to what is called the real man, the real you or the self-conscious individuality.

When we study this idea further we find that fundamental existence is based upon certain laws. That existence is what it is, because certain laws are grouped together in a distinct and definite form of action, and this action must necessarily be changeless. If it were not changeless, the individual would not be himself all the time; part of the time he would be someone else. But through individuality, as we all know, he continues uninterruptedly to be himself. We conclude, therefore, that those laws that work together to produce the individual, or, in other words, those laws that are used by the individual in maintaining continued individuality, must always continue in the same mode of action. That this mode of action always continues in a state of perpetual health is evident, because, to perpetuate the same individuality, that particular mode of action would have to act in harmony with the basic laws of life, and anything that continues to act in harmony with those laws will always be well.

We, therefore, conclude that fundamental existence is always in a state of health; and since the real man is the man that exists by virtue of fundamental existence, we also conclude that the real man is always in a state of perfect health.

Those who reason clearly will understand from the above that we speak the perfect truth when we declare that the real man is well. There are, however, a score of other lines of reason through which the same truth can be demonstrated if it were necessary. The most convincing evidence, however, on any subject is always that of personal experience, and we shall find that personal experience in connection with the subject under consideration, will demonstrate exactly that the real man is well.

To gain a better understanding of this part of the subject it is highly important to understand the real nature of the soul. When speaking of the soul we usually refer to it as something we possess instead of that something which actually is the possessor. We generally say "I have a soul" though the correct statement is "I AM a soul." The cause of this mistake is found in the fact that the ordinary person is only conscious of the surface. To him the outer man is the only real man, because he is not conscious of the deeper and more permanent principles of his being. He, therefore, thinks of the objective person as the true self and refers to what is distinct from the person, as something that is possessed by the person; but when the mind begins to expand, and consciousness becomes aware of the deeper and finer things in life, the discovery is made that the outer mind is not the basic mind, and that the person is not the real self. The first discovery that is made through this mental growth is, that there is a subconscious mind, and if no further step is taken the conclusion is formed that the subconscious is the soul. There are many scientific minds today who have discovered the subconscious and believe they have found the soul, but they are mistaken. The subconscious is only the inner side of the personal mind and is, therefore, not any more a part of the soul than the outer mind. To find the soul, therefore, we must go beyond the subconscious into that state of consciousness that deals exclusively with the real, the permanent, the perfect and the absolute.

When you discover the soul, as you will through the cultivation of the finer states of thought and consciousness, states that are created in the likeness of the absolutely real, you will no longer say that you have a soul. You will then find that you yourself are the soul, and that the soul constitutes the sum-total of all the principles of individualized and permanent self-conscious being. When you make this discovery you will no longer have to depend upon reason, logic, or the statements of others to prove that the real man is well. Your own consciousness will constantly reveal the fact to you, and you will know that the real man is well, just as clearly as you know that you exist. In fact, existence and wholeness will then become inseparable states. To be, and to be well, will become as one in your thought.

You will then have discovered through actual conscious experience that individual existence is impossible without perpetual health, and also that that part of you which is life must therefore be perfectly well at all times. As you grow in the consciousness of your own individual "I AM," this truth will become clearer and clearer, until finally every thought you think will be actually permeated with the realization that the real man is well, and that you are the real man.

Whether you are conscious or not of the fact that you are the soul, and that the soul or the real man is well, you can easily reason the matter out. Pure reason will convince you that there is something in man that is always well; and when you examine that something, you will find it to be your own individuality the self-conscious "I AM" the real you.

The statement "As a man thinketh so is he" does not refer to the soul or to the self-conscious individuality. It refers solely to the personal man. The real man is created in the image of the Supreme, and is above thought, therefore cannot be changed by thought. The real man is the thinker, the creator of thought, and that which creates thought can neither be influenced nor changed by thought. The personal man, however, being an expression of thought, can be changed or modified by thought in any way or at any time; though it is evident that all those changes and modifications can only take place within a certain sphere of action, and must take place through the laws that govern the real man in our present state of existence.

The different functions of the personal man are the products of race development, and race development is the product of change in thought, subconscious as well as conscious; therefore, every function in the human body is the result of ages of thought along a certain line. This can be readily demonstrated, and a complete exposition of this law would clear up a thousand mysteries. What the different functions of the personal man are to do, and how, are also matters that are determined by the lines of thought continued for long periods of time. When certain habits of life or actions change, certain organs and faculties change their functions altogether; and it is changes of thought that produce changes in habits and actions.

When we come to the chemical life of the system we find that every mental state produces a certain chemical effect upon the body. When the mental state under consideration is weak, no susceptible change may occur, but when that state is strong and deeply felt, a decided chemical effect will positively take place. You may partake of the most wholesome food that can be prepared and yet turn the entire contents of the stomach at the time into poisonous elements simply by an intense fit of anger; and it is a well known fact, a fact that has been proven by scientific experiments, that worry and mental depression during meal time can cause the most digestible food to become wholly indigestible. To be afraid to eat certain things has a tendency to cause those very foods to become indigestible and injurious to the system in case they should be taken. On the other hand, it has been proven that a cheerful, joyous mind entertained at meal time can change indigestible food into elements that the system can digest and assimilate with perfect ease. In fact, psychological experiments along this line have forced the conclusion that the mind can do almost anything with anything that is taken into the system; and also that the fear of any particular condition or effect will tend to produce that condition or effect.

The fear of any disease will tend to produce that disease in a measure; if not physically, then mentally. Entertaining fear of smallpox has been known to develop smallpox germs in a body that was thoroughly pure, healthful and wholesome, when there were no such germs in the vicinity. Other contagious diseases have been produced in the same way, proving that the actions of the mind can and do effect the chemical life of the body. To expect health and to believe with a full faith that you are becoming well can, and in thousands of instances has, produced perfect health in cases that all physicians had given up. These are interesting facts, facts that are being demonstrated every day, and that every person can demonstrate through his own personal experience.

The better we understand mind and body the more clearly we understand that every condition in the body is the result of certain continued lines of thought, personal thought or race thought; but since each person can think his own thought, the race thought continues because it is not eliminated through the person's own original thought.

The effect of nature's elements and forces upon the human body depends largely upon the state of mind at the time. In a certain state of mind a draft of fresh air will produce a cold, while in another state no ill effects whatever will follow that particular cause.

But it is not only in the physical personality that these facts are noted. It can also be demonstrated that character is the direct result of certain lines of thought; and therefore character can be changed completely by producing a change of thought and mental action. In recent years it has been discovered that anyone can increase his ability through the scientific application of mind and thought to his various talents and faculties; and that even rare genius may be developed in the same way is now accepted as strictly scientific.

The fact that character, mental capacity as well as the personal man, is the result of the way the individual thinks, the understanding of how to think and what to think becomes exceedingly important. What we think about anything depends upon understanding what we have of that particular thing. Therefore, to think correctly we must not only understand things; we must understand the process of thought. The principal cause of wrong thinking in this age is found in the ignorance of the nature of thought itself. We may understand things in a general way, but we do not always understand thought or the effect that thought can produce upon things. The scientist may think correctly about every element in the universe, according to apparent facts, and yet be thinking detrimental thought a large part of the time; that is, he might be giving the same creative power of thought to the negatives in life as he does to the positives. The negatives and positives both exist and they have certain natures of their own. We should understand these natures and think correctly about them at all times, for whenever we think about anything, we employ mental creative energy and thereby tend to create in our own minds a likeness of the things which we think about. For this reason the average person generally produces just as many weak qualities as strong ones. He permits his mind to create the weak as well as the strong.

There are metaphysicians who declare that it is wrong to even admit the existence of evil, that it is wrong thought to believe that evil has existence but this attitude, though seemingly helpful, is, nevertheless, detrimental. There are evils in the world, there are empty places in the world, and there are weak negative places all about us. To deny that they are here would be to delude ourselves, and delusion cannot give the perfect freedom. It is not wrong to admit that evil exists and you will not necessarily create detrimental thought through such an admission; but it is wrong to permit your mind to create thought that is just like those evil or weak conditions that you have recognized. You can admit the existence of a thing without producing a picture of that particular thing in your own mind. If you have perfect control over your creative energies you can recognize the existence of all the negatives and, wrongs in life and not produce a single one of them in your own mind, character or personality. Right thinking consists in creative thought that is patterned after the good qualities of life. Wrong thinking consists in creating thought that is patterned after the perverted conditions in life. All creation of thought is in the subconscious, therefore you can think objectively as much as you like about the ills and wrongs of life; you will not reproduce those conditions in yourself if there is no subconscious action at the time. In other words, what you think about or recognize will not be created in yourself, unless you permit your ideas or beliefs of those things to sink into your subconscious mind; and this you can prevent by refusing to give deep feeling to those ideas that you do not wish reproduced in yourself. Only those ideas or mental states that have deep feeling can enter the subconscious. This is a fact that is extremely important and should be observed most rigidly in every mental process.

From this law we learn that our thought is the result, not only of our understanding of things, but of our understanding of thought itself and its effect upon things. When we understand thought and the creative process of thought we learn to create only right thought, without having to deny the existence of anything that may exist. When we understand the effect of thought upon things we will know what thought to think under all sorts of circumstances and conditions, and thus produce the very effects we desire.

The personal man, all told, is the exact likeness of the sum-total of all our ideas, thoughts, beliefs, mental attitudes, mental states, our understanding of things, and our entire mental world. Our mental world is the exact likeness of our understanding, defining the term in the largest and broadest sense; and our understanding in itself, or in its real nature, is like the thing understood; in other words, when we understand a particular thing we reproduce in the mind all those elements that constitute the nature of that particular thing.

Therefore, since the real man is well, to understand or to be conscious of the real man, is to produce perfect health in the personal man. This is a fact that will be clearly understood when we remember the law, that whatever we become conscious of we will express in the personality. When we understand any particular thing we become conscious of its qualities, and, according to the law just mentioned, we will express those qualities in our own nature. When we understand the real man we become conscious of the qualities of perfect health, because the real man is always well, and, therefore, we will naturally express perfect health in our own personal system. It is a well-known fact that the most stubborn disease will vanish immediately when consciousness fully realizes the great fact that the real man is always well; and it is being demonstrated more and more that those who live habitually in the realization of the fact that the real man is always well are always in good personal health. We should also realize in this connection that that attitude of mind that constantly recognizes the perfect wholeness of the human being is an unfailing preventive of all kinds of human ills.

As previously stated, thought can do practically anything to the body or its conditions; and what the thought is to do will depend upon what it is in itself; therefore, a thought that is created in the likeness of health will be healthful and will convey health to the system, and when all thoughts are healthful the entire person will be made perfectly well, because every condition in the physical body is determined by the sum-total of our thoughts and mental states. When your mind is filled with the conviction that the real man is well, and that you yourself are the real man, every thought will be thoroughly wholesome, elevating and upbuilding; and conditions of health, strength and wholeness must invariably come to the entire person. There is no darkness where there is light, and there can be no unhealthful thought in the mind that moves and lives in the full conscious realization of absolute health. Every thought is patterned after some impression; therefore, if all the impressions of mind convey the idea of perfect health of real being, every thought we think will be a power for health, and will give only health to the system.

Here we should remember that every thought is a vibration and that it sends its silent thrill throughout the entire system. Every thought you think will in this way impress every atom of your being with itself and with its own life and power, and will therefore carry its life and power to the minutest cell. It is therefore clearly evident that when we live and think in the understanding of the real man we will think only health producing thought, and thus produce complete and absolute health in every part of mind, body and personality.

Chapter 9

Realizing the Perfect Health Within

From whatever point of view we may approach the subject, from that of pure reason, from that of experience, or from that of higher consciousness, we must conclude that there is something in man that is always well. Whatever may happen, this something will positively never get sick; and the reason is that this something contains the principle of absolute health. Principles never change; therefore, the principle of health being health, will never be anything else but health, and nothing can cause it to change from its perfect and original state. This principle of health permeates every atom in the being of man, and so long as everything in the human system acts in perfect harmony with this principle, there will be perfect health throughout the being of man.

The secret of perfect health is to train the elements and forces of the system to act in harmony with the principle of health, and this training may be promoted by growing into the consciousness of the real nature of the principle of health. The elements and forces of the human system are governed by the actions of the subconscious; therefore to train these elements to act in harmony with the principle of health the mind must steadily grow into a subconscious realization of health. Whatever is deeply realized in the mind will become an active force in the subconscious, and this force will express itself through the elements and forces of the body, reproducing its own nature in the body. When the mind grows in the realization of health, the force of health will become active in the subconscious, and conditions of health will in consequence be produced in every part of the body. To cause the mind to grow into the realization of health the principle of continuous advancement should be applied in the attainment of health; that is, the mind should advance constantly in the conscious realization of the real nature of the principle of absolute health.

Conscious advancement into the realization of absolute health will eliminate every form of disease, because to advance into health is to enter more perfectly into the nature, the conditions and the domains of health. To enter into health is to be IN health, and there can be no disease in the human system when every part of the system is IN health. Every part of the system will be in health when all of the elements and the forces of the system act in perfect harmony with the principle of health; and these will act in harmony with that principle when the subconscious is permeated with the realization of health. To establish more and more perfectly in the subconscious the realization of health, the mind must continue to grow into the consciousness of absolute health. This growth in health must be continuous, for to live is to live more, and the more life lives, the greater will necessarily be the capacity of the health required.

To retain perfect health it is absolutely necessary to grow steadily into the conscious possession of more and more health. Continuous advancement is the purpose of life, and everything, to be in harmony with life, must advance in like manner. To promote continuous and conscious advancement into the realization of health, attention should be concentrated frequently upon the inner world of health, harmony, and wholeness, or the principle of absolute health. We grow into the conscious realization and possession of those states, conditions or qualities that we think of the most; that is, when such thinking has feeling and depth. It is therefore evident that by keeping your mental eye single upon the inner principle of perfect health, the mind will steadily grow into perfect health, and thus gain conscious possession of that perfect health. When the mind gains conscious possession of health the subconscious life of the system becomes thoroughly healthful, and as is the subconscious life of the system, so is also the system itself.

When attention is being concentrated upon the inner principle of health, the mind should deeply feel that this principle permeates every atom in one's being, because this feeling of health in every part of the system will impress the subconscious with the life of health; and when the life of perfect health becomes active in the subconscious no form of disease can exist anymore in the human system.

Whatever you become conscious of, that you will manifest or express throughout your mental or physical system. In other words, whatever is involved in consciousness will be evolved through the personality. This is one of the greatest of all metaphysical laws, because it places the entire personality in the hands of individual consciousness. Through this law we can bring forth any quality or condition desired by simply becoming conscious of its interior or potential existence. What consciousness perceives the mind creates, and what the mind creates will be expressed in every part of the human personality. The present conditions of the body, be they health or disease, harmony or discord, strength or weakness, are the results of the recent thought of the individual, with possibly a few exceptions in some instances; while the character is the result of all that the individual has thought and all that he may have inherited from the race. The same is true of talents, tendencies and desires. The entire personality, including character and mentality, is but an effect of what the mind has been creating up to the present moment; and what the conditions of the personality are to be in the future will be determined by what new creations the mind may produce. When new creations come forth from the mind the old ones disappear. For this reason it is possible to largely modify physical appearance and change bodily conditions, mental tendencies and desires, while the character can in most instances be transformed absolutely.

In all our efforts to produce any desired change in ourselves, physically or mentally, we should always remember the law that whatever we become conscious of, that we will express through ourselves; and what we express, gradually becomes a part of ourselves. Whatever you constantly see in the great within, the vast field of consciousness that the mind will create and express in the personality. This is a law that never fails. Whatever you continue to see yourself become that you will gradually and surely become, and no obstacle in the world can prevent it.

The mind is constantly creating. It cannot cease to create so long as life continues. To live is to think. All thinking is creative in some sense or form, and all that the mind creates will come forth sooner or later unless it is recreated before expression takes place. Personally you become what you mentally create, provided your creations are completed and permitted to come forth undisturbed; and the secret in this connection is to keep the eye of consciousness single upon the ideal which you realize, create and express, and continue to keep it there until you get what you want, no matter how many obstacles will come in your way. If you continue thus you will positively succeed.

What you continue to see in the within becomes a mental image. All such images act as models for thinking, and the mind will create thoughts, states, conditions and actions that correspond exactly with those images. Every idea that comes into the mind becomes an image, and while it lasts millions of mental creations may be formed in the likeness of this idea. All these creations will appear in the person unless they are recreated before expression takes place. We therefore understand why it is so extremely important to have the right idea about everything and why our ideals should be kept before mind constantly.

The more deeply an idea or belief is impressed upon consciousness, that is, the more thoroughly it is felt, the longer it remains as a model for the mental creative processes. Consequently, the more thoughts will be reproduced in its likeness, and the greater will be its effect upon the person. This is the reason why the life of a person is ruled by his predominant ideas, and why the person who has simply a few small ideas becomes narrow, one-sided, fanatical, and finally superficial. Whatever you continue to feel deeply in the within, that will positively come true in the without, for what is inwardly felt in consciousness will, according to law, be created and expressed. To become conscious of truth is to deeply feel the very soul of truth, and consequently to express only true states and conditions in the personality. When you become conscious of truth you establish a true state of affairs throughout your entire system. Everything will be right and well and all the functions of your being will work together for your highest welfare. The remarkable changes for the better that have taken place in the lives of those who have entered, even to a slight degree, the conscious realization of truth are due wholly to this fact.

To become conscious of health is to feel the existence of health in the within, to realize that there is a source of unbounded health in the inner life, and to come into perfect touch with this source. Every effect must have a cause, and, since health is expressed more or less in every person, it must, like other expressions, come from some source. Health does not come to some by mere accident and depart from

How to Stay Well

others in the same way. Health comes through a definite law and departs through the violation of that law.

The universe is based upon law. Everything that appears, appears through law. It has a definite source and there are definite methods through which various degrees of expression may be secured. The leading minds of every age, those minds that have understood the inner principles of real life, have been aware of the great truth that there is an abundance of health in the interior life of every personal being; that there is actually a fountain of unbounded life and wholeness in the soul of every man; and that by placing the mind in perfect touch with this inner source of health an abundance of health will constantly flow into the personality.

To place the mind in more perfect touch with the inner source of health we must become conscious of this interior health; that is, we must deeply feel the perfect health that is within us the health and wholeness that permeates every atom in existence.

The consciousness of health is attained by keeping the mental eye single upon the real life of the soul. Know that the soul is the very essence of health, that it not only contains health, but that it is health. The soul is health and wholeness. The soul is power and purity. The soul is love and wisdom. The soul is everything that is in the supreme. Turn consciousness, mind, thought and attention upon the perfect health of the soul and enter more deeply, and ever more deeply, into the spirit of this perfect health. Gradually you will feel more and more keenly the real life and power of this absolute health, and what you feel will be expressed through every fiber of your being. Think only about the perfect health that is within you. Refuse absolutely to talk about disease or to think about disease. Keep the mental eye single upon the wholeness of the spirit in which you live and move and have your being, and realize that this same wholeness is in you. Before long you will know that it is. Then you will feel it and express it with so much power that all disease must vanish from your system like darkness before a strong light.

Consciousness develops naturally and steadily along those lines to which we give the greatest amount of thought and attention. Therefore, by thinking constantly about the perfect health and the unbounded health that is within us, we shall soon feel and become conscious of that health; and what we consciously feel, that we shall invariably express through every fiber of our being.

The real life of everything is in a state of health. Everything is in a healthful condition when in a normal condition, and the inner cause of the normal always is normal. In other words, the law that produces normal conditions must always be normal. It must be changeless, as all other laws in nature, and the principle from which health proceeds must always be in perfect health. We, therefore, conclude once more that there is a state within us that is always well, and that there is a law in the human system that is always ready to produce health if applied.

No matter how much sickness or weakness may appear in the body or in the outer mind, there is a state in the deeper life within that is always well and strong. The fountain of health and life and power is always in action in the great within. The inner source of health and strength is constantly giving health and strength to every part of mind and body, and sickness or weakness can begin only when the force of health and strength is misdirected or wasted. The inner source of health is constantly producing health throughout the system; therefore, if the force of health were never misused or wasted the entire system would always be in health. To prevent the misdirection of the force of health the mind should live constantly in the realization of the inner source of perfect health.

To be conscious of real health is to express real health, and if this consciousness is perpetual, the expression of health in every part of the system will be perpetual. To produce this realization, all thinking should be trained to work in perfect touch with this inner state that is always well, and the mind should always live so near to this state that it should constantly be aware of its existence. When the body is in a condition of ill health the first step towards healing is to recognize the existence of that absolute state within that is always well. The second step is to impress upon every thought the fact that this state does exist, and that it has its being in every atom throughout your entire system.

To continue to impress upon the mind the fact that the entire system is now, and always, filled through and through with a state that is well, always well, is to develop the realization of health; and as this realization is developed the force of health will begin to express itself in every part of mind and body. When the mind gains a full realization of this state of health you will feel that you are in health, and when you are in health you are well, absolutely well, through and through. When you are in the realization of health every thought that you think and every word that you speak will also be in that same realization. Such words and thoughts will be permeated with the life of health and will consequently have healing on their wings.

Every thought that is formed in the mind while the mind feels the state of absolute health will be a health producing thought. It will be as natural for such thought to produce health, wherever it may go in the system, as it is for fire to produce heat, or for a sunbeam to produce light. Herein may be found the secret power of affirmations and constructive suggestions. To suggest health to one's self, or to affirm a statement of health, while the mind is in touch with the inner source of absolute health, is to give that statement the power of health, and the thought or the word that proceeds from that statement will produce health just as surely as the sunbeam will produce light. However, those affirmations that are made while the mind is not in touch with this state of absolute health will be powerless to produce health, no matter how determined or sincere we may be at the time. The more superficial the mind is while making affirmations, the weaker and the more deficient in health producing elements will those thoughts be that are formed at the time, while the more deeply the mind enters into the state of absolute health the more power will every thought contain that is formed during such a realization.

The secret of metaphysical methods in all their phases, is found in this law, and the same is true of the power of the mind over the body. Any mind that gains a perfect realization of that state of absolute health that permeates every part of the system will give the power of health to its thoughts; and by concentrating the power of those thoughts upon the body, health will be produced in the physical system.

The power to cure yourself or prevent disease in this manner may be steadily developed by training the mind to live more and more deeply in the realization of that state in the being of man that is always well; and to train the mind in this respect think constantly of this inner state of absolute health, and think with deep feeling. When thinking of this state impress upon the mind the fact that absolute health permeates every part of the system. Know that you are actually filled through and through with a life and power that is well, always well, and that you literally live and move and have your being in a living sea of perpetual health. Should your mind form tendencies to doubt this truth, know that this truth can be conclusively demonstrated by anyone; then impress upon your mind the fact that it is so. After a time your mind will know that it is so, and will at the same time discover that sickness and weakness have mysteriously disappeared.

The mind that is superficial has very little power over the body; but as consciousness deepens into the realization of the fact that there is extraordinary power in the mind limitless power in fact the mind finds that the body will respond almost instantly to any desire that may be expressed. When the mind lives in perfect touch with the inner source of power, every thought will be given more power, and will consequently have the power to produce any cause or change in the body that is desired. Such thoughts will actually be power, because they were created while the mind was IN power; and the thought that is power can produce in the system any effect that would naturally come from that power.

It is therefore evident that when the mind lives in the realization of the inner state of absolute power, the power of the mind over the body will be complete; and the desire of the mind to produce perfect health in the body will invariably be followed by the realization of perfect health.

Chapter 10

Purity of Mind and Body

That the body must be pure in order that health may be maintained is self-evident, and most systems of prevention and cure have given due attention to the insuring of physical purity; but physical purity is not sufficient to perfect health. There must also be mental purity, and mental purity means not only wholesome thought and right thought, but also the right mental conception of purity itself. We must know what purity actually is before the mind can be pure, because a false belief about purity would constitute mental impurity, just as much so as any form of unwholesome thought or desire.

A certain view of purity has declared that "To the pure all things are pure," implying the idea that things in themselves are always pure, and that impurity can exist only in the human mind. This view, however, though true in a certain sense, does not from the ordinary viewpoint express the whole truth; and the reason why is evident when we realize that it would be impossible for a mind to conceive of impurity that was living in a world where all things were always pure. This same view has led many to the conclusion that if you are pure in motive, or mean well, you can do what you like; your action will be pure and right and good. In other words, so long as you think the action is pure it will be a pure action, regardless of what the moral code may decide in the matter; but such a conclusion can come only from a mind that does not understand the real meaning or the real purpose of purity.

When we know what purity means, we know that every thought or action that does not conform to the law of purity will be impure, no matter whether we think it pure or not.

How to Stay Well

Our influence cannot make a natural cause modify its natural effect, and our thoughts cannot change the inevitable action of law. It is only superficial thinkers who believe that every action will be pure if we think it is pure, and that they can accordingly do as they please. However, the power of thought is immense, and in the last analysis constitutes the cause of every condition that appears in the personal being of man. Nevertheless will any line of thinking be pure simply because you think it is pure? That is the question; and it is a question that the majority have neglected to consider.

When we say that thought is the cause and the only cause of whatever transpires in the personal man, we refer to the thought of the heart; that is, subjective thought action. Mere objective opinion cannot be cause, and has no effect whatever upon the forces of mind or body, nor does it affect circumstances or things in the least. You may think objectively that a certain action is pure, and at the same time there may be impure subjective mental states in your mind that are causing that very action to be impure. In other words, if there are impure subjective states in your mind, the actions coming from those states will be impure, no matter how much you may objectively think and affirm that those actions are pure. As long as there are impure states in the within, there will be impure actions in the without, and your objective thought, or opinion, or belief about the matter will count for naught. This should be clear to everybody, and those who see it clearly will realize that a great deal of the thought that passes as profound metaphysics today is nothing but illusion; in brief, foundationless ideas that have sprung from minds that could not see the difference between objective opinion and subjective causation.

It is subjective causation that determines whether things are to be pure in your world or not. What you think of the matter in your outer mind will have nothing to do with it.

True, you can so direct your objective thinking that it will gradually change subjective causation, but to do this your objective thinking must be according to mental laws, and not according to opinions.

The statement, "As a man thinketh in his heart, so is he," might read, "Everything in the mind, body or environment of any man is the direct or indirect result of the subjective causations that are active in the being of that man." This being true, whatever change we wish to produce anywhere in life, the desired change must first be made in the causations within the subjective mind. There are many minds that change their opinions, only permitting subjective causes to remain unchanged, and then wonder why everything in their lives continues in the same way as before. Most of these changes that are made in the objective opinions are not made according to the psychological laws, but according to the passing views that come from the various sources in the without. If you have changed your thought, but find no change for the better in your life, you may know that it is only your outer thought, your objective opinions that you have changed; the subjective causes remain unchanged.

Whenever your subjective or subconscious mind is changed, there will be a corresponding change in your life, no matter how that subjective change was brought about, whether it came from old fashioned conversion, modern metaphysics, esoteric experiences, or profound scientific thought. But in this connection we must bear in mind that subjective changes, though coming in many ways, can be permanent only when we fully understand the laws of mental change and act accordingly. This is why so few systems have fully satisfied, why nearly all of them have developed one-sidedness in their disciples, and why they have, in nearly every instance, become creed-bound. The full understanding

How to Stay Well

of life is lacking in nearly all such systems of thought, because that full understanding is not sought. Nevertheless, they all possess a power for good, having the power of changing for the better subjective causations in one or more places.

To find the great laws through which subjective causations may be changed as we desire, it becomes necessary to learn what is really meant by the statement, "To the pure all things are pure." Since the statement was made by one of the greatest psychologists in history, it must possess absolute truth when understood from that viewpoint of consciousness from which it was expressed. To find the true meaning of that statement is not difficult, however, when we realize that purity means to be in the proper place, and that impurity means to be out of place. In the last analysis, elements, forces and substances are not impure, but impure conditions may be formed amongst them when something transpires to cause those elements to be misplaced.

Since all impurity comes directly from the misplacement of things that are in themselves pure, we can readily realize that all things could be pure to those who are pure, because those who are absolutely pure would have the power to cause all things in their lives to be properly placed. Things would not be pure because those pure minds believed all things to be pure, but because they would naturally, through their superior power, change impurity into purity. When you attain such a complete mastery of yourself that all the elements, forces, functions and activities in your being are always in place, always doing what they are created for, and are never misdirected, you will have the power to properly place everything in your world. Your understanding of purity and the proper placing of things will be so thorough that you will know exactly where everything belongs, and will have the power to place it there. Having become conscious of the true order of things, and being master of the situation, you will be able to establish true order, both in the within and in the without.

Having established absolute purity in your subjective mentality through your consciousness of absolute purity, everything that enters your system will naturally become pure at once, though it might have been impure before coming in contact with your life. Everything becomes warm when it enters a warm room, provided the heat is sufficient to overcome all opposite conditions; that is, when the heat in any place is absolute heat, everything that comes into that place will become warmth, no matter what it was before.

In the same way, when the purity in any place is absolute purity, everything that enters that place will also become pure. In other words, when everything is properly placed in a certain place and held in place by an irresistible power, everything that enters that place will also properly place itself. Negative conditions are powerless when in the presence of such positive conditions as are completely positive; and disorder cannot possibly exist in the midst of order when that order is complete.

When we realize the transmuting power of positive forces, we shall soon understand the full truth of these statements. It is a well-known fact that a strong personality naturally appropriates and makes a part of himself any force that he may come in contact with, provided that force is not as strong as the predominating positive force in himself, and he naturally transforms that force so that it becomes similar, both in quality and action, to the predominating states of his being. A personality that is in perfect harmony, and that continues in harmony, becomes stronger and stronger, even when passing through conditions of extreme discord. The forces of discord are transformed as they come in contact with the system of a strong, well-poised personality, and become harmonious forces which he can appropriate and use. He meets the enemy, so to speak, and makes it his own. In like manner, the mind that remains unshaken in his convictions increases in power, influence and supremacy the more opposition he encounters.

It is the mind that falls down in the midst of opposition that fails utterly, while the mind that remains untouched and undisturbed becomes a giant; he not only retains his own power, but adds to his own the power of the losing opposition. Consequently, when the subjective states are properly placed, in harmony, in order, and in absolute purity, and you hold all those subjective states in absolute purity, the force of purity in your system will be so strong and so positive that it cannot be disturbed or changed by anything. Whatever may enter your system while it is in this condition will become pure, no matter what it was before. The most impure elements and conditions will crumble into atoms in the presence of a force of purity that remains unshaken, and then reassemble again in a new compound, substance or condition that is absolutely pure. Whatever comes into your system, therefore, or into your world, will be transformed into purity at the very door, provided you continue in the consciousness of absolute and irresistible purity.

Upon the arch, above the entrance to the mansion of your life, you may safely write: "Whatever enters here leaves impurity behind." The demon becomes an archangel the very moment he passes through your door, metaphorically speaking, and the poison becomes a nourishing food the very moment it enters your system. The wrong thoughts and hatreds, and the ill-will that may come to you from minds that do not understand you, will be transformed at once into valuable energies that you may use to develop yourself or build up your health, strength and power.

Those who do not accept this extreme conclusion, and it is certainly extreme, should suspend their judgment until they have examined those laws in nature that govern transformation and transmutation in the realms of nature. When we experiment in the chemical world, we can readily demonstrate that one force can entirely transform another force and make it a part of itself, provided the ruling force remains unshaken while the new combination is being made; and when we look into the human world we find innumerable illustrations to prove how an undisturbed mind, a mind forever standing firm upon his convictions, finally sweeps everything before him; but it remains for the new psychology to reveal the real secret back of these phenomena.

It has also been demonstrated through recent experiments that a positive mental force can, by remaining positive, transform every negative force or condition that may come into the same sphere of action; and when we know that all phases of impurity are negative conditions, perpetuating themselves simply through the indifference or the inactivity of the positive forces about them, we understand clearly the real truth that is back of the whole matter. Then it becomes clear to any mind that the pure can cause all things to become pure, and that in the world of him who is pure, everything else will naturally tend to become pure. It could not be otherwise. He is the master when he chooses to be; and there is no greater mind than the pure mind. We conclude, therefore, that in this sense the statement is true, "To the pure all things are pure," because, in the life of the pure, impurity is at once transformed into purity.

Looking at the subject from a still higher viewpoint, we find that the pure mind enters that state of consciousness where everything is discerned in its original nature, and in that state everything is in place; that is, everything is right and in perfect order. In other words, the pure mind, having become conscious of absolute purity, can see all things as they are in that original state, or before they became misplaced, or misdirected by ignorant minds. The pure mind naturally dwells in that sublime state, therefore to such a mind all things are pure, not because he simply thinks so, but because in that higher field of consciousness all things are properly placed; that is, in the realm of pure reality, everything is pure, and right, and good. By becoming pure, he has entered that loftier realm where everything is pure, and consequently he sees everything as such.

Every thorough student of life will eventually learn that there is an inner world back of the exterior, phenomenal side of things. It is the cosmic realm, and this realm, being beyond the interference of the human mind, understanding always remains pure. To enter this realm is to see everything as it is in a pure state of being, as in this realm everything is forever in its pure state; but no mind can enter this inner state and discern cosmic life until purity is attained, both in physical and in mental action. The disturbed, misplaced mind can discern only the discord on the surface, while the calm, serene, absolutely pure mind gravitates naturally to its own higher plane and enters the consciousness of that state of existence where everything is absolutely pure. To train one's self to consciously dwell in that world within, beyond the turmoil of the personal man, is of the highest importance, not only to the health of the body, but also to the development of all the higher qualities latent within. It is ideal living; and it is not simply imagination; it is profoundly real and indescribably beautiful. Back of the disturbed surface of life there is a pure, calm, beautiful state of being, as tangible and as real as reality itself. It is the kingdom within, and the source of all the unbounded possibilities in man. When one becomes pure, he enters that pure world; therefore "to the pure all things are pure"; because when one becomes pure he enters a state of being where everything is pure, always was, and always will be. In perfect health there is always purity, and in absolute purity there is always perfect health. Disease can thrive only in the impure, and the impure always tends to produce disease. Therefore, one of the royal paths to health is to be absolutely pure in all things and at all times; that is, to be pure in body, in mind, in thought, in feeling and desire. There is strength in purity, because in purity there is no waste of life; and in strength there is wholeness and health. The clean body becomes vigorous and virile. The clean mind becomes able, forceful and brilliant; and clean thoughts, feelings and desires invariably lead to greater and better things. Purity means life in abundance, and when life is abundant all the good things of life are invariably added.

Chapter 11

The Happiness Cure

Health is harmony. Disease is discord. The more perfect the harmony in the human system, the better the health; and happiness invariably produces harmony. When the forces and elements of mind and body work together in harmony, wholesome conditions are naturally produced; and if the creation of wholesome conditions is continued for any reasonable length of time, all disease will finally disappear. There can be no discord when the harmony is full and complete; there can be no darkness when the light is sufficiently strong.

The happier you are, the less energy you waste, because added happiness means added harmony, and the system wastes no energy while it continues in perfect harmony. The less energy you waste, the more vitality you will possess, and the greater your supply of vital energy, the less liable you are to sickness. When your system is absolutely full of vital energy, you will contract no disease whatever, not even diseases that are said to be contagious. Retain all your energy and you will never be sick; but to this end harmony must be perfect, and perfect harmony is possible only when happiness is continuous.

When the human system is thoroughly harmonious, every particle of food that is taken will contribute its full nourishing power, and to properly nourish the system is one of the chief secrets of health. In the average system, however, a great deal of the food taken is not digested, there being too much discord among the digestive forces, and, therefore, actual starvation obtains in the midst of plenty. There are millions of cells in the majority of human bodies that are daily starved to death, regardless of the fact that three full meals are eaten every day. Those starved cells wither up and become waste matter, clogging the system, thus giving extra work to the forces of elimination and reconstruction. And the more energy you use up in getting rid of useless matter, the less energy you will have for your work, your life and your thought.

A fit of anger, or prolonged excitement, is frequently followed by a cold; and the reason is that agitation, in every form, tends to prevent proper digestion and assimilation. Most of the food that is taken at the time, or that has been taken within the last eight hours, will simply become waste matter; and all the starved cells will, in like manner, become waste matter; the system is thus clogged from two sources, and what we call a cold must naturally follow. The system, however, would have been clean and well and properly nourished through and through if there had been no anger or excitement, but harmony and happiness instead.

There would be but few cases of indigestion if happiness and harmony were continuous in every mind; and when you prevent all the ills that come directly or indirectly from imperfect digestion, you prevent fully three-fourths of all the ills known to human life. But the powers of happiness and harmony do not end with the digestive functions; their effect upon the nervous system is just as far-reaching and beneficial. Make continuous happiness a part of your life, and your nerves will be as good as new as long as you live. The same is true concerning the mind. Nourish your mind with happiness as you nourish your body with food, and the ills of mind will never gain a foothold in your life for a moment. You will be mentally vigorous and strong every day, even though you should live as long upon earth as those worthy examples of ancient days.

How to Stay Well

The forces of growth, recuperation and reconstruction are all given a healthy stimulus by happiness. No matter how tired out the system may be, it will recuperate in a very short time, if you are thoroughly happy; but this the average person fails to do. When he feels tired he permits himself also to feel downcast, weary and depressed; and, therefore, instead of helping nature to restore normal conditions, he places every possible obstacle in her way. When your horse is wearied by one load, you do not expect to give him a rest by having him hitched to a heavier load; but this is the very thing the average man does to his own personality. When the body is tired from physical burdens, he gives it a mental burden instead, and is blind enough to think that he is giving his body a rest. Mental burdens exhaust more vital energy than the hardest kind of physical work; and mental burdens are always useless; but they can be removed completely by the power of happiness. But there is happiness and happiness; there is the genuine and the counterfeit; the former produces harmony, health and virility; the latter produces weakness, depression and hysterics. When you are bubbling over with joy, and feel like shouting, you are not happy; you are mentally intoxicated; and intoxication, whatever its nature, is an enemy to health. True happiness is calm, deeply felt, composed and contented. It is not merely intellectual, nor is it lacking in feeling; it is not necessary for the mind to run riot in order that it may feel deeply, or express the full warmth of tenderness and emotion. Those emotions that are deeply felt and calmly serene are always the most tender; they are what may be termed the full emotions, because they express all that is tender in body, mind and soul; and they therefore give the highest and most satisfying form of joy. True happiness enjoys all things deeply, but serenely; and you can always know when you have had such happiness, because it makes your countenance radiant with a restful sweetness.

To gain real happiness, the first essential is to train yourself to think constantly of the great value of such happiness, and especially with regard to its health producing power. Such thinking will tend to produce a subconscious desire for happiness, and what the subconscious begins to desire it also begins to create. Train yourself to think of happiness as a mental necessity, just as food is a physical necessity, and you will gradually train every element and force in your system to work for the creation of happiness. By creating within yourself a constant demand for happiness, you will inspire the elements of your own nature to produce the desired supply, and ere long the happiness you desire will become a permanent part of your life.

Every moment of joy that comes to you should be entered into with a deep, contented calmness. Do not permit your happy moments to bubble over on the surface, and do not permit yourself to be wrought up when occasions for great joy come into your life. Make it a point to turn your attention to the richer depths of every joy that you feel, and your enjoyments of all things will not only multiply many times, but the effect of your joy will be most beneficial both to mind and body. Gradually your happiness will give you that calmly sweet contentment that makes the whole universe look good. And so long as you dwell in the mansions of that form of contentment, sickness can never enter your door.

Learn to look upon life as a privilege instead of a hardship. View all things, not from the valley of discontent and limitation, but from the mountain top of all that is rich and great and marvelous in the sublimated nature of man. Learn to think that everything must come out better and better if you only do your best; then proceed to do your best. Have no fear of results so long as you do your best; and believe firmly that whatever comes to him who always does his best must of necessity be good. If it does not appear to be good, it is only temporarily disguised, and will soon reveal itself to be the greatest blessing that could have been desired. No person can be unhappy who lives in this thought; and he who lives constantly in this thought will not only become happier, and thus healthier, but he will also discover that things always turn out better and better when we do our best.

Do not think that it is necessary to carry such a weight of responsibility. The universe is held in position by the law of gravitation; do not wear yourself out trying to hold it up. Do not think that the human race will be saved through your anxiety, and do not think that your own welfare or success in life will depend upon how much you worry. Do your best, and leave results to the laws of life; do not worry for a minute, and do not be anxious about anything; do your best in the present and everything will be better for you in the future; this is the truth; then train yourself to deeply realize that it is the truth, and you will always be happy.

Do your part in the world as well as you possibly can, and let nature carry the responsibility; she is not only able, but most willing; in fact, that is what she is here for. You are not required to carry anything on your mind, and you are not called upon to be anxious about results in a single field of action anywhere in the universe; you are just called upon to do your best NOW; but to do your best you must be happy. It is easy, however, to be happy when you know that everything will be better so long as you do your best. Make it a point to be happy just as you make it a point to be clean, to be presentable, to be properly dressed, to work well, to be efficient, to be worthwhile, to be true to all that is in you. In brief, make the attainment of continuous happiness and greater happiness a permanent part of your strongest ambition. You will soon find results. Your unhappy moments will become less and less frequent as well as less and less significant, while your happy moments will become so numerous as to almost become one continuous moment, and the richness of your joy will increase daily to a most satisfying degree.

Avoid all unwholesome mental states, such as fear, anger, worry, depression, disappointment, discouragement, gloom, sulkiness, moroseness, pessimism, sadness, harshness, resentment, remorse, anxiety, and states of a similar nature. Find fault with no one, condemn no one, antagonize no one; but first refuse to be anxious. Anxiety saps more life and energy in a day than work does in a week; we all know this; and as anxiety cannot possibly be of any use at any time, we are not justified in being anxious for a single moment. To remove anxiety, however, we must view life, not in the old way, but in the new way. That is, we must learn to know that all things contain possibilities for greater and better things, and that we have the power to bring out those greater possibilities at any time and under any circumstances. When we begin to preach and practice the gospel of strength instead of the gospel of weakness, we shall not be anxious any more.

To be happy constantly in this deep, calmly contented manner, is to steadily increase the power of harmony in your system; and the more harmony there is in your system, the more energy, the more vitality and the more wholesome conditions there will be in your system. Finally, the power of the wholesome will become so strong and so completely established in every nerve and cell and atom that all disease, if there was any, will have to leave. And if you wish to hasten this great day of freedom, you can do so through a very simple exercise.

Whenever you feel this deep, calm contentment, turn your attention upon those organs or parts in your body that require better health. Try to impress upon those organs the same deep, serene happiness that you feel, and you thus produce in those organs a greater degree of harmony. Repeat the exercise as frequently as you can. Try to feel happy in that organ that needs health and strength. Where you feel real happiness you produce harmony; and when you give nature perfect harmony she can restore perfect health every time, no matter what the ailment may be. A little practice will convince you that the healing power of happiness is very great indeed; and it becomes doubly so when combined with temperance. We should therefore write the rule of life in this fashion: Be temperate in all things. Be happy at all times.

Chapter 12

How to Rest and Recuperate

When we know how to rest, we do not have to rest that is, not in the usual sense of that term. Complete inactivity is never necessary; in fact, it is impossible; and every effort to produce complete inactivity is more or less injurious. Every moment of attempted inactivity is a moment of waste, and therefore leads to weakness and ill health. It is possible for the different parts of the system to be temporarily inactive in an objective manner, but it is not possible for you to be inactive at any time. You must eternally act: and to act, you must act upon something. Therefore, if you wish to give rest to a certain part of the system, you must go and act elsewhere. Make no attempt to become inactive in yourself; it is not possible. Besides, such attempts simply prevent the exhausted parts from receiving the peace and rest that are required for natural recuperation. In the human entity, absolute standstill is impossible. If you are not going forward, you are going backward. Regardless of this fact, many people seem to be at a standstill, but they are taking one step backward immediately after having taken a step forward; so, therefore, they are always in action, but never getting anywhere.

It is the current belief that no one can rest without stopping all personal and mental action, but the fact is that to try to stop all action in the human system is much harder than the hardest work, and uses up more energy than the most strenuous kind of work. To proceed to do something else is the one secret in the art of resting. When you want to rest and recuperate one group of muscles, begin to use another group. When you want to rest one part of the brain, think of something entirely different. When you want to rest the objective mind, use the subjective; and this is easily done, because we use the objective mind while fully awake and objectively active, and we use the subjective while asleep or when in an attitude of calm and deep serenity.

In this connection, it is well to remember that you will get greater good from your sleep if you give your subjective or subconscious mind something definite to do before you go to sleep. While the outer self is resting in sleep, the inner self should build up the subjective or subconscious side of our talents and faculties, and thus increase constantly the capacity of the mind and the strength of the body. When you give the subconscious mind nothing definite to do during sleep, it will spend the night creating meaningless pictures and situations, a few of which you remember and call them dreams; but when you give the subconscious something definite to do during sleep, this waste of energy in the subjective field of creation is avoided, and that energy will instead be used for constructive purposes that will prove of advantage to you in the coming days. Besides, you will in this manner secure perfect rest during sleep. The idea, therefore, is this: if you want to rest the objective, have your consciousness go and do something definite in the subjective. Never fall asleep in the attitude of weariness, because by so doing you will impress the condition of weariness upon the subconscious and that condition will be reproduced and brought forth into the personality in the morning; and here we have the cause of that tired feeling that so many people have when they wake up.

Go to sleep with the purpose of going into the subconscious and doing something there that is constructive, upbuilding and wholesome; but as you entertain such intentions, place your mind in an attitude that is perfectly serene. We should approach all work in the serene attitude, whether we are to act objectively or subjectively. Perfect rest for any part of the system during the waking state can be secured by learning to withdraw consciousness absolutely from one part and causing it to act wholly upon another part. Consciousness is the result of the I AM expressing life, thought and being, and therefore consciousness acts on a certain plane, or in a certain part, so long as the I AM gives expression to itself upon that plane, or in that part. Consciousness is always active. An inactive consciousness is as impossible as a dark ray of light. When anything is conscious, it must do something, and it continues to do something, either objectively or subjectively, so long as conscious existence continues. Since consciousness means action in every instance, it is evident that no part of the system can rest until we become unconscious of that part. So long as we are conscious of that part, we will act upon that part, and the energy in that particular place will continue to be used.

The purpose of rest is to recuperate or regain that energy that has been used up in work; but it is not possible to regain energy in any part of the system so long as we continue to use up energy in that part; and energy will continue to be used up in any part so long as there is conscious action taking place in that part. To be simply quiet in any part of the system is not necessarily to be unconscious of that part; therefore such rest is not complete. This explains why so many people recuperate so slowly. The reason is that while trying to rest they continue to be conscious of the entire mind and body. Any person who can become wholly and instantaneously absorbed in some other line of thought or action will recuperate rapidly, and so long as he will practice that art intelligently he will not wear out; neither will he find it necessary to retire from usefulness at four score and ten. He will then be in his prime, both physically and mentally; and on account of his extensive experience his service will be of the highest value.

To turn consciousness into another channel, reposeful or well-poised action is necessary. When we work in the attitude of poise, we concentrate well and naturally without trying to do so. We thereby give our whole attention to the present action, and all other things are given a complete rest, and on account of our perfect control of concentration, we can give our whole attention to something else at any time desired. When we act or think in a nervous, excited attitude, consciousness moves rapidly through every part of the system, and no part of the system is left free for many seconds at a time. Recuperation, therefore, is impossible under such a condition, and if such a system is in a rundown condition it will continue in that condition until the nervousness is overcome, while if the system is in fairly good condition, it will, through nervous action finally become so weakened and so confused that natural rest will be difficult to attain that is, unless perfect poise is first secured.

That inactivity, or, rather, attempts at inactivity, will waste energy and thereby produce weakness and disease, is readily understood when we examine the process involved. So long as you try to make a certain part inactive, you continue to act upon that part. That part, therefore, is just as active as it ever was, and it continues to use up its energy. Ere long there is not sufficient energy remaining to even carry on the work of repair in that part, and then we have decay, or that clogged-up condition that is always a forerunner of disease.

It is therefore clearly understood that a great deal of premature senility comes simply because we do not know how to rest. There is no reason whatever why brain workers should lose their mental brilliancy after they pass their sixtieth year, or any other year; nor is there any reason why the physical strength should diminish in anyone at that age. The physical organs are constantly being rebuilt, so that we wear out simply because we do not give them the proper rest; and our mental activities become dull for the same reason.

To master the art of resting, the first essential is never to attempt to become perfectly quiet in the entire mind or body while you are awake. The second essential is to withdraw consciousness absolutely from those parts of mind or body that need recuperation, and become vitally interested in something else. In other words, give your thought and your attention to something that does not require the activity of those organs or faculties that need recuperation. The third essential is to take physical exercise whenever the whole brain needs rest. Such exercise will rest the brain completely in a very short time, and this method, therefore, is infinitely superior to the old habit of lying down and continuing to think about how tired you are. The fourth essential is to give your attention to something that is delightfully interesting to the mind whenever the body needs rest, though at such times we should remember not to give the mind anything to do that may demand heavy or profound thought. At such times light reading of a harmonious nature, or light music, will prove perfect in restoring the body to normal strength and vitality.

To enter the loftiness, the beauty and the life of spiritual thought, is the best method of all for recuperating mind or body, provided you are sufficiently conscious of the sublime to touch those lofty realms whenever you desire. But if you have not attained to that consciousness, you will find it most profitable to begin at once and gradually develop that power in yourself by which you may rise to the calmness, the splendor and the beauty of the sublime whenever you may wish to get above the usual physical or mental action.

When you wish to rest any part of the system, do not try to take your consciousness away from that part. To make this attempt would simply be to concentrate your attention on that part, and thereby continue to be conscious of that part just the same as before. The proper course is to direct your attention elsewhere and become so completely interested in the new object of your attention that you forget completely the part that is to receive rest. When your whole attention goes elsewhere, consciousness will soon follow, and all action will be removed from that part, which for the time being is to rest in a state of inactivity.

Wherever consciousness acts, there energy will be used up, but when consciousness is withdrawn, nature will be given an opportunity to restore to that particular part the full and natural supply. That is the reason why we must become unconscious of muscles, organs or faculties before they can completely regain their strength. When we remain conscious of a certain part too long, that part is not only deprived of all its energy, but the elements of that part are also used up, just as a starving man lives for a while on the elements of his own body.

But the converse is also true. When we remain unconscious of a certain part too long, the energies that have been accumulated there will begin to disappear, and that part of the system will decrease in capacity. That is the reason why unused muscles gradually decrease both in size and capacity, and also why unused faculties gradually become more and more deficient in mental power until they are practically useless. Whenever any part of the system has renewed its strength, we should proceed at once to use this new energy for constructive purposes; but as soon as that energy is used up, we should turn our attention elsewhere and do something else, so that renewal may again take place. In this way we use constructively all the energies we accumulate, and as every part of the body is exercised fully and properly, and for the proper time, the general capacity and power of the system will steadily increase.

During those moments when we have nothing in particular to do, we should turn our attention upon the development of mind or body, or upon the building of finer mental structures for the future. At such times the constructive use of the imagination can be carried on to great advantage. There is no need of waste of time, nor is it well for the health and wellbeing of mind or body to ever waste a single moment of time. When your physical or mental labor is over for the day, turn your thought upon something else. Direct your imagination into some other field where you may find new and valuable ideas for future use, or give attention to the further development of mind or body. In this way the tired parts of mind or body that is, those parts that have used up their available supply of energy will receive perfect rest, while your time during this period of rest will be profitably employed along other lines.

The average person throws away several hours every day by simply being partly alive. He thinks he is resting because he is not actively at work, but the truth is, he is working still. He is using up energy by being consciously active in every part of his system. He is not working at something, but is working upon his own energies, and thereby using them up to no account. This is a mistake that everybody should eliminate at once, because we need all the energy that we receive if we wish to retain perfect health and continue to advance in our own work and development.

When you are not working at your particular business, turn your attention upon the building of yourself, or upon some interesting pleasure. When you are not busy at work, be busy at pleasure. Those activities that are called forth during pleasure are produced by entirely new activities in consciousness, so that two desirable objects will be promoted: First, you will call forth new energy and thereby build yourself up along new lines; and second, those parts of mind or body that were active during the working hours will have a perfect opportunity to recuperate themselves. In this manner no time or energy will ever be wasted, and work, rest, development and pleasure will constantly and harmoniously blend throughout the entire system.

Chapter 13

Letting Go of Your Ailments

To let go of those things that we do not desire to hold in mind, may seem to be difficult; and yet it should be just as easy to drop a thought from the mind as it is to drop a stone from the hand; and we must be able to do this if we would set ourselves free from those conditions of mind or body that are not conducive to health, strength and wholeness. In like manner, it usually seems difficult to prevent undesirable impressions from entering the mind, though any person should be able to refuse undesirable mental impressions just as readily as he refuses undesirable food.

But the reason why these things seem difficult is because we have attempted them in ignorance of the fact that both the act of letting go and the act of holding on are subconscious processes. So long, therefore, as the subconscious mind is holding on to a thought or any particular condition, physical or mental, you may spend eternity in trying to get rid of it with the objective mind and secure no results whatever. Likewise, if the subconscious is attracting a certain thought or condition, you cannot possibly keep it out by fighting against it with the objective mind. The importance, therefore, of knowing how to direct or change the subconscious in this connection, is very evident. The movement of every muscle in the body is preceded by a subconscious action. The involuntary movements of the body, such as breathing, circulation, digestion and assimilation are subconscious processes that have been established in the subjective nature of man during ages of human evolution; but the voluntary movements of the body are also subconscious, in the sense that the objective acts upon the subconscious, and the subconscious causes the body to move as directed by the objective.

When you move your arm you do not cause the arm to move by willing to do so with objective action. You might try to move your arm by objectively willing to do so, and try for any length of time with no results; in fact, the more intensely you will the arm to move by mere objective action, the more rigid will the muscles become. When you wish to move your arm, the objective will must act upon the subconscious with a desire to move the arm, and it is the subconscious that will carry out that desire. In like manner, when you wish to drop something from your hand, the objective will must impress upon the subconscious the desire to let go, and the subconscious will cause the hand to let go of its object. The same process must be employed when you wish the hand to hold on to an object. The objective will must impress upon the subconscious the desire to hold on, and the subconscious will cause the hand to do as the objective will desires. The hand will thus hold on until it is subconsciously caused to let go. The reason for this process is simple when we know that the subconscious governs all the forces in the system. No force in the human personality can act unless the subconscious causes that force to act, and the subconscious will cause any action that the objective will may direct. It is the function of the objective mind to direct the subconscious, and it is the function of the subconscious to carry out whatever the objective may direct.

When the subconscious undertakes to give directions, we have misdirections, or what may be termed abnormal conditions, attitudes or actions of mind; and when the objective undertakes to carry out its own directions, we have simply waste of energy with no action whatever. Therefore, whenever the natural functions of the two phases of the mind become mixed, we either have perverted, unwholesome and abnormal actions, or none at all.

The mixing or misplacing of these two functions may be caused by ignorance, or by continued false thinking along any line, but the proper replacing of these functions may be readily accomplished when we understand what each of the two phases of mind has been designed by nature to do. The objective mind is the conscious, wide-awake mind, therefore it knows what should be done each moment, and for that reason is competent to give directions. The subconscious mind is the creative mind, therefore it has the power to produce anything that may be required, and being in full possession of all the underlying forces of the system, it alone can cause the forces to proceed in action or to cease action.

It is therefore evident that to produce the desired results in any sphere of action, physical or mental, the objective mind must be trained to give the proper directions to the subconscious. In many respects this training has already been perfected, especially those that are called natural physical movements; but in many other respects, such as the removing or producing of any condition desired for mind or body, this training has as yet only begun.

When we wish to move a muscle, the proper directions are given by the objective to the subconscious, because we have been trained to do so in the school of experience. The child learns to walk by training the objective to impress the subconscious with that purpose in view through repeated attempts, and that training is promoted through the acts of attention and interest. When the objective mind is interested in the doing of any act, attention is naturally directed to the subconscious, because interest always causes attention to act upon the subconscious. This process, however, can be perfected to the very highest degree, and this is done whenever skill, art or proficiency is attained. The child learns to talk through the use of the same process, and it is through this process that the musician, the artist, the artisan or the acrobat gains control over mind and muscle.

The training of the objective mind to properly direct the subconscious is generally a slow and gradual process, due to the fact that imperfect methods are usually employed. We make many mistakes before we strike upon the correct methods, and we continue to make more mistakes before we find new and improved methods. The cause of this is found in ignorance concerning the true functions of the two phases of mind, and also in a limited scope of consciousness. When we begin to employ the principles of the new psychology and a more thorough knowledge of consciousness, both in our daily life and in our educational institutions, we shall find that the process of training along any line, physical or mental, will be perfected to a remarkable degree. In consequence, less time and less effort will be required to secure any particular result, and what results we secure will be far superior to what have been gained before.

The subconscious mind controls all the forces employed in the movement of mind or body. Whatever we wish to have done, therefore, the subconscious holds the necessary power, and by properly directing the subconscious, that power will be given the required action and will do what is desired. In the art of letting go, it is this principle that must be employed. The objective mind must not try to drive things out, but must properly impress the subconscious to let go, and when that is done the undesired thoughts or conditions will be dropped at once.

It is the subconscious that holds, therefore it is the subconscious that must be directed to let go. To cause the subconscious to let go of certain habits, tendencies, tastes or undesirable conditions, sometimes requires months or years, simply because we do not know how to direct properly the subconscious in this respect; but when we understand this process, very little time will be required to accomplish our purpose.

It is therefore not scientific to think that a certain amount of time will be required to produce certain results. We usually require considerable time in finding the way, but after the way has been found, the time required to secure results is usually insignificant. When the individual is in possession of clear mental insight, the proper way is readily found, however, even though the sphere of action be entirely new.

To acquire the art of letting go, the first essential is to understand that it is the subconscious that holds, and that the subconscious will let go only when properly directed to do so by the objective mind. The second essential is to train the objective mind constantly to act in the closest touch possible with the subconscious at all points of consciousness. In this connection no effort will prove more valuable than that of broadening and enlarging the scope of wide-awake consciousness along all lines.

To enlarge the scope of wide-awakeness, the mind should aim to discern the larger reality and beauty that exists in all tangible things, and should at the same time aim to discern the reality and the beauty that exists in all the finer qualities of life. More attention must be given to the finer elements, the finer feelings and the finer experiences that are met in the world of consciousness, because this will cause the mind to gain possession of new fields of conscious action. It will also cause the objective to touch the subconscious at many new points of contact, and wherever the objective touches the subconscious, at that point the subconscious can be directed properly and instantaneously at will.

The average person disregards practically all thought concerning the subconscious, looking upon the subject as visionary, and yet he cannot take a single step without first directing his subconscious mind to produce the necessary muscular action, nor can he advance mentally until he trains the objective to impress the subconscious with regard to the action of that advancement.

We are absolutely dependent upon the subconscious for everything we do. Instead of ignoring the subject, therefore, we should study every part of it with the greatest of care; and we have everything to gain by so doing. We do a great many things without knowing why we do them, therefore if we can secure certain results through a limited, unconscious action of mental laws, we can certainly secure far greater results through those laws when we employ them intelligently and in the consciousness of perpetual mental expansion.

To use the objective and subconscious phases of mind in their true places, and to aim to bring the two minds into contact, at as many points of consciousness as possible, is to use the entire mind intelligently and progressively; and since the objective can properly direct the subconscious wherever the two minds consciously touch, we understand readily how the possibilities of mind become unlimited, and we also understand how every condition in mind or body can be changed completely in the same way.

The subconscious has the power to make any change in the human system that it is directed to make, and the objective mind has the power to direct the subconscious in any way that may be desired. Whenever there is anything that we wish to eliminate from mind or body, we should direct the subconscious to let go, and the subconscious will be properly directed to let go whenever we express this desire in the attitude of fine feeling and deep interest. Feel deeply that the subconscious is letting go of the condition that you wish to eliminate, and you have given the subconscious the proper direction in that respect.

Through this simple method the human personality can be caused to let go of any disease, any perverted condition, any detrimental desire, or any abnormal state of being. The art of letting go, therefore, is an art that is practically limitless in value.

Chapter 14

How the Subconscious Creates Health

To give the subconscious mind definite and systematic training along the lines of health-building is one of the first essentials in the attainment of permanent conditions of health throughout the human system. As the subconscious mind is, so are the conditions of the body. What is active in the subconscious is active in the body; but no condition can exist in the body that does not exist in the subconscious. The subconscious mind permeates and fills every atom in the physical body, every fiber in the nervous system and every cell in the brain. In fact, the subconscious mind is the real power that is back of every force and every element in the personal being of man. Therefore, every change and improvement that is desired for mind or body must begin in the subconscious.

So long as every action in the subconscious mind is positive, harmonious, wholesome and health-producing, there will be perfect health in the body; and as the subconscious is more and more thoroughly trained in such actions, physical vigor, physical vitality and physical endurance will increase in proportion. By giving a few moments every day to the training of the subconscious in health-building, the body will finally become so brimful of vigorous health that it will become practically immune from every ailment that was ever known.

To proceed, employ only such mental actions as tend to impress health upon every thought, feeling and desire. Every mental action that conveys the idea of health, the desire for health and the feeling of health will impress health-producing power upon the subconscious. In other words, when the idea of health is impressed upon the subconscious, that impression will place in action forces that are health-producing.

When you habitually think health into the subconscious mind you give the subconscious a system of training in health producing; and accordingly, the subconscious will produce better and better health as it is more perfectly trained. When you habitually talk health to the subconscious mind, you are causing all the forces and elements of the subconscious to focus their actions upon the idea of health. Health becomes the model for all the creative forces of your system, and therefore these forces will create wholesome conditions in whatever part of the system they may act.

The principle is to literally fill the subconscious with health ideas of health, desires for health, suggestions of health, mental actions of health, thoughts of health and impressions of health. Fill the subconscious with every manner of health, and the subconscious will fill the body with every manner of health. From every mental action that is turned into the subconscious there will be a reaction that will be felt in every part of the human system. And as the action is, so will also be the reaction. When every mental action that goes into the subconscious is an action of health, the reaction will contain the power of health, and as it comes forth from the subconscious into the body, it will produce health.

To turn mental actions of health into the subconscious it is not sufficient, however, to simply desire health, or to suggest to ourselves that we have health. There are many mental actions, both good and otherwise, that produce no impression upon the subconscious, and, therefore, a good many who continually employ health-producing suggestion fail to get well. If you can only impress health upon the subconscious, you may know that the subconscious will express health through every part of your body in return. But the problem is, to get your health-producing suggestion into the subconscious. To solve this problem, you must learn to distinguish those mental actions that do enter the subconscious from those that do not.

The difference between those mental actions that readily and naturally impress the subconscious and those that do not is well illustrated by the statement of a would-be metaphysician: "I AM suggesting to myself all the time that I will not have the hay fever this summer, but then I know that I will." Here we have two actions of mind; the one that "knows" will impress the subconscious; the other will not. When you know that you are going to get well, or that you will stay well, you impress health upon the subconscious, and the subconscious will respond by producing health in every fiber of your being.

You may continually suggest to yourself that you are getting better and stronger and more vigorous, but if you doubt, "deep down in your heart," whether your good suggestions will produce results or not, those suggestions will not reach the subconscious; and, accordingly, there will be no results. This feeling of doubt, however, can be gradually removed by repeating your good suggestions as often as possible, and by trying to give as much deep feeling to those suggestions as possible. In other words, let your good suggestions "sink in."

What you feel "deep down in your heart" will invariably impress the subconscious; and here we have the simplest and most direct route to the vastness of this inner mental world. Whatever you feel "deep down in your heart" will develop and grow, because every feeling of this nature plants its seed in the subconscious; and every seed that is planted in the subconscious will, without fail, bring forth after its kind.

To apply this principle thoroughly and systematically, make it a practice to impress health upon the subconscious for a few moments several times every day. Think health into the subconscious, and try to feel "deep down in your heart" that you are steadily growing in health. Talk health to the subconscious, and try to feel "deep down in your heart" that every word you speak contains the power of health. Fill your subconscious mind with good, strong, positive, health-producing suggestions and try to feel "deep down in your heart" the health-producing powers of these suggestions. That power is there. Every health-producing suggestion contains health-producing power; and that power will impress itself upon your subconscious mind if you will let yourself feel it "deep down in your heart."

If there is some ailment in your system, suggest to yourself that you are going to get well, and know that you will. Tell your subconscious mind that you are getting well; that you are getting stronger and more vigorous every minute. Use any number of such suggestions, and let them all sink in. Think health and talk health to yourself constantly, and try to feel "deep down in your heart" that you are steadily growing in life and the power of health.

But if you are already reasonably well, do not become indifferent as to how you impress the subconscious; continue to impress health and strength upon your subconscious mind every day, no matter how well and strong you may be. Make it a point to train the subconscious to become more and more proficient in the building of health, and increase continually the health-producing power of all the forces in your system.

Do not permit the garden of the mind to become overgrown with weeds; in fact, do not permit a single plant to grow in that garden unless it is from the best and the strongest seed that you can secure. Do not permit a day to pass without reseeding this garden with the best seeds of every description that you can possibly find. In other words, fill your subconscious every day with the best, the strongest, and the richest thoughts that you can create. Talk health, talk harmony, talk power, talk success, talk happiness to your subconscious mind continually and let all of this talk sink in. When you talk to the subconscious, feel "deep down in your heart" what you say; thus every word will enter the subconscious, and the subconscious will proceed to do what every word may desire or direct. Sometimes the results are instantaneous, while at other times frequent repetitions are required; but the subconscious is so constituted that it will reproduce every impression it receives, and express in the physical personality what it has reproduced. When you fail to get results, you may know that you have not succeeded in getting the impression into the subconscious; but you finally will succeed in doing this if you continue to repeat again and again the suggestion that conveys the condition that you want.

The subconscious mind has the power to give your body perfect health, and in a short time, even though you are literally full of ailments. And in training the subconscious to do this, you would not be calling upon its power to do something new. It is the subconscious mind that controls all the functions of the body, and all the involuntary actions of mind or body when we are asleep and when we are awake. The power of the subconscious mind in you and the powers of "nature" in you are one and the same thing. Therefore, when you are dealing with the subconscious you are not dealing with something out of the ordinary. You are simply dealing with the deeper and greater powers of nature in yourself. These powers, however, can be trained more thoroughly and more extensively than we ever dreamed; and the process of training is so simple that anyone can apply it whether he has any scientific knowledge or not. In fact, everyone is training these powers constantly, though not always in a manner that is conducive to health and happiness. Whenever you have formed a habit you have trained the subconscious powers to do something they did not do before. When you change that habit, you turn those same powers in a different direction. When you cultivate likes or dislikes of various kinds, you train the subconscious along those different lines. You do the same whenever you form tendencies or desires along any line whatever.

The subconscious mind responds readily to your suggestions, desires or repeated actions. When you do a certain thing a number of times, you can do that particular thing henceforth without thinking about it; you do it automatically; it acts of itself. The reason is, you have trained the subconscious mind to do it for you. When you desire a certain thing over and over a number of times, that desire will soon come of itself; and it may become so strong that you can hardly control it. You have trained the subconscious mind to continue to keep that desire alive; and, accordingly, that desire will live and grow regardless of the fact that you may frequently try to suppress it or destroy it entirely.

But the only way that you can remove that desire is to begin to desire something of an entirely opposite nature, and continue to repeat that desire until you have trained the subconscious to give its life and power to the new desire instead of the other one. In the same manner all kinds of habits can be readily and easily removed.

When you continue to suggest certain things to your subconscious mind, and repeat those suggestions over and over a number of times, the subconscious will soon take them up and act upon your suggestions. And the time required will depend upon how easily you let each suggestion sink in. Suggestions that are made mechanically, or in a half indifferent manner, will not reach the subconscious, no matter how many times they may be repeated; but any thought or desire that you feel "deep down in your heart" will impress itself upon the subconscious at once.

The fact that we can train the subconscious to produce and perpetuate any desire whatever in the human system, should prove that it could also be trained to produce and perpetuate any condition whatever. An active desire is a condition, the same as a condition of life, strength, vigor or virility. We conclude, therefore, that the subconscious mind can be trained to produce all those things; and what is more, this idea has been proved any number of times. You can train the subconscious mind to keep your system in perfect health under all sorts of circumstances; and all that is necessary is to keep your thought of health and your desire for health deeply alive in your subconscious mind constantly. Train your subconscious mind to think only of health and strength; never of disease and weakness; and what the subconscious mind thinks of constantly it will produce constantly. Remember, whatever the subconscious mind thinks about, it will produce. This is a psychological law that is demonstrated every minute in the life of every person; and it is a law which, when applied intelligently, will enable a person to change and improve his nature and his physical conditions almost as he may choose.

The subconscious powers are producing powers; they invariably produce and express in the physical personality whatever is constantly brought before their attention;

therefore, nothing but that which we actually want should ever be impressed upon the subconscious. You do not want weakness, discord, sickness, failure, unhappiness. But if you think of those things and let your thoughts sink in, you will impress those things upon the subconscious; you will sow weeds in your mental garden, and you will reap accordingly.

Any thought, however, is liable to sink in; therefore, think only of the good things that you wish to see grow in your nature, your body, your mind and your character; and let all of those thoughts sink in. You want the subconscious to be deeply impressed by all those good things, to constantly think of them, and constantly produce them.

In the beginning, however, there are a number of ideas, desires and suggestions of an undesirable nature that will find their way into the subconscious unawares; and to counteract these, as well as to train the subconscious more thoroughly in producing health, strength, harmony and happiness in greater measure, it is necessary to make it a practice to give the subconscious mind definite training every day. Give your subconscious mind a full supply of good, strong, health producing thoughts and suggestions just as regularly as you give your body a full supply of wholesome food. And look upon the one as being just as necessary to your personal welfare as the other. You will soon gain perfect health, and as long as you live you will continue to retain perfect health. In the study of the subconscious, we find that the sensitive mind is the mind that receives the best and the most immediate results in directing or modifying subconscious actions. We also find that most minds are more or less sensitive; in other words, impressible; but that the good qualities of that sensitiveness are usually misdirected, and are not employed to advantage in the training or the changing of the subconscious.

To understand this subject, therefore, is highly important in connection with the attainment of physical health and mental wholeness. Besides, what is called sensitiveness may, if not understood and properly protected, lead to a multitude of mental and nervous ills, which may in turn be followed by physical ills, or a decided decrease in physical vitality. The reason why the sensitive mind is so important in this connection, is because it is the most highly organized mind, and therefore, when properly protected and directed, may so apply the finer mental elements as to secure the greatest possible results, and also become a great mind. But when not given this proper protection and direction, the sensitive mind becomes a source of disease, misery and failure.

The reason why is found in the fact, that the sensitive mind is so easily impressed, both by that which is for, and that which is against. When placed in the midst of adverse conditions, the sensitive mind will be filled with adverse and detrimental impressions, and will consequently think, do and say many things that are entirely at variance with the real character back of that mind. This fact explains why so many persons do things under certain conditions that they would not even think of doing under more favorable conditions.

When placed in the midst of conditions that are favorable, constructive, ennobling and inspiring, the sensitive mind, will be filled with impressions of high worth, and will consequently rise beyond itself, both in thought and action. At such times the mind will not only be its best, but will transcend its best, frequently acting as if it had gained some superhuman power, or was under the control of some extraordinary intelligence from exalted spheres. We do not have to account for such phenomena, however, by assuming the existence of superhuman entities, and their power to act through man, for unlimited power and intelligence is latent in every individual mind. When that power is aroused, the mind may ascend to heights of greatness that we can only describe as superhuman; and this has been done a number of times in history.

That exalted beings exist in various parts of the universe is probable; in fact, to be consistent we must admit it; and there are many who claim they know. But the inhabitants of this planet do not have to depend upon the power or the intelligence of other entities in order to scale the heights. We have sufficient power within us to do everything that has been done before, and much more. This has been the declaration of all the prophets, and all the superior minds of the ages; and the new psychology is verifying every statement that was made by those wonderful minds.

To cause those prophecies to come true prophecies that are now becoming scientific facts it is only necessary to awaken, protect, and properly develop the marvels that are already latent in the human mind; and the sensitive mind contains those elements upon which, or through which, we may act when attempting to arouse and develop those greater things in human nature. The sensitive mind is in that condition where all the finer elements of mentality can be brought into action, and is also in that condition where it can receive those impressions that are necessary to produce action among the finer elements. Thus we realize the importance of having sensitiveness of mind in order to apply mental and spiritual means in gaining or maintaining health, as well as in directing the subconscious for any other purpose we may have in view. The sensitive mind can be inspired by the superior and the sublime as no other mind can; but it can also go farther in the other direction than any other mind if not protected.

The sensitive mind is most fertile. It is therefore necessary to genius and richness of thought. But this same extraordinary fertility can also produce an abundant crop of weeds if such seeds be sown, and as the conditions in which the mind is placed determine to a very great extent what seeds are to be sown in the mind, the conditions in which the sensitive mind is to be placed should be selected with the greatest of care.

The sensitive mind is sensitive because it is highly organized, and is alive with all the finer forces those forces that can produce emancipation and lead man on to greater things when properly applied. Therefore the person who has a sensitive mind has a rare prize; but to turn his treasure to good account he cannot live like ordinary people.

To properly apply the finer elements and forces of the mind, all thought must be wholesome, optimistic, and of an ascending nature. Every desire must have a greater goal in view, and every action must be animated with the spirit of aspiration. To rise in the scale, to work up to greater things, and to reach the heights these must be the ruling ambitions; and to advance perpetually in every conceivable manner must be the real purpose of life.

The sensitive mind should be impressed only with those things that will promote its higher aims and greater desires; therefore every person who has a sensitive mind should learn scientific thinking at once, and never permit any other mode of thinking. Such a person must never get angry nor permit destructive actions of the mind, as sensitiveness of mind also produces tenderness of mind. The finest things in life do not permit of rough treatment; they must be handled with care. The sensitive mind must never worry nor permit depressing states of mind, because such states will impress mentality with descending tendencies. For this reason a person with a sensitive mind always goes down more quickly after the downward action has begun, and also loses ground more quickly in the same way.

When the mind is in a sensitive condition the subconscious is easily reached, because it is through sensitiveness that the objective mind must act in order to attain that deeper feeling of action which is necessary to impress and direct the subconscious. To possess a sensitive mind, therefore, is great gain in this respect, provided, of course, only favorable, wholesome, health producing and inspiring impressions are placed in action in any part of the mind. To give the sensitive mind proper protection from adverse impressions, associations should be sought that are elevating, and that tend to increase the ascending desires, and only such people should be associated with intimately whose words and actions tend to give everybody faith, encouragement and determination. Persons who criticize and antagonize should be avoided, and there should be no actual contact with the pessimistic element anywhere in life.

The sensitive mind should aim to live with superiority and worth, and there is an abundance of such to be found, both among persons and things. The sensitive mind is such a rich field that no person with such a mind can afford to use anything but the best of seeds, and therefore only the best conditions and environments should be sought, both in the within and in the without; though in this connection it is well to remember that all minds require an abundance of mental sunshine if the seeds sown are to grow, develop and mature.

The sensitive mind, however, should never be permitted to become supersensitive; that is, that condition that may be termed being "touchy" should be positively avoided, and anyone with a sensitive mind should never think of being easily affected. The person with a sensitive mind should live in the midst of circumstances that are growing and expanding, that are rich with opportunities, and that are working for greater things; but when adversity is met, the mind should be protected with such care that not a single undesirable impression can enter; and so long as there are no undesirable impressions there will be no undesirable thoughts or undesirable conditions of mind or body.

That person who habitually declares, "I AM so sensitive," is simply producing nervousness, "touchiness" and a tendency to ill temper. Such a person is not sowing good seeds in the mind, but is instead filling the mind with autosuggestion of weakness, nervousness and uncontrolled susceptibility. Such a person, by dwelling on the adverse side of sensitiveness, will cause the mind to be continually impressed by everything that is adverse, and will in addition cause the mind to create adverse conditions within itself. When a person suggests to himself that he is sensitive, he intensifies his susceptibility to external conditions, and will consequently be affected almost constantly by those conditions against his will. He will also impress his mind more and more with the belief that he is constantly being affected by external conditions, and will ere long be almost entirely controlled by environment.

The sensitive mind, therefore, should never think of sensitiveness, but should aim to continue in the attitude of full self-mastery, and should seek only such environments and associations and thoughts that tend to produce a high order of mental impressions. The sensitive mind should live the life of the sensitive mind, but should never think of itself as being sensitive. It should not be sensitive to its own sensitiveness nor sensitive to undesired impressions from any source whatever, but should be so sensitive to all that is high, worthy and ideal that it may respond immediately to the touch of everything that is wholesome, worthy and superior.

There are thousands of minds in the world that are highly sensitive, but on account of their ignorance of how to care for such mental qualities, they are victims of fate, instead of being instruments through which the symphonies of the beautiful life may find expression. They may all become the latter, however, by giving the foregoing ideas thorough attention; and they will not have to wait for results. The sensitive mind is already prepared for a life of freedom, power and superior worth; it requires only scientific direction.

Those people who are associated with a sensitive person should realize that they are in the presence of a highly-organized mentality, an instrument that is tuned for greater things, and they should act accordingly. And this fact is especially important in dealing with children. Thousands of children have lost their health on account of their sensitiveness not being properly protected, and other thousands have failed to become what nature has given them the power to become, because that same sensitiveness was permitted to respond to inferior impressions instead of being directed to respond only to the superior. In this connection we should remember that what we do for others we also do for ourselves. When we open the door of greater opportunity for someone else, we always find that that same door has caused the opening of another door through which we may pass to better things. It is, therefore, giving our best and receiving the best in return; and the more we practice that great principle the richer will life become in everything that has value and worth.

Practical Methods

(1) When you feel weakness, or do not feel as strong as you wish, think deeply of the fact that you are filled through and through with a subconscious state of life and that this vast interior mental field has layers beneath layers of unused power and energy ready for use. To think of this limitless amount of energy with deep interest and with a feeling that you are coming into more and more perfect touch with it, will cause your mind to come in contact with, and to enter into those layers of extra energy and thereby arouse and gain possession of a larger measure of this power. Thus you will feel more and more of this power coming forth into mind and body and you will actually feel yourself gaining in strength and vitality every day.

(2) When some ailment seems to threaten, proceed at once to direct the subconscious to give your body added strength and vitality, knowing that no ailment can gain a foothold in your system so long as there is a full supply of vitality. Proceed by realizing two important facts; first that there is any amount of energy and vitality latent in your subconscious, and second, that the subconscious will bring forth into your body more and more of this energy, provided you give the proper direction. To direct the subconscious in this matter, therefore, is the secret, and you do this by thinking deeply of the subconscious as you desire more energy from within while fully expecting the desired supply. Or better still, as you deeply desire the subconscious to fill every atom of your body with added life and energy, imagine that you are feeling this added energy come forth from within and accumulating in every part of your system.

(3) Another excellent method is to talk mentally to your subconscious mind, giving your directions just as if you were speaking to a living person. And in a sense you are speaking to a living person. Your subconscious mind is a part of yourself, a living person, and has intelligence without measure. To apply this method, proceed as before, by thinking deeply and attentively of your subconscious. Then, as you seem to feel that you are becoming conscious of the existence of the subconscious, begin to give your directions as follows:

"You are my subconscious mind. You are amenable to my direction and desires. You always do as I direct and suggest. You obey my wishes absolutely. You always do what I want you to do, and you can do anything. You have unlimited power. You can produce any condition in my system that I may desire, and you can change any condition in my system whenever I wish you to do so. I simply have to make my wishes known to you and you proceed at once to comply. You have both the power and the inclination to change anything for me and to produce anything for me. Just now I want more strength and vitality in every part of my body. You can give me this added life and energy for your supply is limitless; and as I wish it I know that you will bring forth the desired supply this very moment. I know that you can and I know that you will, for you cannot possibly fail. You will give my body more strength and vitality now. You will restore perfect health and vigor to every atom of my body at once. This I know. My faith in your power is limitless, and you always respond the very moment you receive my directions. You have now received my directions, and I can already feel more life and vitality coming forth into my system. I AM beginning to feel stronger. Every part of my body is gaining in strength. I can feel it more and more every second. I AM being filled through and through with the limitless life and power from within. You have received my directions. You have responded at once to my wishes. I knew that you would. You always do. I have received what I asked you to bring. My system is now teeming with life and vigor, and I feel the fullness of perfect health in every fiber of my being."

(4) The above method may also be used in any other way desired in the cure of any ailment or in the changing or eliminating of any condition of mind or body. It is only necessary to change the wording of the above directions in a few places to correspond with the results you desire. That is, if you want health, direct the subconscious to produce health. If you want strength, direct the subconscious to produce strength. If you want peace of mind and harmony of the nervous system, direct the subconscious to produce those conditions. If you want a better circulation, a perfect digestion, pure blood, good assimilation, complete elimination of physical waste, red blood, good lungs, a strong liver, healthy kidneys, abundance of vitality and virility, or whatever you want for your body, direct the subconscious to produce it, using in the main the directions given above.

(5) Never direct the subconscious to remove disease, weakness or adverse conditions. To do so would be the same as to sow weeds in your garden. Always direct the subconscious to produce what you want, knowing that when health and strength are coming forth in abundance every form of sickness and weakness will completely disappear.

(6) Always expect results from the subconscious according to your wishes and directions, and always imagine those results coming as soon as you have given your directions. When you expect the subconscious to respond you place yourself in perfect touch with the real life of the subconscious, and when you imagine the desired results coming, you actually enter into the subconscious fields of those results, thereby going into and gaining those results in the same way as you get into and receive warmth when you enter a warm room. These things are very important because the subconscious always receives your directions when you enter into perfect touch with its real life; and the subconscious never fails to respond to those directions that it actually has received.

(7) In most instances the response from the subconscious is immediate; in fact, it always is immediate when you fully expect the results desired and imagine that you feel the coming of those results. When results do not seem to come at once, however, pay no attention to the matter, but proceed again and again to give the subconscious new directions, knowing that as soon as the subconscious receives those directions you will positively secure the health and strength you desire.

Chapter 15

The Power of Mind Over Body

Every action of the mind produces a certain effect in the body. When the mental action is weak or superficial, the physical effect may be too slight to be noticed, but when this action is both deep and strong, the results will be so clearly in evidence that anyone can detect them. These effects, however, are not simply functional, nor is it the nervous system alone that is acted upon. The power of the mind can and does affect everything in the body, frequently producing chemical changes which we have believed were possible only through the use of most powerful drugs. But the action of mind in the body always follows exact law; therefore when one knows the exact physical effect produced by each mental state, physical conditions can be largely determined by the intelligent use of the mind. A few illustrations of this law will prove both interesting and profitable. That selfishness should contract the cells of the physical body does not only seem plausible, but has been demonstrated to be scientifically true. The selfish attitude is contractive. It has a tendency to draw one's self within one's self, and also to live for this isolated self alone. When the cells are contracted, what may be called a dried-up condition invariably follows, which in turn produces weakness, old age and decay. The contraction of the cells frequently produces disease, because the contracted or dried-up cells are useless, and all useless cells become waste matter. The contraction of the cells also interferes with the healthful normal actions of the system, which, if not always producing disease, will always produce weakness; and a weakened system cannot long remain in perfect health. The effect of selfishness upon the cells of the brain is similar. The selfish mind is always a cramped mind, and such a mind cannot attain greatness, because greatness demands mental expansion. The development of the brain and the mind through the methods of subjective concentration methods of exceptional importance cannot be promoted with any degree of satisfaction so long as selfishness is marked and strong. Brain development requires the constant expansion of the cells, while selfishness invariably produces contraction of the cells.

It will not be necessary to draw upon one's imagination to realize that a sour mind produces a sour stomach, because this fact has been demonstrated so frequently and so conclusively. It is true that certain kinds of food may not always agree with us, but as a rule the fault does not lie with the food. Sometimes the food is at fault, but in the majority of cases the fault is in the state of mind. Those who do not believe that the mind can affect the stomach or interfere with digestion, will be required to explain why sudden and shocking news will destroy the appetite completely; also why a vivid description of the most luscious eatables will make anybody hungry, even within an hour after a hearty meal. Why the mouth should water when we think of good things may seem somewhat mysterious, but it proves conclusively that the actions of the mind can increase or retard the flow of the various juices of the system.

Those who have been observing have discovered that a person with chronic sourness of mind, and who maintains habitually a surly disposition, is very frequently troubled with sour stomach. His food does not digest, because the gastric juices are not only retarded in their flow by this disordered mental state, but these juices are chemically changed in many instances by these same states of mind. That the opposite state, cheerfulness, should help digestion, is therefore evident. A sluggish mind produces a torpid liver, while a dull, heavy mentality produces costiveness, the reason being that the various nerve centers become almost inactive when the mind is dull, heavy or sluggish; and since these nerve centers control the different organs and functional activities of the body, a corresponding sluggishness will take place in many parts of the system. To stir up all the dormant cells, therefore, both in the brain and in the nerve centers, would aid remarkably in promoting good digestion.

Nervousness has the same effect upon the digestive process, because nervous attitudes waste energy, thereby depriving the natural functions of their necessary supply. Anger produces uric acid in the blood, and uric acid produces rheumatism. All rheumatism, however, does not come from anger, but anger does indirectly produce rheumatism; therefore it is wisdom to train oneself to gain absolute control over one's temper. Intense fits of anger will cause confusion and consternation among all the vital energies. These energies will accordingly go on the rampage, and will tear up millions of the weaker cells in the body. All of these destroyed cells will be drawn into the circulation as waste matter, and will clog the smaller blood vessels, thereby causing pains and inflammation. Anger also overheats the blood, excites the action of the heart, and nearly always causes the circulation to be too strong in some parts and too weak in other parts. This, however, is not all the damage that may be wrought by anger. Anger actually burns up vital energy, and that is the reason why one feels weak after having indulged thoroughly in this expensive luxury of the smaller man.

The stubborn attitude of mind produces unconscious resistance to the natural forces, thereby preventing those forces from proceeding with their normal functions. The action of everything in the human system is more or less retarded when the mind becomes stubborn. It is therefore evident that a stubborn mind cannot become a great mind;

neither can the best physical and personal development be promoted while such a mental state is permitted.

The attitude of pride has a tendency to produce artificial conditions in the system, and these in turn may produce artificial growths. A person who is full of pride does not try to improve his appearance by improving himself, but by adding something artificial to himself. Frequently this desire to add the artificial becomes so deep and strong that it takes root in one's subconscious activity. Nature herself will accordingly imitate these subconscious activities, which nature is doing all the time, and will try to add artificial growths to the physical form. In many instances she will succeed. We do not mean, however, that all abnormal growths in the system come from pride. There are various causes for these things, and a very common cause is the clogging of waste matter coming originally from such causes as overeating, lack of vitality, poor circulation, anger, or other disturbed states of mind. The mental attitude of pride will produce a tendency to add something artificial to the human form, and then this tendency becomes very strong it will do what it has all the time threatened to do. We should say farewell, therefore, to pride and vanity of every description, and proceed to improve ourselves by bringing forth the greater perfection of life from within.

The attitude of hatred implies the act of separation, and this action will express itself more or less in every part of the system when that feeling of hatred is strong. The system will thereby be divided against itself. Equilibrium will be disturbed. Nerves that should work together will be driven apart, and no two functions will be able to work in that perfect concord that is necessary to health, wholeness and harmony. To secure the greatest results, all things in mind and body must work together, but hatred tends to drive them apart, and therefore may cause both disease and failure.

Indignation, whatever its motive, may produce the same results. For this reason indignation can never be righteous.

The attitude of worry tends to dry up, harden and ossify the cells, both of the body and of the brain. It is, therefore, one of the chief causes of old age and those conditions of lessened ability and vitality that come with old age. Worry acts directly upon the nervous system, depressing the nerves and thereby producing not only pain in the nerves, but also every imaginable form of nervousness. In fact, there is no cause that produces so many nervous disorders as worry. Such mental states as gloom, despair, despondency, discouragement and anxiety produce the same results. They are all different forms of worry, however, sometimes mixed with selfishness. Their tendency is to depress not only the mind, but the physical tissues. This depression causes the tissues to dry up, harden and ossify, and here we have one of the principal causes for that stiffness in the human framework that we mistake for old age. When we eliminate worry, we shall eliminate one of the principal causes of disease and weakness, and we shall find it an easy matter to prolong life many, many years, and stay young and vigorous as long as we live.

Envy and jealousy proceed from the desire for things that do not belong to us; that is, things that have no place in our world. It is therefore not strange that the envious person should be very susceptible to germs, epidemics, contagious diseases and the like. Jealousy repulses what we want, but attracts what we do not want. A jealous mind is repulsive, and thereby causes good things to depart from us; but it also has a weakening effect upon the body, and it is the weakened body that is the most susceptible to the ills that may exist in our environment. The attitude of grief wastes the tissues, both in the body and in the brain, though especially in the brain. The thought of grief is loss, and as like causes like, the thought of grief will naturally produce loss wherever it may act; that is, it will cause the tissues to waste away, and will cause the system to lose much of its life and energy. Those who have grieved much have felt this loss among the elements of their own system, and when we look at those who grieve we discover the wasting process at work in every fiber. Nothing is gained, but much is lost through grief. To "dry those tears" is therefore the height of wisdom; and we all can learn how.

To enter the attitude of fear is to become negative, and to place the mind in a state of incapacity; that is, a state where you are much less than you can be. The person that fears does not hold his own, but opens his entire system to the enemy that may be at hand. To fear an adverse condition is to give that condition permission to take full possession of the system. The same results would take place if that adverse condition were purely imaginary. That which we fear we impress upon the mind, and what is impressed upon the mind will be created in the mentality, to be in turn expressed in the personality. This is the reason why the things we fear come upon us; we create them in ourselves. Fear is always negative in its action, and a certain form of fear when very intense will entirely remove the resisting power of the physical system, thereby rendering the system extremely susceptible to any adverse condition that may exist in the body or in one's environment. In fact, in the attitude of fear we absolutely give in to everything that in any way may tend to gain a foothold in mind or body. To live in fear, therefore, is to place yourself in an utterly helpless condition. Among all the undesirable states of mind, fear has the greatest power, the reason being that it is so deeply felt, and what we feel deeply we impress deeply upon the subconscious. Fear can be entirely removed, however, by directing the subconscious to have faith perfect faith in all things and at all times.

To remove the effects of adverse mental states, the opposite states should be impressed upon the subconscious in every case. This practice will in a short time also remove the tendency to wrong thinking, and will increase the power of right mental states. The first function of right mental states is to reestablish normal conditions in the system. The second function is to chemically change the system so as to gradually produce more perfect actions among all the organs, functions and faculties; in other words, to steadily develop and refine every part of the mind and body so as to produce a higher order of personal and mental action. The personality can be refined through the exercise of right mental action in the body, and as this is being done the joy of physical existence will increase correspondingly. The tendency to disease, weakness and physical inharmony will decrease, while the personality will become a more and more perfect instrument through which the limitless possibilities of the great within may be expressed.

Chapter 16

The Relation of Mind and Matter

In this great study, one of the most important of all things is to be able to relate one's self properly to the powers that be, and the elements and forces of this sphere of existence. In fact, this may well be termed the greatest of all problems in human life. To solve it means to solve practically everything; and many are they who have tried. The majority, however, have either approached it wholly from the physical or wholly from the metaphysical point of view. The former have declared that all cause and all reality exist in matter, while the latter have declared that all reality is in mind. The materialist believes that all will be well when we obey fully the physical laws of nature; the metaphysician, or idealist, believes that through right thought alone can we enter into harmony with life; and both sides are right as far as they go, but only as far as they go.

The one great mistake of the materialist is his belief that physical forces and elements alone can produce actual effects upon human life. Mind to him is a physical force generated by the chemical action of other physical forces, and, therefore, to his mind, all causes are primarily physical. The one great mistake of the idealist is his belief that matter has no power of its own, and that its seeming effect upon us is, after all, produced not by matter, but by our belief about matter. According to his view, elements have no natures or qualities of their own; a physical element or a physical force will do to us only what we think it can do, and nothing more; and there are many experiences in life that seem to prove that this view of the idealist is right. However, there are many sides to the subject, and we must see all sides to understand the whole.

In order to relate ourselves properly to all things, there are three principles that must be considered, comprehended and applied. The first principle is, that all things in the external world have natures of their own, and that they can, under right conditions, impart those natures to the person of man. The second principle is, that every individual thought that man thinks has a nature of its own, and that it can, under the right conditions, impart this nature to the person of man. The third principle is, that the mind's conception of external things, and of its own thoughts, produces a cause, the effect of which will be different, both from the external things themselves and the thoughts themselves; and this cause can also affect the person of man according to its nature and power.

We therefore find three great causes in the life of man, each one affecting human conditions in its own way; and these three causes are external things, internal thoughts, and the mind's present conception of these two. To know which one of these causes brought about certain effects is sometimes difficult to determine, unless we have a thorough knowledge of the whole subject, which is hardly possible under every circumstance. Frequently a certain effect comes from the combined actions of these three causes, and at other times from only two, while in many instances there is only one cause that is responsible.

To illustrate the subject, we will combine the external force of a cold draft, the internal state of discord, and the mind's fear of both the draft and the discord. The draft will be a cause from without; the discord will be a cause from within; and the fear of both will be an adverse mental conception. The effect of these three will be a severe cold; first because the cold air closes the pores of the skin; second, because discord wastes physical vitality, thereby rendering the system incapable of throwing off the adverse condition;

How to Stay Well

and third, because the fear produces a mental picture of a cold, and as we well understand, every mental picture that is deeply and vividly impressed upon mind tends to reproduce its nature in physical conditions.

These three causes when combined will naturally produce a cold, but anyone of them, or any two of them, can also produce a cold; and the process is simply understood. When the cold air strikes the skin, the pores close themselves up because they desire to protect the system; but in so doing the waste matter in the system is prevented from escaping, and is thus thrown back on the system to clog and obstruct; but nature, in her effort to get rid of this waste, compels it to escape through the mucous membranes, thereby producing the various conditions that go with a cold.

Thus we understand how a cold can come from a draft, and why a cold acts as it does, regardless of the presence of any other cause. But suppose there is no cold draft, but only discord in the system, the result will be that a great deal of vital energy is wasted, so that the power of the system to keep itself clean is impaired to such an extent that a great deal of waste accumulates in the system and begins to clog. Nature, again, in trying to remove that extra waste, naturally compels a great deal of it to escape through the mucous membranes, which are the most porous of all membranes, and we have the same conditions as before, that is, we have a cold; and in this connection we should also remember that in addition to the accumulation of waste in the system produced by a lack of vital energy, this same lack of vital energy renders the system unable to keep the pores of the skin open, so that we have again the same clogged condition as the one produced by the draft.

It requires a great deal of vital energy to expel waste matter through the pores of the skin, because this is a function of the circulation, and the circulation must be full and strong in order to perform this function; but when vital energy is lacking the circulation becomes weak, and does not act fully in every part of the body nor at the surface of every part of the body. The skin, therefore, is not kept clean and open, and waste matter begins to clog more or less. We understand readily, therefore, how we can bring upon ourselves a regular cold by wasting our energy through worry, depression, anger, excitement, discord or any other disturbed state of mind. We shall now illustrate the third cause in this same connection, that of fear. When you fear a cold, you picture upon the mind all the conditions of the cold; that is, you impress the idea of the cold so forcibly upon mind that it becomes a pattern for your creative energies. The result is as we have explained before, that you actually create in your system those very conditions that are contained in the idea that was impressed upon mind; that is, you create in your system all the causes of a cold. You compel the pores of the skin to close more or less, because you place your system under the influence of a negative attitude of mind, and a negative attitude always has a contractive effect upon all the muscles and fibers of the physical system. You destroy a great deal of vitality because you are in fear, and you actually increase the amount of waste matter in your system, because through the destructive action of fear you cause a great deal of healthy tissue to become waste.

In addition, you impress upon the subconscious mind what we may term a clogged-up condition, which always accompanies a cold; and what is impressed upon the subconscious, will be expressed in the person. When you originate forces in the subconscious that tend to clog, those forces will clog wherever they are expressed, and all subconscious forces will, sooner or later, come forth into the body and act according to their nature.

This brief analysis proves conclusively that cold air alone can, under certain conditions, produce a cold; that the discord of the mind alone can produce a cold; and that the fear of a draft, or the fear of weakness from the discord, or the mere fear of the cold itself, can alone produce a cold. And it is evident that when two or three of these are combined, as they usually are, the effects will be proportionately worse.

However, the question is how to prevent these three causes under every circumstance. To prevent discord in the mind is possible, and with the knowledge we now possess along metaphysical lines is becoming comparatively easy. To prevent fear and perverse conceptions is likewise becoming one of the possibilities of nearly every mind; but to always keep away from a cold draft is something that is not possible. The question, then, is what we shall do under that circumstance.

In the first place, we must properly relate ourselves to the atmosphere, both physically and mentally. To relate ourselves properly in a physical sense, it is necessary to provide the right protection through clothing; and to relate ourselves properly in the mental sense it is necessary to provide an increase of vital energy. It is a well-known fact that a cold draft cannot possibly close up the pores of the skin so long as the system is full of energy. A full supply of vital energy will keep the pores open at all times, and will prevent the cold air from coming in through the skin; but the question is, if it is possible to increase our vital energy to such an extent that this can be done. And the answer is, that we need not increase our present supply of vital energy, but save it, or rather, prevent it from being wasted. The physical personality generates many times as much energy as we usually employ, therefore, if we prevent all waste through the cultivation of poise and harmonious mental and physical action, we shall always have sufficient energy to protect the

How to Stay Well

system from within from any changes in the atmosphere that may be met.

We realize, therefore, how the three causes of an ordinary cold can be avoided at all times and under all circumstances, and we shall find that the corresponding three causes of all other physical ailments can be avoided in the same way. A number of illustrations from daily life could be mentioned that would prove conclusively the power of man to prevent external causes from affecting the system, and also his power to change his mental states, or subconscious thoughts, so that nothing but good effects could come from their expression. But the most important problem is to prevent the formation of wrong conceptions, both concerning ourselves and concerning the things that exist about us.

Every idea that is impressed upon mind exercises a great power over human life, because every idea formed in the mind becomes a pattern for our creative energies; and in consequence all kinds of mental states, tendencies, desires, forces, conditions and thoughts will be created in the exact likeness of that idea. It is a fact that the conception we form in mind concerning the things we meet in life determine almost entirely what we are to become or pass through. The powers of nature, the forces and elements about us, can affect us in a measure, because they have a power of their own; but man can modify that effect so completely as to absolutely change it if he understands nature and properly relates himself to her laws.

Our subjective thoughts and our mental states, both those that we have inherited and those we ourselves have or are creating, can also affect us in a measure; but when we understand ourselves and gain the right conception of our real nature, we can so modify the effect of our thoughts and mental states, that effects, the very opposite to what were indicated, may be secured. The laws, the elements and the forces of nature are easily directed, and can be so modified by man that their power to act will act only in accordance with the wishes of man.

Likewise, the mental states and the subjective lines of thought are easily directed or changed, because it has been thoroughly demonstrated that the subjective side of mind responds both easily and readily to every new thought or every new direction that may be given to the subconscious. By impressing new ideas, new desires and new purposes upon the subconscious, you will receive in return an absolutely new mental life, and it will correspond with the ideal you have in view. The effect of this new subjective mentality will be precisely like the new mental life created, and that effect will appear both in the objective mind and in the body.

Our conclusion, therefore, is this: First, the external world has a power of its own, but man can direct that power for good, and according to his own desires. Second, the subjective world has a power of its own, but man can direct that power so that it becomes wholly constructive and conducive to the purpose he may have in view.

But man's ideas about these two worlds are not so easily determined or controlled. This third cause, therefore, or power in human life, is what requires our closest attention. To illustrate further the power of mental conception, and demonstrate more clearly that our thoughts about things have more power over us than the things themselves, we may mention the ordinary events of life and the way we meet them. We shall find through this examination that a great many difficulties have no existence whatever outside of our own minds, and that the most troublesome troubles never take place except in imagination. We shall also find that the majority of the people are affected more by the false, imaginary world that they themselves have created, than they are by the real world in which they live.

Take the simple matter of noise, and observe how differently it affects different people. Some become indifferent, some become nervous, and others become strenuous under its influence; and the reason is because they form different mental conceptions of the nature or possible effect of the noise. Accordingly, it was not the noise that made the person nervous, but his thought about it. When you think that noise is confusing, you create confused states of mind, and a confused mind will make you nervous. And here you should remember, that the only thing in the world that can possibly make you nervous is a confused state of your own mind. Avoid mental confusion, and you will never become nervous.

We do not mean, however, that the noise itself is powerless. It produces a number of vibrations that are confused in their actions; and those vibrations, as they enter the human mind through the sense of hearing, have a tendency to produce mental confusion. But if the harmony of your mind is so full and strong that no confused vibrations from without can disturb that harmony, you will not be affected by the noise. It is always the strong and the more positive force that wins, therefore, if the vibrations of harmony in your mind are well fixed, established and positive, they will be stronger than any number of confused vibrations that may enter from without.

But strength does not consist of volume; it consists mainly of direction and control. The problem with you, then, under the circumstances, is to direct your attention upon the idea of harmony and control your mind so perfectly that you remain constantly in harmony with the idea of harmony. When you do this, harmony will have such full possession of your system that no noise or confusion can disturb you.

When you complain that you are disagreeably affected by the scores of disturbed conditions that are all about us in the world, you are simply proclaiming the fact to the world that you have not attained self-possession, and that you have not entered into the permanent consciousness of real peace. When you have entered into the consciousness of real peace, no confusion from without can affect your life, and the reason why is simple. You may hear the noise, but its effect upon you is not confusing, because you are in a state where peace and harmony exercise complete mastery over conditions.

When your own room is warm, the chilly blasts upon the windowpane do not affect you; in fact, they add to your comfort, through your consciousness of the contrast. It is the same way with noise and confusion. When you are in harmony you feel more peaceful than ever before when you contrast that state of harmony with the confusion that may exist about you. The reason is, you have formed a new and true conception of the subject. You know that noise is a confused state of vibrations, but you also know that your system is full of harmonious vibrations, and you have adapted yourself to the latter; therefore, you are at peace. Instead of thinking that you are at the mercy of external vibrations, you know that you can create and maintain your own vibrations of perfect harmony; and when you positively know this, you have results accordingly.

This same subject can be studied with great profit in connection with the effect that environment exercises over human life; and when we discover how differently the same environments affect different people we must realize that the cause is not wholly in the environment, but largely, if not entirely, in the people themselves. When the environment seems hard, many people become stronger by passing through it, while others would go down into physical and mental distress. In such cases it is not the environment alone that produces the effect, but the mental conceptions that the different people form of that environment. What one man calls hard luck, another man calls opportunity; and the one who calls it opportunity wins the day.

When you do not like certain people, you are miserable in their company, though in many cases those people may be much better than you are, and far more agreeable. It is, therefore, not the people that make you miserable under those circumstances, but your mental conceptions of them. Yesterday a certain task seemed very difficult, but today it is a pleasure; and why? Because you have just been told that as soon as you learn to master that task you will be given a better position with larger recompense. In that case the work did not change, but your conception of it and your attitude toward it did change. You thought of it yesterday as drudgery. Today you look upon it as a great opportunity, and the effect, therefore, upon yourself, is produced entirely by your own idea of the situation.

Your sister may ask you to go out in the rain on some important household errand, but during all the time you are gone, and for hours after you have returned, the world seems cold and disagreeable. You did not want to go, and the condition of the weather caused your mind to look upon the forced action in such a way as to make you picture it far more disagreeable than it really was. But at another time, when the rain and the sleet and the slush were far worse, and you were asked to go out somewhere to accommodate some girl that was all the world to you, how differently you accepted the invitation. You were in such a hurry to go that you almost forgot your rubbers and umbrella; and what a pleasure it was to tramp through the mud. How supremely happy you were, and what sweet dreams you had that night. But the rain was the same rain, and the mud was not of a holier clay. The difference was in your own thought, and there only.

When people meet what they call trouble, they usually take the worst possible view of the subject, and thereby actually make it much worse than it is. When you see a little trouble, you usually begin to think trouble, and so much so that you are soon in a state of chaos. Then everything goes wrong, because when you are confused everything you touch will be disturbed or upset. In many instances what appears to be trouble would not trouble you in the least if you took hold of it in a calm, self-possessed attitude and corrected the matter in the beginning.

It is impossible, however, for people to correct troubled conditions in this way if they become troubled and confused, or go into hysterics at the first sight of it. How can we calm troubled conditions when we ourselves are trembling with fear and anxiety? The trouble that has entered your life may look serious enough, but if you think of it as more serious than it really is, and magnify the matter many times, you actually create a world of trouble in your own imagination that will be many times as large, and many times as distressing, as the one that you have met in external circumstances. But this imaginary sea of distress is real to you, and you suffer just as much from it as if it had actual or tangible existence. This proves conclusively that we can create a great deal of trouble and misery in our own lives by simply magnifying with the mind every little adversity that we may meet, so that it is not so much the adversity we meet that is adverse, as the thought that we form concerning the nature of that adversity.

We might illustrate this matter further by taking up every experience that we meet in life and thereby demonstrate again and again the same principle. But repetition is unnecessary. When we study the subject to any extent at all, we realize most clearly the great fact that what we think of things and what we think of ourselves has a greater power over us than anything else in existence. When a person meets adversity, he should realize that the power of that adversity is very limited, and also that that power is subject to his direction. When he takes this view, he is reducing the effect of that adversity to a minimum, and may, if he understands the conditions, eliminate its power completely. Then when he considers in the same connection the supremacy of his own being, and realizes that so long as he remains in the absolute no wrong can harm him, he has formed the correct conception of the circumstance in his own mind.

The result will be that he will have no fear, and will form no false mental creations. His power will not be wasted, but will be directed upon the circumstances at hand, and since those powers are coming from a mind that is poised in the absolutely right, those powers will also be right, and will naturally tend to set the circumstances right. To understand how this thing will naturally work will be simple to everyone, and all will realize that it explains the true conditions of any situation in which we may be placed.

But the problem is how to form the true mental conception of everything; in other words, to see everything as it is and then know how it should be dealt with. This may seem difficult, but it is not, because when we recognize the three causes that have been mentioned, and study the natures of those causes, we shall soon understand. The reason why most people have the wrong conception of things in general is found in the fact that they believe in only one underlying cause of human conditions instead of three. When we study life from the three viewpoints of cause, that is, from the viewpoint of the objective or the outer world, from the viewpoint of the subjective or interior world, and from the viewpoint of the world of ideas, or our own mental conceptions, we shall understand the world of cause as it is, and form correct conceptions of all things that may exist or act in our sphere of existence.

The objective world and the subjective world are both real, and have enormous powers of their own facts we must well remember. But what those powers are to do to us will depend largely upon what we think of them, how well we understand them, and how well we can direct them. The objective and the subjective worlds are based upon laws that are permanent, and, therefore, always produce the same effects under the same circumstances; but man has the power to change those circumstances by relating himself differently to objective and subjective laws; and he does this by forming correct or superior mental conceptions of everything with which he comes in contact in life.

When man's conceptions of things are false, he is not properly related to the subjective or the objective worlds, and consequently his contact with them will produce adverse conditions. But when his mental conceptions are correct, that is, based upon the truth of all things as they are in his own world, he is properly related to the objective and the subjective, and accordingly his contact with those worlds will bring only good results.

In the average person, mental conceptions are partly right and partly wrong, therefore, he receives from life both the bitter and the sweet; but the moment he causes his mental conceptions to be wholly right, the bitter must disappear and the sweet alone remain. To make the subject clearer if possible, we might say that a man's mental conceptions of things are right when he understands the truth, both about the objective and about the subjective, which would mean that he understands the nature of the objective in the concrete and the nature of the subjective in the abstract; and he will be properly related to both those worlds so long as his thought world is right, because man acts as he thinks.

When man understands things, he knows how to use those things for good, and when he understands himself he knows how to apply himself in such a way that the results desired are secured. Therefore, to gain the correct mental conception of both worlds, we must study and understand the external as well as the internal. We must study them both as real worlds, and we shall find that the reality of the one, though different from the other, is a counterpart of the other. To study the one as real, and look upon the other as unreal, is to form wrong conceptions. We have done this too long, and have never become properly related to the various things, laws and principles of existence.

It has been the fault of the materialist to look upon the objective as the only real world. It has been the fault of the ultra-idealist to look upon the subjective as the only real world. Both of those extremes, therefore, must be avoided; and we shall find that when we study both the objective and the subjective as real, our mental conceptions will be composed of pure objective facts and absolute subjective truth. We will see all things, both external and internal, as they are. Both the great without and the great within will be subject to our direction. We will be in harmony with the external and at one with the internal. The powers that be will serve us, and of all that is good, both from within and from without, we shall have abundance.

In connection with this study of the power of mind over body, it is highly important to understand exactly what effect is produced upon the system by what is taken into the body. The question of what to eat and what to drink is ever before us, not only because we desire to be nourished in the best manner possible, but also because we do not wish to partake of anything that may interfere with the advancement of mind or personality; and it is believed by many that certain foods can retard or promote human progress. But here we must remember that it is not what we eat or what we drink, but what we think at such times, that must receive our chief attention. It is not what enters the system, but what comes forth from the mind, that is of first importance. Nevertheless, what enters the system has some power over the system. If it had not we would not have to eat. If food did only what we think it can do, as some idealists claim, it would be needless to eat. We could think the same effect with or without the food; but the fact that we eat for a purpose, the fact that every element has its own nature, and in proportion to its strength imparts that nature to whatever it may enter into harmony with, makes this subject one that is decidedly important.

It has been said that the power of mind over body, and what enters the body, is so absolute that a man with a strong, well directed mind could eat anything and cause only good results to follow. In fact, it is claimed that he could take injurious elements or poisons and not be harmed in the least. But in this connection we may well ask if the power of the mind is created for the purpose of fighting and destroying what has no right in the first place to enter the system? A study of the whole nature of man reveals the fact that the powers of man, even though they can in the case of absolute necessity neutralize or overcome the effects of injurious elements that may enter the system, are created directly for the purpose of building up and developing the larger, the higher and the better in human nature. And through this same study we learn that we increase our powers, not by trying to overcome the wrong, but by using our powers fully and constructively in building up the right, the good and the ideal. That we receive indigestion from "this" food or "that," is not true, because when a certain food is not digested the cause is usually in the system and not in the food. When your system is disturbed or weakened by anger, fear or other adverse thoughts or actions, it is not in a fit condition to properly care for the food taken into the system, and, therefore, at such times indigestion will usually be the result; but when the mind is right and wholesome in every respect, it is in a position to aid nature in all natural functions, and practically all the ordinary articles of diet can be taken and digested with perfect ease. The problem of what to eat is, therefore, reduced to the elements of simplicity; but there remains this fact: Whatever is done should be done properly, and eating is no exception. The food should be wholesome and well prepared, and no more should be taken into the system than is required.

There are thousands of people who waste so much energy trying to digest heavy meals that they have little energy remaining for thought and achievement. In order to do good work the brain needs all the energy that we can provide. All waste or misuse should, therefore, be eliminated. Here we should remember, however, that fretting, anger, worry, discouragement and similar states of mind waste more energy than any misuse that we can make of the body or its functions. So to be on the right side we must avoid not only physical causes of waste, but the mental causes as well. To discuss this subject thoroughly, volumes could be written, but there is a simple rule that everyone can apply in his own case, and a multitude of words are not required to explain it. It is simply this: Whether in eating or drinking or living or thinking, do nothing that will waste energy. So live and so regulate everything in your life that all your energy is employed constructively in giving health and strength to the body, ability and capacity to the mind. Growth, progress, attainment and achievement are the objects we have in view; but if we are to promote them fully, completely and constantly, we must not place obstacles, physical or mental, in our way. Neither must we permit ourselves to think that such obstacles as may come in our way cannot be overcome.

That certain foods can promote or interfere with human progress is an idea that has not been proven, and where experiments have been made the conclusions have not been conclusive, because if a man expects a certain food to make him finer in mind, character or soul, he will receive from each food the very results that he expected. Whatever the effect of food may be upon the nature of the human system it is itself so slight and so easily modified by the mental attitudes entertained at the time that it fails to prove itself of sufficient importance to be considered. The sensible course to pursue, therefore, is to partake of all wholesome foods that the system seems to require, and to try to improve constantly the quality and effectiveness of the food employed as far as possible; and in addition, to always expect the best results from all food that is taken. In brief, select the best, the cleanest, the most wholesome and the most nourishing. Then use all things in moderation, cheerfully expecting all foods taken to give strength to the body, refinement to the personality and health, virility and wholeness to your entire system.

When we constantly think about disease, or habitually fear disease, we create states in the mind that are unwholesome. These states will gradually, and sometimes instantaneously, work themselves into similar conditions in the body, just as immoral thinking will produce immoral desire. Every mental state acts in the human system exactly as the seed acts in the soil where it is placed. The seed will grow, take root, and produce fruit after its kind. Likewise, a mental state will establish itself and produce conditions to correspond to its own nature. It is possible to produce a certain disease by constantly fearing or expecting that disease; and it is possible to produce health by constantly expecting health, or dwelling in the conscious feeling of health. What you think of a great deal with deep feeling you impress upon the mind, and mental impressions act exactly like seeds. They will grow and if not disturbed will reproduce their kind. Through this same law you can produce virtue and high personal worth by constantly thinking of virtue, quality and superiority; or, you can completely undermine your character and your mental capabilities by constantly looking forward to weakness, inferiority or defeat. Turn your thoughts towards that which you wish to accomplish, that which you wish to become. You thus create mental states that are wholesome, constructive and inspiring. Those states will steadily reproduce themselves in body, mind and character. They will work themselves out through and through your entire system. You will thus become what you wish to become, and you will gain that strength, that worth and that efficiency through which you may accomplish what you have in view.

The prevention of disease and the maintenance of health is largely a matter of self-control. The more fully the individual controls not only his actions and his conduct, but also his thoughts and his feelings, the more perfectly can he live and act in harmony with nature, and in consequence maintain that order of mind and body that is necessary to perfect health.

Whenever you take something for your ailments or resort to outside help physically or metaphysically, you depend upon something else instead of upon yourself; and accordingly you ignore, in a measure, the power of self-control. There are times when outside help may be needed, but to make it a habit to resort to outside help for every little difficulty is to lose more and more the power of self-dependence; and it is the constant application and cultivation of this power that alone can produce self-control. Whenever you feel symptoms of any form of ailment, do not give in to them. Control yourself so perfectly that you scarcely feel them, and that you suffer no inconvenience. The power of this method is well illustrated when there is a tendency to cough. When you feel like coughing, refuse to cough. Control the muscles of your throat so that you will not cough. In many instances the desire to cough is produced by a slight irritation of the throat, and the more you cough the more you irritate the throat, and thus feel the necessity of coughing more. Practically all coughing, however, can be stopped in the beginning by self-control; that is, by simply refusing to cough; and many a serious throat trouble would be prevented, or nipped in the bud, if this practice were applied faithfully. The same idea holds in nearly every other condition that may arise in your system.

Chapter 17

The Greater Powers in Man

Whatever the methods may be that we employ in any system of metaphysical, mental or spiritual healing, the power of thought is the power that heals. The great essential, therefore, in metaphysical therapeutics is to apply every conceivable process through which the power of thought may become as strong as possible, as wholesome as possible, and as conducive as possible both to the production of health and the maintenance of health.

To increase the power of thought, live in the realization of the fact that there is any amount of power within you that has never been used before; and impress, more and more deeply, upon your inner convictions the idea that you can draw upon this power for as much as you may require, no matter how great the occasion or how extensive the needs may be. To live constantly in the conviction that you have within yourself all the power that you may require for any purpose whatever, will in itself increase the power of your thought to a remarkable degree because you will constantly be thinking more power, and to think more power is to charge every thought with more power.

Place the mind in the closest possible touch with this inner power; try to feel the real living expression of this power, and try to feel that every thought you think is created in the very life of this power. Live mentally in the consciousness of all the power that you can imagine as existing within you, and desire, from the very deepest depths of your being, to appropriate more and more of this power according to the ever-growing needs of your advancing life.

The more you think of the greater power within you the more power you think into your thought, provided you think with feeling, faith, and deep soul conviction. This law works on the same principle as the well-known law the more you believe in yourself, the more you develop in yourself, and the more you become accordingly. To continue to give full, conscious attention to that vast realm of life, energy and power that is within you, is therefore most important. You not only charge your every thought with more and more power in this manner, but you also enlarge perpetually your own life, you own capacity and your own permanent possession of an ever-increasing measure of power. But your thinking must have depth; you must believe in the greater power within, and live so close to the great interior world of power that you can feel its supreme existence every moment.

Realize more and more that the supreme life within you is greater by far than any disease in existence, and that this life, when aroused can remove absolutely every disease that can possibly enter your system. The more this great truth is realized the stronger becomes your thought, and the more effectively you can apply the power of your thought, either in healing yourself or in building up within yourself a greater measure of health, life and energy.

When you are thoroughly convinced of the fact that the supreme life within you is greater than any disease that you can possibly meet, you charge all your thought with this supreme life; and, therefore, in like manner, the power of your thought becomes greater than any disease that you can possibly meet. That which is born in supreme life will possess the power of supreme life; and all your thoughts will be born in supreme life so long as you live in the deep soul-consciousness of such a life.

How to Stay Well

To consciously and continuously live in harmony with the Infinite will increase the power of thought to a greater degree than anything else that we can do. To learn how to connect with the life and the power of the Supreme is one of the greatest of secrets, not only in the healing of disease with mental and spiritual means, but also in the living of a greater and a greater life. To establish this sublime unity between the human mind and the Infinite mind, the first essential is to continue to think, under every circumstance, that we are with the Infinite and the Infinite is with us. And as we enter more and more deeply into the inner conscious of this supreme thought, we should place ourselves in perfect harmony with the spirit of that thought; that is, we should inwardly feel that we are in harmony with the very spirit of the Supreme.

When we feel that our minds are connected with the life and the power of the Infinite, we can feel supreme power in every thought; in fact, every thought becomes the vehicle of supreme power, transmitting that power to every atom in the system. Any disease can be removed at once, or almost at once, with the power of thought, provided this power is sufficiently strong; and the power of thought always is sufficiently strong when we connect our minds with the Infinite before we begin to think. This being true, and anyone can prove it to be true, we should never proceed to use mind or thought for any purpose whatever until this supreme harmony with the Infinite has first been established. Undertake nothing until you feel that you are with the Infinite and that the Infinite is with you. This is the greatest secret in the world; and he who never fails to apply the principle of this secret shall never fail in anything, no matter what may be his goal in view.

To have faith in the power of thought; to have faith in the greater power within; and to have faith in the power of the

How to Stay Well

Supreme working in man this is most important. In fact, there is no increase in the power of thought unless there is an increase of faith in every power that can enter into thought; and the more faith we have in every power that does enter thought, the greater becomes the power of thought. The reason why is found in the fact that faith awakens the finer and the more powerful forces of mind. Faith breaks bounds; it expands the mind in every direction, and thus gives mind the possession of a greater world of life, force and power. The more faith you have in everything that is within you, the more fully you arouse everything that is within you; and, in consequence, the larger, the stronger and the more powerful you become in every state of your being. And the more strength and power there is alive in you, the stronger becomes your thought.

The finer forces of mind those forces that are awakened through faith invariably give soul and spirit to thought, and, therefore, not only cause the power of thought to become immensely strong, but also cause that power to become so penetrating in its actions that it undermines completely every physical condition that is not in harmony with the true order of things. When these finer and more penetrating forces are fully awakened, all that is necessary is to concentrate the mind upon that part of the body that is not in health, and to deeply desire health; the finer forces of thought will penetrate that part of the body and absolutely consume everything that is wrong. What you deeply desire the power of thought to do, the power of thought will do; and if you have unbounded faith in your own greater power within, and in your sublime unity with Supreme power, you will give your thought sufficient power to do whatever you may wish to have done.

The true faith is not a mere belief, but a higher order of consciousness a state of consciousness that actually connects the mind with the limitless power of the Supreme. Such a faith awakens all that is large, all that is great, all that is superior, and all that is masterful in man; and, in consequence, gives man the power to banish from his life everything that is adverse, inferior, detrimental or wrong. And such a faith anyone can attain by thoroughly believing in the great truth that the power that is within things, back of things, above things, is infinitely greater than anything that can ever happen or appear in the world. To steadily grow in this faith, however, it is necessary to have faith in faith; that is, to enter into the soul of faith, the spirit of faith, the hidden secret of faith, whenever we think of faith, or, in any manner, exercise the power of faith.

When you are healed by faith you are healed by the power of thought, because it is only the power of thought that does heal; but your faith has so increased the power of thought that the power has become sufficiently strong to fully banish every ill from your system. When you have faith in the healing power of something that exists outside yourself you are, through that faith, giving more power to your thought; faith always increases the power of thought, no matter what the faith may be or the object of the faith may be; and it is the increased power of your thought that removes the ailment.

When you actually believe that you will be healed by a certain element or power, you animate your own mind with healing power; your own thought becomes charged with this greater power that is aroused by faith; and if this greater power is sufficiently strong, you will become perfectly well. To have faith in anything whatever is to increase the power of mind and thought, because the actions of faith invariably expand the mind and arouse the more powerful forces of the mind. Indirect faith, however, is limited, and does not always arouse all the power that the occasion may demand; but when we express direct faith in the real, the true and the limitless that exists in all life, and have faith in faith, we shall so increase the power of thought that every ailment in the system must positively disappear the very moment our thought is directed, with the desire to heal, toward that place in the body where the ailment may happen to be.

Chapter 18

The Higher Curative Forces

Realizing the great fact that every thought is a power, that every state of mind produces a distinct effect upon the system, and that every mental change is followed invariably by a corresponding physical change, we conclude that we can through the complete control of the process of thinking, secure any effect desired in the human personality; and this includes not simply the body, with all its various functions, but also mentality, character, talents, faculties and every phase of consciousness. Every thought created in the mind becomes a distinct vibratory action, producing a certain tangible effect in the human system, complying invariably with the law of like causes producing like effects. Metaphysics, therefore, is a science in fact, an exact science. The laws of mind, thought and consciousness are absolute laws, invariable laws, invariably acting in the same way under the same conditions. Consequently, the person who understands these laws and will take the time to apply them may change his whole life to a remarkable degree. Through the intelligent use of these laws, there is not a single thing in body, mind, character, ability, capacity, conditions, environments or destiny that cannot be changed for the better.

When we deal with the power of thought, we should remember that there are three grades; namely, objective thought, subjective thought, and thought charged more or less with spiritual thought. Objective thought is that thought that is created in the more superficial states of the outer mind. Accordingly it has neither depth nor feeling, and produces no real effect upon the mind or body. Objective thought, however, should not be ignored, but it should be trained to act along right lines under every circumstance, because every objective thought may, under certain circumstances, become subjective. Subjective thought is what Solomon called "the thought of the heart" It is the thought we create while more or less in subjective consciousness. It is the thought of feeling and depth that is individualized and that produces a distinct effect wherever it may act in the system.

Every subjective thought produces, not only general effects upon the system, but in many instances produces chemical effects in the body. In fact, subjective thought can affect the body chemically just as readily and completely as the most powerful drugs. Subjective thought also affects the mind and the nature and actions of ability. A person, therefore, may gradually decrease his intellectual power and mental brilliancy with wrong subjective thinking, or he may, as many are learning to do at the present time, constantly improve his ability through the practical use of a constructive system of subjective thinking. Every subjective thought produces a certain tendency in the mind which will not only affect character, but may change a number of creative energies from their present courses. When this change is not desirable, it may lead to abnormal conditions that may prove very detrimental. A fact to remember, however, is that every subjective thought is a power, and that the same subjective thought always produces the same effects in the system of an individual; also, that a subjective thought never fails to produce a certain effect upon body, mind or character.

The two greatest questions, therefore, in this connection, would be how to cause all subjective thinking to be right, and to give all subjective thinking the greatest power possible. The first question may be answered by training the mind in the art of right, constructive and scientific thinking; and the second question may be answered by learning to give more spiritual power to subjective thinking. How strong the power of subjective thought will be depends upon how much spiritual power the mind contains at the time the thought in question was created. And this leads us to a simple solution of one of the greatest problems in the world today.

We all admit that the living of life in any or all of its phases is almost wholly determined by the way the individual thinks; therefore when we learn exactly how life, conduct, attainment and achievement, are affected by the power of individual thinking, we have the secret through which every condition in human existence may be changed, and changed according to our own desires.

Every problem in life must be brought face to face with the real power of thought before a solution can be secured. Man can do nothing without his thought. To live is to think; and the process of thinking is the channel through which he is to act, no matter what his work or purpose may be. Since man must depend upon the power of thought in one or more of the many forms of that power for everything that he intends to accomplish, it is simple to understand that when he knows the whole power of thought and the real power of thought, he will be in a position to do that which he desires to do. That man can solve the problems of life and accomplish what he has in view, is impossible so long as he has only a vague idea of the power of thought, because it is only through the use of that power that his purpose can be fulfilled. The moralist attempts to better the life of man by trying to persuade people to change their thoughts along certain lines, knowing that if their thoughts are changed their actions will be changed. But does he know the whole power of thought; is he familiar with the laws of mental change; has he discovered what particular changes in mind produce the desired changes in character? He evidently does not know these things, because though he tries to persuade people to change their modes of thinking and living, he does not tell them how.

The scientist aims to better the life of man by increasing the general fund of exact knowledge, which is an indirect attempt to change the minds of the world; but does he understand what effects will follow each particular change that may thus be made? He certainly does not, or he would change his methods in many ways. All the institutions of learning are dealing with thought, changing thought and attempting to improve upon thought; but do they understand the real power of thought? In the light of modern metaphysical research, many of them are groping more or less in the dark. Sometimes they make a lucky strike, but too frequently they are throwing time and energy away. All these attempts, therefore, to change the thought of the world and thereby promote the welfare of the race, must consider the real power of thought, and to understand that power we must investigate the metaphysical and the spiritual realms of thought.

We are all dealing with thought; we are all trying to accomplish things through the use of the power of thought; but most of us have no idea what the real power of thought may be. We therefore miss the mark in too many of our attempts. The discovery of the fact that thoughts have real individual power, and that the mind does produce chemical changes in the body, constitutes the basis of the science of modern metaphysics, both in its application to everyday living, and in its application to the prevention and cure of disease; and as metaphysics is an exact science, it is a system that does possess rare virtue; but it can be made far more effective than it ever has been before.

Those who employ metaphysical methods, however, do not always succeed, nor do all those who employ metaphysics understand what mental laws are called into action when results are secured. The metaphysical scientist is, therefore, in many instances, in the same position as the physical scientist; he misses the mark too often because he is dealing with something that he understands but vaguely. The average metaphysician knows that thought is power, and that the power of thought will cure disease; but what kind of thought is required; and how is that particular kind of thought to be created? These are important questions. We know that different kinds of thought are created during different states of mind. It is necessary, therefore, to enter the right state of mind before certain mental actions can be produced; but it is also necessary to know what mental actions to apply for the various forms of human ills.

The science of metaphysics as applied to the cure of disease, therefore, is an immense study, but as a science it is not confined to the cure of disease. It is also the very foundation both of mind building and character building. A number of metaphysicians think themselves channels of some higher spiritual power, and believe that it is this power that produces the cure; and though they are not always right in this conclusion, still that particular idea gives us the key to the situation. Every physical change is preceded by some mental change, but how great the mental change may be depends upon the power that was in the mind at the time. All cures secured through the metaphysical process are produced by the change of mind. To this there are no exceptions. Those who succeed in producing cures through metaphysical or psychological methods do so through the use of some mental law. If they understand that law, they will always have results when that law is employed, but if they do not understand that law, only occasional results will be secured. Those who grope in the dark will once in a while find something, but, as a rule, they do not find anything.

The principle is this, that all healing through metaphysical, psychological or spiritual means is produced by subjective thought; and the results depend upon how much spiritual power or soul there is in that thought. The first secret of such healing is, therefore, to enter subjective consciousness so as to create subjective thought; and the second is to enter as high a spiritual state as possible, so as to give that subjective thought the largest measure of spiritual power. It is subjective thought that produces the change of mind; and it is the change of mind that heals; but whether the subjective thought is strong enough to produce the necessary change in mind, depends upon how much spiritual power the mind contains at the time. This is the great secret, not only in the use of mind for restoring health, but also in the use of mind along all other lines of activity. Every thought produces its own effect. If the thought is weak, the effect will be slight; if the thought is strong, the effect will be greater in proportion. Since every thought produces its own effect, to secure a certain definite result we must create that thought that always does produce that effect; and the thought must be subjective; that is, it must be produced by our acting in the subconscious mind. In addition, that thought must be charged with spiritual power if we desire the largest and best results possible.

To secure more power for mind and thought, spiritual consciousness must be developed; but this is something that nearly everybody has ignored, and for this reason the power of the average mind is not very strong nor effective. Power comes from within and from above, therefore we must gain a larger consciousness of the interior and the higher states of our being if we wish to secure more power; and we must enter into as perfect harmony as possible with the real source of power, whenever we desire to accomplish something that is above the ordinary.

How to Stay Well

The average metaphysician secures results in healing simply by bringing about a mental change in the patient. The average physician secures results in the majority of his cases through the same law; but in neither instance has any higher power been called into action. Accordingly, the results gained in such instances are never above the average. Occasionally, however, a metaphysician who is inclined towards higher consciousness may temporarily and in a measure touch the enormous power within, and thereby secure almost miraculous results; but such experiences are not numerous, simply because we have ignored the attainment of spiritual consciousness. When this consciousness is highly developed, however, such experiences will happen regularly, and there will be practically no failures in metaphysical healing.

If you are in spiritual consciousness when giving a metaphysical treatment to yourself or to someone else, you are in touch with limitless power, and will consequently charge your thought with so much power that any physical condition can be changed completely. Any physical disease can be absolutely removed by the right thought, provided there is enough power in that thought. This is a great truth we all should remember and fully understand. Another truth equally great is that unlimited power will be given to your thought if you are in spiritual consciousness while your thought is being created. The power of every thought increases as consciousness is expanded, elevated and refined; and to refine consciousness is to gain a more and more perfect consciousness of the soul or spirit of all power.

It is not only the thought that we employ in healing that may be increased in power through development of spiritual consciousness, but all thought will increase in power in the same way, thereby adding immensely to the power of mind and intellect. By developing spiritual consciousness you add quality, worth and power to every talent and faculty you may possess. Your physical and mental capacity will increase, and your genius will become greater than it ever has been before. You may think that your reasoning power is perfect, but spiritual consciousness will add remarkably to the brilliancy of that reasoning power and enable you to clearly understand problems, principles and laws that you heretofore could never comprehend. You may have special talents along certain lines that are considered exceptional, but spiritual consciousness will steadily improve those talents until you will be able to accomplish far more than you ever could in the past.

We must remember, however, in this connection that to secure these greater results we must create the right kind of subjective thought in each instance, through which the greater power from within may be expressed, and no form of thinking that tends to interfere with the constructive process must be permitted. From these facts it is evident that whatever one may be trying to do, he must first create subjective thought, because it is subjective thought alone that produces effects in the system. Second, he must create the thought that produces the exact results desired; and third he must develop spiritual consciousness so as to give his thought as much power as possible.

The process of thinking must be carried on according to exact metaphysical laws, so that the proper mental cause may be formed for every effect desired, and to give each mental cause as much power as possible, consciousness must dwell in perfect touch and in perfect harmony with the inner realms of limitless power.

The secret is this: Think scientifically and give soul to your thinking. Through scientific thinking you will secure the exact results desired, and by giving soul to your thinking those results will be large, even extraordinary at times. When we attempt to develop that inner state of mind called soul, we must remember that the term "soul" signifies the real, the perfect, the absolute and the limitless that exists within all things. It is the source of everything, and is the foundation of existence itself. Through the development of the conscious realization of soul, we gain possession of that power that contains unbounded possibilities, because we enter into that larger state of life, where everything is complete, perfect and limitless. However, whether or not we can at the present time realize the absoluteness of the real, and the reality of the limitless, we can begin where we are and apply the three essentials just presented. We can learn what the exact effect of each thought actually is and think accordingly. We can learn to think subjectively by giving depth of feeling to every thought created, and we can increase the power of every thought by living constantly in that faith that feels the unbounded life within us and all about us. Whatever our field of action may be, we shall find that results from our efforts will constantly increase if these three essentials are applied as thoroughly as possible. A great many people have tried to practice right thinking according to the laws of metaphysical science, but they have failed to give more power to their thinking. Results, therefore, have been limited. The next step is the development of spiritual consciousness, through which greater quality, greater worth and greater power may be given to every thought. We shall then, not only receive what we desire, but we shall receive the best in abundance.

Chapter 19

The Use of Spiritual Power

We must eliminate the idea that the metaphysical process requires hard work and strenuous effort on our part. We must also eliminate the idea that the cure is performed by the exercise of personal power. All of this work is performed by the higher spiritual forces coming into personal expression; but our personal selves do not produce those forces; neither will hard personal work bring them into evidence. It is the consciousness of the spiritual side of life that produces true emancipation and the absolute health and wholeness we have in view; and this is natural because the spiritual alone contains absolute wholeness. That which is not health and wholeness cannot produce health and wholeness, but since spirit is health and wholeness, perfect health and wholeness must manifest wherever the power of the spiritual is expressed.

It can truthfully be said that the spirit is at hand waiting at the gate of every mind. All that is required of us is to open, and the spirit will come in, filling the entire mansion of man with its peace, its power, its healing and its light. But to open the door for the spirit to enter does not require hard work, agonizing prayers, nor efforts that tear both mind and body, as so many of our personal efforts do. To place ourselves in the consciousness of the spiritual attitude is the secret of the highest and the most perfect form of healing, and when we place ourselves in that attitude we shall find that peace, health, freedom and power will inevitably come; because the spirit is peace, the spirit is health, the spirit is freedom, the spirit is power.

When you are in the spirit of health you cannot be sick; and to be in the real life of the spirit is to be in the spirit of health, because spirit is health. When you are in freedom you cannot be in bondage; and to be in the spirit is to be in freedom, because everything that is in the spirit must necessarily enjoy absolute freedom.

When we try to help others with these higher powers, we frequently begin as if it were hard work. We think that we have to do this personally. We forget that it is the spirit and the spirit alone that has the real power. Our work is to place the matter in the hands of Infinite Wisdom, Infinite Power, Infinite Love; and we do this, not through hard personal efforts, but through pure spiritual faith. It is riot the will of the Infinite that anyone should suffer pain or distress of any kind, but it is the will of the Infinite that all should be in the perfect freedom of spirit and truth. It is the will of the Infinite that everybody should be well now; therefore, whoever is placed in the hands of the Infinite now will be healed this very hour.

In this connection we may ask if we are not already in God's care, since we live and move and have our being in His spirit; and what more, then, can we do to place ourselves in His hands? To answer this question, we will simply say that we are in the spirit of the Infinite now, but we do not all know it; and we must know the truth before the truth can make us free. To place ourselves in the hands of the Supreme, is to enter consciously into divine presence, so that we do not simply believe in God, but also feel the life and the power of His spirit in every fiber of our being. Where the spirit is felt, there peace, health and power will also be felt, because where the spirit is felt, there the spirit is; and where the spirit is, there peace and power are also. When you enter the spirit you feel that what you desire to have done is being done, and it is being done by a power that can do all things.

When you actually and sincerely believe that healing and emancipation is taking place in your system, you open the door for the spirit to enter; and when the spirit comes in, the spirit will do at once whatever we desire to have done. While the spirit is at work, we are simply to be silent and receive, that the power of the spirit may take full possession and make us every whit whole. Whatever we desire the power of the spirit to do, that the spirit will now proceed to do, provided we do not interfere; but we do interfere with that work whenever we think about it, or whenever we become strenuous, trying to push the power.

To leave all things in the hands of the Supreme is to leave all things in those hands that will do things right, and that will do just what is best for us. What the Supreme thinks is best for us will give us far more good than anything that we could have planned for ourselves. And here we should remember that the Supreme does not think it is best for us to be sick or in trouble. God thinks it is best for us to be as He is, and He knows neither sickness, nor pain, nor sorrow. Therefore, when you place yourself absolutely in divine hands, you will positively regain perfect health and wholeness.

Many a parent thinks, "If I place my sick child in the hands of God and ask His will to be done, He may desire to take my child away"; but do not believe this for a moment. God wants you to have your child. He does not wish to give you sorrow; and if you are perfectly willing, He will heal your child so that both your child and your joy may remain. But you must be perfectly willing and have no doubt. We all have the privilege to live our own lives so that not even the Infinite will interfere with our individuality; and in order to enjoy this privilege it is necessary that we remain here for a long time and continue in health and freedom during that entire period.

In this connection we should remember that we do not have to leave the body in order to go to God. God does not have to take us out of the body to take us to Himself, because He is everywhere. We may go to God and be with Him absolutely and completely while still living in the visible form. When we understand this, we realize how absurd it is to believe that God wants to take us away from our grieving friends in order to have us to Himself. The truth is, God does, not wish to deprive anyone of anything, and His way will never give sorrow to a living creature. The Infinite is radiant with supreme joy, and it is His will that we should be as He is; but as we are individualized beings, we of course have our own will in all these matters. Nevertheless, the sooner we combine our will with Infinite will, the sooner we shall have freedom and gain possession of the highest and best that life can give. When we take this step, we soon discover that the ways of pleasantness and the paths of peace are found only when we place ourselves unreservedly in His hands, and open the door for the spirit to come in and make all things right.

To clearly discern this conception of the Infinite is of extreme importance if we would heal with the power of the spirit, because the more completely we enter the spirit, the greater is the power of the spirit in us; and when the spirit is strong in us, then it is that we reach that state where our prayers availeth much. Every word of truth that we speak while in this power has healing on its wings; and every just desire that we may express at such times will surely be fulfilled. When the spiritual physician is confronted with threatening failure, there is a tendency to become anxious, and the belief that harder work is required will almost invariably arise; but such beliefs should be put away at once. It is not harder work on our part that is required; it is more faith in the power of the spirit that should be sought; and that faith is never disturbed by appearances, but remains beautifully calm, because it knows. It is the power of the spirit that gives health and emancipation. We are the instruments through which that power is to find expression, therefore we should place ourselves in that high, silent, spiritual state through which the unbounded power of the spirit may find full and free expression.

Our anxiety is always a hindrance. Our intense personal effort takes us out of the hands of the spirit, and we cease to be instruments of its power. In this way failure is usually the result, though remarkable demonstrations of healing could easily have been attained. When we know that the power of the spirit is always at hand, always ready to do anything that we may wish to have done; when we know that the power of the spirit is limitless and can do all things; and when we know that it is the will of God that all should be healed now, what have we to fear or to be anxious about? What more do we need than this sublime truth to give us unbounded faith? And as our faith is, so shall it be; therefore when our faith is unbounded every prayer will be answered, every desire will be fulfilled.

When we are in this perfect faith we find the real secret. We discover that it is the power of the spirit that heals; that the spirit will heal whenever we enter into the spirit; and that we enter into the spirit whenever we pass through the door of pure spiritual faith and place ourselves absolutely in the hands of Infinite Wisdom, Infinite Power, Infinite Love.

To become a good spiritual physician, or to apply the spiritual powers within us in gaining and maintaining health, there are several fundamental essentials to which we should give our fullest attention. These are peace, love, faith, spiritual consciousness, and the understanding of truth. To cultivate these five essentials to the very highest possible degree, is to gain possession of that something within us that will not only give us the power to realize and express the power of the spirit, but will also give us the power to help others in the same way.

The necessity of perfect peace is evident, because without such a peace we cannot enter into the deeper realization of truth and life. The disturbed mind dwells on the surface and has little or no knowledge of absolute reality, therefore cannot understand that something within that is perfect and well at all times. What we realize in the within we express in the without. For this reason, everything that is necessary to our realization of the perfect health within must be fully supplied; and peace is one of these essentials.

A metaphysical treatment should never begin until we have become absolutely still in mind and thought, though this stillness must not simply be a passive stillness. It must be a state wherein you feel very still and very strong. When you feel that the power within is awakened in peace, you are ready to begin. During the treatment, the same peaceful attitude should be maintained, and the feeling of a strong calm should permeate all thought and effort.

The attitude of real peace is one that can be cultivated to a very high degree, because it does not consist in simply being quiet. It is a living peace, and since life is boundless this living peace can be deepened, and deepened for an indefinite period; and the greater the peace the greater the power when the power is surely awakened, because to enter that peace that is a living peace is to enter the higher life and the greater power of the spirit.

Before we can help anyone through spiritual and metaphysical means, we must realize a spiritual oneness between ourselves and those whom we desire to help. We must enter their world, so to' speak, and must feel that we are in perfect touch with their inner and true selves. We must be able to spiritually touch the perfect life within them before we can awaken that life, and it is the awakening of that life that we have in view. The perfect life within is health and wholeness, therefore when the inner life, the life more abundant, takes possession of the person, every phase of sickness or pain must vanish.

To enter into spiritual oneness with another mind, or to produce perfect oneness between the outer life and the inner life in ourselves, love is the secret, because love is spiritual unity. No one can heal to any extent, or realize the power of the spirit in himself, unless he loves much; loves everybody, and loves with the whole heart and soul. But in this connection we must remember that pure spiritual love is not in any way related to ordinary sympathy. Ordinary sympathy sympathizes with sickness and distress, and enters into the world of discord and pain, thereby making evil more real than it previously seemed to be. This, however, is never done through real spiritual love. This love sympathizes with the divine in man, and this makes the divine seem more real and far stronger than it ever seemed before. The result is that the true and the perfect side of man is. recognized and accepted as real. When man recognizes the divinity within, he admits divine qualities into his consciousness; and whatever is admitted into consciousness is expressed in the person. Consequently, by recognizing the divine that is within us, all that is true, all that is real, all that is wholesome, and all that is perfect in the soul of man will be brought forth into actual, tangible expression. The new life thus enters the body, and as this new life is health, all disease must vanish. When health comes, disease is no more; and health does come whenever the inner life is awakened and expressed.

The mission of true spiritual love is therefore very High, and what is more, it is indispensable to this great work. You cannot heal anyone without entering into a spiritual unity with that one's soul life; and this unity is attained only through pure spiritual love. The love that we speak of is impersonal, a love that can love every creature without effort, and regardless of appearance or present conditions of life. The person, therefore, who has such a love, is a perpetual benediction to everybody, and could heal at any time by simply wishing to do so.

The necessity of faith in this connection is so evident that nothing need be said as to why we must have faith in order to heal; but a great deal could be said and should be said concerning the real meaning of faith. Faith is not a mere belief, but a gift. It is a high state of mind that transcends all limitations and discerns the real, the perfect and the good everywhere. Faith knows that all things are possible, because it has the power to see and understand the limitless life and power that is working in man and all about man. Faith makes all things possible because it awakens the greater, the larger and the superior in man. No one can fail who has faith, because faith gives to the mind all the wisdom and all the power that is necessary to realize the object in view. Faith has constantly greater things in store, and keeps the mind on the verge of higher revelations and more beautiful experiences every day. To have faith is to live on the heights, and to constantly ascend to greater heights. When faith comes, all despair, all discouragement and all disappointments disappear for all time. No dark conditions can remain after faith has taken possession, because faith positively proves to the mind that all things are possible, that we can accomplish what we have undertaken, that destiny is in our own hands, and that the future is just as bright as we may desire to make it.

In metaphysical and spiritual healing, faith is not disturbed about threatening symptoms, because it knows that there is a power at hand that can put to flight all kinds of symptoms and diseases at once. In this conviction faith works, consequently it cannot fail. Faith sees the real man and knows that the real man is well, therefore there is nothing to fear, nothing to cause anxiety or unrest. What we inwardly know, that we become conscious of; and what we become conscious of, that we express in mind and body. Therefore, to know that the real man is well, is to bring the health and the power of the real man into the personal man; and since faith does know that the real man is well, anyone who has faith will accordingly be healed through faith.

Spiritual consciousness is the consciousness of the soul, the divine in man, or that which is created in the image of God. The value of this consciousness, not only in the work of healing and emancipation, but in all important or higher attainments, as well as the further development of man, becomes very evident when we realize that it is only those things that we become conscious of that find expression through us.

The great truth that man is created in the image and likeness of the Infinite, is the foundation of pure spiritual metaphysics; and from this great truth we conclude that man is in reality what God is. Not that man is equal with God, because God is infinite while man is individualized; but the same attributes and qualities that exist in the Infinite exist also in man the real man. To be conscious of the real man, and to know and feel that you yourself are the real man, is to have spiritual consciousness.

You are spiritually conscious when you know that you are a spiritual being. Many people believe that they have souls; others believe that they are souls; but this is not sufficient. You should actually feel that you are a soul; and this feeling should be based upon actual conscious realization. When you know that you are a spiritual being; when you know that you are created in the likeness of God; when you know that you are living in a spiritual world; when you know that you are one with the Infinite, and that you are in your real being perfect, good, true and absolutely whole, as God is, then you have attained spiritual consciousness. This consciousness is not mere intellect, but a realization that is felt and known without the aid of ordinary intellectual processes. It is not something that is arrived at through logical reason, but comes as a special illumination to the mind that has been developed up to that necessary state.

When you become fully conscious of your spiritual nature, you enter into the wholeness, the life, the peace and the power of the mind. You no longer live in conditions of discord, sickness, weakness or confusion. You have entered the perfect world which permeates everything, and have appropriated all the high states of the perfect world. To believe in the spirit, and to be conscious of the spirit, are two wholly different states of mind. Many depend upon the former, and depend in vain. It is the latter that we must secure. To be conscious of the spirit is to be in the spirit; and to be in the spirit is to be in peace, health and power, because the spirit is peace, health and power. When you attain spiritual consciousness, you know that you are one with the Infinite, and to know this is surely the greatest thing in the world. To know that you live, and move, and have your being in the Supreme; that you are so near to God that God is closer than breathing; to know that you are inseparable from God; and that you shall never, never be separated from His life or presence, but continue to be one with Him through all eternity to know this is to know that which is greater than all other things in the world. It is a thought too beautiful for tongue to ever describe, and many believe this thought because it is so very beautiful; but when you enter spiritual consciousness you will absolutely know that this thought is the truth; and that realization alone should be sufficient to inspire every mind to seek the spiritual heights this very day.

The value of spiritual consciousness in healing is found in its power to illumine the mind with the light of real truth, and thus reveal man to himself. The average man looks upon the body and calls that himself. He looks upon the beliefs and the opinions that he has inherited and calls them his light and his understanding. The result is the blind leading the blind, mental illusions and false beliefs creating more illusions and false beliefs, and thus perpetuating discord, sickness and failure.

When spiritual consciousness comes, man discovers that he is not the body or the mind, but that he is an eternal soul, a spiritual being, the exact likeness of the Infinite. He discovers that he is neither sick, nor weak, nor depraved, but that he has in the reality of his being the purity of God, the health of God, the power of God, the light of God. He finds that though he is manifesting himself in a visible universe, he is actually living in a spiritual universe; and he learns that this spiritual universe is the kingdom of heaven that is within everybody and within everything. In other words, it is God's own true world, where all is well always well.

When man discovers that he is actually living now in a spiritual world where everything is perfect and absolutely good, he realizes that everything must be well with him; and this is the truth that can make him free. When man becomes conscious of the great truth that all is well with him now because he is the image of God, and is living in God's world, where all is well, the counteracting evidences of the senses must be dealt with. The real and the seeming frequently contradict each other. At any rate, they seem to do so; and to establish perfect peace throughout the system, harmony between the without and the within must be secured. This requires a clear understanding of truth, both spiritual and intellectual, because what is true to spiritual consciousness must be true to objective reason; and it will be true to objective reason when the mind can see truth so clearly that a perfect and immediate discrimination between the true and the false is made possible. When we see the truth clearly, the light of truth so fills the mind that there is no room for darkness. Even reason becomes illumined, accepting conclusively what the spirit has to reveal.

One of the greatest essentials in securing emancipation for the personal man is to be able to prove to the senses and the outer mind that the real man is well, because as soon as the outer man receives this truth there will be nothing to perpetuate disease. Disease and discord can live in the human system only so long as we continue to recognize their existence. Disease does not exist by itself or from itself. It is an effect; and the underlying cause of disease is the belief that man is a material being, subject to all kinds of ills. Therefore when it is demonstrated through the intellect, and to every phase of consciousness, that man is a spiritual being, and that he is always absolutely well, the outer mind will no longer create false beliefs; and when false beliefs cease to be, the effect of false belief, that is, disease, must also cease to be.

False beliefs, created by the outer mind, are the causes of the conditions of disease that fill the body; consequently, when the outer mind discerns the truth, that the real man is well, false beliefs about man will no longer be created. The result is that the cause of disease is taken away, and therefore the disease itself must of necessity disappear also.

It has been said that the senses must be blinded if we are to see pure spiritual truth, and that reason must be held in abeyance when we try to comprehend the reality of the spirit; but this is not true. The physical senses can be trained to work in harmony with the spiritual senses and reason can be educated to corroborate the revelations of spiritual consciousness.

The universe is one with many parts but within each part we find spirit pure, perfect eternal spirit. The being of man is one with many parts and all parts are necessary to each other, and each part has a spiritual basis. When all the faculties of man are trained to function properly, they will all work together to demonstrate the one truth. The spiritual faculties will recognize the physical side of all things, and the physical faculties will be able to demonstrate the reality of the spiritual side of all things. This is the true harmony of being, when all parts of being work together for the larger life and the greater good.

The senses should not work against the spirit; neither should we imagine that the senses are nothing in the eyes of the spirit. When the senses refuse to recognize the spirit they are not properly trained; and that reason that cannot logically demonstrate the existence of the spirit lacks true cultivation.

In the understanding of the truth, therefore, three things are implied: First, to know the real, that which is eternal and absolutely perfect; second, to know the nature and the exact purpose of the temporal; and third, to know the law through which the within and the without may work as one for the greater good of man.

To combine these three essentials in the understanding of truth may seem to be an undertaking too large for the average mind; but it is very simple, and when it is accomplished, man's entire world is illumined. Everything becomes clear, for he can see things as they are. To see things as they are in themselves is to know the truth; and to know the truth is to gain freedom, harmony, health and peace. To simplify the understanding of truth we should base all thought upon the statement that man is a spiritual being, created in the likeness of the Infinite, and that every part of the mind and body of man is created for the purpose of perpetually unfolding the divine qualities and attributes that are inherent in the spirit of man. By realizing that man himself is perfect, absolutely good, and every whit whole, all thought will be the thought of truth, and will produce only true conditions in the life of man. By trying to unite all the senses and faculties, physical and spiritual, upon the one purpose of building a larger life, complete harmony will be established throughout the human entity, and the within and the without will become as one. The result will not only be perfect health and wholeness to body and mind, but also the unfolding of a greater and more beautiful soul.

Chapter 20

How to Enter the Silence

The right use of what is called the silence is highly important, both in the prevention and the cure of human ills, and there are several reasons why. To prevent disease and maintain continuous health, it is necessary that the human system be full of vital energy. Most people, however, waste more than two-thirds of the energy generated in their systems, so that they never possess the required amount for perfect health. The cause of this waste is found in a lack of poise, or in a condition of nervous agitation in mind and body, which is almost continuous in the majority. To remove this condition and attain that perfect calm and serenity which is necessary to poise and the conservation of vital energy, the use of the silence becomes absolutely necessary.

In the cure of disease through metaphysical methods, the use of the silence is vitally important for two reasons: First, the system must be brought into a state of peace, harmony and serenity so as to give nature sufficient energy with which to restore the true order of things; second, when the mind is in the deeper and more serene states of the silence, the upbuilding power of right thought, affirmation and wholesome thinking goes deeper into the subconscious life, thereby producing better as well as more immediate results.

The attitude of the silence is a state that is quite distinct from the usual attitude of mind, and therefore the greater part of the human race has not arrived at that state of consciousness that is necessary to produce the silence. They may be physically quiet at times, but the nervous system is seldom absolutely still, and the mind usually moves according to the call of external suggestion, regardless of the attempted control of the individual. Such is the condition of the majority; in fact, it is the condition, more or less, of nearly everyone. The exceptions are very few, and in those exceptions the more desirable attitude of which we speak has not been attained to a perfect degree. We have many minds that can be still at times and thus conserve more of their power, but they do not live habitually in the silent, well-poised attitude. The degree of stillness and poise that they have attained, however, enables them to occupy the highest and most important positions in the world. The real power of silence is to be found, first, in the conservation of energy, as already stated, and second, in the deeper consciousness of power. We know that the generation of energy in the system will increase as we become more deeply conscious of power, and that this deeper consciousness invariably follows deep thought; but it is not possible to think deeply so long as the mind is in chaos. Confusion of mind tends to make thinking superficial, while harmony and peace tend to make thinking deep and high. It is consequently the still mind that attains the greatest insight into principles, laws and great truths; not the mind that is inactive, but the mind that combines high action with deep stillness. Therefore whenever there is confusion in mind we should never attempt to solve problems that require keen judgment, and we should never make important resolutions nor final conclusions while upset or disturbed.

It is not only deep thought, understanding and truth, however, that come to the silent mind. As stated above, an increase of power comes in the same way. All psychologists now admit that the subjective side of mind is the great reservoir from which proceed the waters of life, power and thought, and so great is the subjective that its supply is inexhaustible. Consequently, if we would bring forth more abundantly the life and power from within, we must enter more deeply into the inner life; or, in other words, the outer mind of action must come into closer touch with' the inner mind of power and life. The electrical motor will receive all the power it may require to perform its work when connected with the dynamo. In like manner, when we connect the outer mind the mind that does things with the inner source of power, enough power will be received to accomplish whatever we may desire. This is perfectly rational, because it has been conclusively demonstrated that the subjective, or subconscious mind is inexhaustible. The outer mind therefore can receive just as much power as it can use, provided it is properly connected with the source the great within. To bring the outer mind and the inner mind together so that the latter can give fully and the former receive fully, is the high art of which we speak, and it is usually called entering the silence; but the result of the silence is more than this. Through the cultivation of the silent attitude, we not only establish a perfect unity with the mind that works and the mind that supplies the power; we also develop that perfect poise which prevents the waste of power. To receive more power from the subjective, and to use properly all this power in the objective, is the twofold purpose; and both are attained through the silence.

The fact that the average person wastes more than two-thirds of the power generated in his system, is a fact that must necessarily cause the deepest possible interest in this subject; and the fact that the lack of poise is the principal cause of this waste will necessarily cause everybody to take up the practice of the silence who has better health and greater things in view. There is no profit in gaining more power from within so long as we are unable to conserve it and properly employ it in the without. The cultivation of poise, therefore, becomes an absolute necessity in all this work. By poise we do not mean inaction, but perfect harmonious action. It is a state wherein all the forces and elements of being are working together for construction.

There is no energy thrown away. All is profitably employed in building up body, mind, character or talent. In the attitude of poise you realize that you have full possession of all the forces of your being, and that you have full control over them, not by trying to control them, but by virtue of the fact that you are in the attitude of poise.

To be in the attitude of poise is to control yourself without trying to do so. In the nervous, restless, disturbed attitude, your forces leave you and you are always weaker, but in the attitude of poise your forces accumulate in the system, and at times to such an extent that you feel as if you were a living magnet. That such an accumulation of energy, with a knowledge concerning its proper direction for use and development, can make any mind great and cause the body to become brimful of health, vigor and virility, must certainly be evident to all. There are many minds that think they are well poised who are simply quiet in a physical sense. They will usually find various states of restlessness in mind that are just as wasteful as the tangible confusion on the surface. That person who lives in constant nervous agitation is no worse off than the quiet individual who trembles in the within. Both lack poise, and both are throwing their precious energies to the winds. To attain poise we should not simply enter a silent state of mind every day for a definite period of time, but should cultivate a still state of living, thinking, acting and speaking. Special effort should be made to do all things in harmony and in order. Gradually the attitude of poise will establish itself more deeply, until before long we can actually feel poise; and to find a greater joy than the feeling of poise would be difficult.

To take a brief period every day for silent thought and deeper realization is of the highest importance, but to make it a practice to be mentally still just before we proceed with any particular work, is of still greater importance.

The real purpose of silence is the development of the art of thinking and working constructively. However, it is a well-known fact that many new experiences and higher states of consciousness may be gained through the cultivation of a lofty and serene state of mind. Though this be true, it is a question if there is anything to be gained by conquering new worlds while the worlds in which we already live remain undeveloped. When we learn to think and work constructively, we can make so much out of this life, this present state of consciousness, that we shall not have occasion to think of other realms for some time to come. Then, it is also well to remember in this connection that we cannot take possession of new mental worlds until our present worlds have given us all the life, all the power, and all the worth that they possess. To develop that attitude of mind wherein all action becomes constructive, therefore, should be the object of the silence, and to promote this object the silence should not be practiced for the purpose of becoming inactive, but for the purpose of becoming poised while in action.

Many have taken silent moments for the purpose of stilling all actions, and this may be required at times, but we shall find that there will be no occasion for absolute mental inaction when all the actions of the mind are in poise. The well poised mind never feels exhausted, nor is it natural that it should. The electrical motor continues to be full of power so long as it is properly connected with the dynamo. In like manner, a well-poised mind, being in perfect touch with the inexhaustible source of power within, and at the same time constantly developing the power already in action, cannot feel otherwise but full of energy at all times. The only reason why we feel exhausted, is because we get out of poise when we work; and to avoid this we must not merely practice the silence in a room by ourselves; we must also live, think and work in the calm, serene attitude.

How to Stay Well

To be in the silence is not to be in a dormant state, but to feel that you are in perfect touch with the fullness of life and the true expression of that life, which is always calm, strong and serene. The silence is a state of consciousness that unites the outer with the inner, and that maintains the outer life in such an attitude that all is harmony and true expression.

The highest activity is possible only in the silent consciousness, and the best work is always done in such a state. You may be very active in the body, and yet be in the silence; you may be in the midst of confusion, and yet be in such perfect mental calm that you are not in the least disturbed. It is not only possible to be in the silence of calmness and serenity at all times, but it is the only true state in which to live, think or act; and to attain this state is one of the greatest essentials to perfect health.

The use of strong, positive and constructive affirmations is the most effective when the mind is in the silence, or in a calm state of deep feeling. To secure the best results from the use of affirmations, place the mind in a quiet attitude and think peacefully of the deepest states of feeling that you can conceive in your mind. Be comfortably seated in a quiet room, by yourself if possible, though this is not absolutely necessary. You can enter this calm and deeply quiet state anywhere or at any time when you are by yourself or in the company of congenial souls. When you feel that you are becoming inwardly still, proceed to repeat your affirmations. Take a number of good affirmations that declare the present health and strength of your entire being, and repeat each one several times with deep and serene feeling. Think of the truth of each affirmation as going directly into the very depth of your system, permeating and making alive with health and wholeness every atom in your system. Then deeply impress upon your mind the fact that what you affirm is true, and you will realize more and more the very life and presence, all through yourself, of that very truth that makes man free.

To those who have undertaken the development of the superior nature in man, which necessarily includes physical health, mental wholeness and personal power, the silence will be found indispensable, but the exact meaning and purpose of the silence is not generally understood. To a large number it means simply silence; that is, being quiet; but of all actions the silent state is the most active. To others the silence means an inner contact with the psychical forces in man, but here we should remember that the silent state to which we refer has absolutely nothing to do with those forces.

The majority possibly believe that to enter the silence is to think of nothing, to keep the mind in a perfect blank, and to be mentally still absolutely; but there is more real thinking in the silent state than in any other mental state that can be produced in mind. To enter the silence is to enter into the consciousness of the absolute; to gain the most perfect realization possible of the real power, the real wisdom, the real wholeness, the real virtue, the real harmony, the real purity, the real health, the real happiness, the real ability, the real talent, the real genius, and the real greatness that is latent in man. To enter the silence is not only to enter into the subconscious, but to place the mind in touch with the absolute life that constitutes the very soul of the subconscious. It is to enter the great within, and to enter even the within of the great within. In other words, to enter the silence is to place mind in perfect touch with the source of all things. The purpose of the silence, therefore, is to penetrate the larger, the greater and the more perfect that is latent in man, so that mind may become conscious of the limitless that exists in the within. That there is unbounded power in man is easily demonstrated, and that man has within himself the capacity to comprehend greater and greater wisdom without end, is evident to all who have been in touch with the cosmic state; and to enter the silence is to enter this immense field of wisdom and power the cosmic or the universal the limitless sea of absolute life that permeates all things. The silence is called the silence, because the outer mind must be stilled before consciousness can enter the inner state of the silence, but consciousness itself at such times becomes more active than it ever was before, though it is an action that is so perfect in harmony and in rhythm that it can only be discerned by the finer perceptions of the inner sense.

To enter the silence is to enter the innermost chamber of mind and close the door. The external is for the time being eliminated in a measure from thought and attention; but a mistake to be avoided is to try to shut out the external entirely. Many do this and fail, and the reason why is simple; when you try to shut out the external, you turn attention upon the external. You resist the external, and thereby cause the actions of mind to move outwardly towards the surface of thought and feeling. To enter the innermost chamber of mind, however, the actions of mind must move away from the external towards the internal. When trying to enter the silent state, no attention should be paid to those thoughts that may try to crowd in from without, nor to the tendency of mind to wander all over the universe. When entering the silence, we are not concerned with the thoughts of the outer mind, and must not try to still them. Such attempts will only cause attention to come out to the surface and scatter its energies wherever the mind may choose to roam. It is not possible to still the outer mind by trying to do so. The tendency of the mind to wander can be removed only by training consciousness to come in constant contact with the silent and peaceful within. When the whole of attention is concentrated upon the peaceful within, all the actions of mind will become serene without any effort being made to make them so; and this is the one perfect method for removing the roaming tendency of the mind.

To enter the silence, picture the absolute life as pervading all things in an inner, finer plane, and picture this life as being the very highest form of activity, though at the same time absolutely still. Then concentrate attention upon this high, still activity that permeates your entire being. To think of this absolute life within you, and within every fiber of your being, visible or invisible, as being both active and still to the most perfect degree, will cause the mind to become deeply interested in that life; and it is deep interest that produces perfect concentration. To concentrate perfectly upon the high, still activity within will in a few moments cause the mind to enter that state of high, still activity, and then you are in the silence.

The consciousness of the silent state has any number of degrees, from the smallest perception of the silence to the full realization of the absolute state itself. The entering of the silence is therefore a process of growth and development that has practically no end. This fact becomes evident when we realize that the silence is not merely being still in mind and body, but the perpetual ascension of consciousness into the absolute. When consciousness grows in the realization of the silent life, then mind and body will of themselves gradually become more serene. The forces of mind and body will move more peacefully and more harmoniously, and will also become much finer and a great deal stronger. Practically all waste of energy will be prevented. The human system will therefore have unlimited power at its command.

At first thought the silence may seem to be a purely esoteric process, having no value in practical life, but a clearer understanding of the purpose of the silence will prove conclusively that it is absolutely necessary to the best results in any form of life, thought or action. In the average person the surface of life is more or less like the rolling sea, turbulent, wild and stormy; but in the depths absolute calm forever reigns supreme; and the problem is whether a person wishes to draw his power, his thought and his life from the discord and the confusion on the surface, or go to the depths of life, where power is immensely strong, thinking clear and comprehension practically without bounds.

Whatever a person may undertake to do in life, he needs clear thought, calm judgment, a serene, well-poised personality, harmony of action, perfect concentration, and all the mental power he can possibly secure, but it is only through the silence that these essentials may be provided. When we realize that the purpose of the silence is to open the mind more and more to the limitless possibilities that exist in the real life of man, we understand perfectly why the silence can give better health to the body, more perfect harmony to the personality, greater power to the mind, clearer thought to mentality, greater brilliancy to the intellect, and greater capacity to any faculty or talent.

To practice the silence is to train the mind to draw upon the greatness that is latent in man; to constantly break bounds; to transcend the limited; and to live more and more in that power that makes all things possible. To practice the silence is to constantly press on towards greater things, because to enter into the more perfect consciousness of that absolute life that permeates all things is to gain possession of that life that produces greater things. In other words, to practice the silence is to learn to use in practical life the wisdom and the power of the superior self.

When entering the silence, no attempt should be made to cause the mind to become a blank. To try to do so is to pervert the actions of the mind, because it is not possible to stop thinking. To live is to think, and since you cannot suspend life, you cannot suspend thought. He who tries to make his mind a blank is simply turning his attention upon whatever ideas he may have of nothingness, and will thereby think just as much about those ideas as he does about tangible things. The result of such thinking will be the formation of a number of false conditions in the mentality, conditions that will interfere directly with clear, consecutive thinking.

When entering the silence, do not think of mystical forces. To enter into those forces is not to enter into the life of the absolute, and the purpose of the silence is to go directly into that life that is absolute. To enter the silence is not to enter into the so-called finer grades of the mental forces or vibrations, but to enter into the consciousness of those principles and laws through which the very finest and the most powerful forces may be brought forth into peaceful, harmonious action. When attention is centered upon different forces or states of being, the mind cannot enter into the consciousness of the principle that lies back of those forces or states; therefore to enter the silence we must turn attention upon the absolute life at once, and continue to hold attention upon that life by being deeply interested in the perfect calm and the high action of that life.

Instead of trying to keep the mind from thinking, proceed to think about the real, the worthy and the superior that is latent in every part of mind and life. Proceed to form higher and more perfect mental conceptions of the real, the limitless and the absolute, and try to comprehend that greatness that is greatness, that harmony that is harmony, that perfect health that is perfect health, that strength and wholeness that is strength and wholeness. Every step in that direction means another degree in the silent state, the state of the absolute life; and every step taken in the consciousness of this state will make the personality more powerful and more serene, while the mind will become larger in capacity and more brilliant in thought.

When entering the silence, all anxiety must be avoided, and no feeling must be sentimental. Every tendency towards the emotional will cause the mind to become confused with psychical forces, while anxiety will cause the mind to think too much about those tangible results that are desired instead of turning the whole of attention upon that power that can produce any results desired. To enter the silence, keep the mental eye single upon the great within, and think only of the absolute life the life that is in perpetual action, action that is immensely strong, very high, yet absolutely still.

Chapter 21

The Use of Positive Affirmations

In the application of the principles and methods of metaphysics for the prevention and cure of human ills, the use of strong positive affirmations, or what may be termed statements of truth, is highly important; in fact, it is absolutely necessary, and the reason why is found in the fact that the subconscious is one of the prime factors in every phase of this work; and to secure subconscious action the use of affirmations in some form is always required.

The subconscious is the garden of the mind and will promote the growth of any kind of seed, be it good or otherwise. Every thought that we think when the mind is in deep feeling will be a seed sown in the subconscious mind and will without fail produce fruit after its kind. This being true we cannot begin too soon to train the mind to think only the truth; and to affirm statements of truth frequently is the simplest, most direct and most efficient method for training the mind in this respect. It should therefore receive thorough attention and should be made a permanent part of life. Affirmations should be used daily, but we should not permit them to become mere mechanical repetitions of words. Every statement of truth should be deeply felt as truth and should be affirmed as absolute truth. When we employ an affirmation as a mere suggestion its greatest power is lost, because it is the conviction that a statement of truth is a truth that causes the thought of that truth to be impressed deeply and thoroughly upon the mind. The more deeply we feel that the affirmation is the truth the more firmly we establish the thought of that truth. When we impress the subconscious with some vital truth the subconscious will respond with mental states that are created in the likeness of that truth. The result will be the expression of true conditions in the entire system.

Another matter of importance is to express the statements of truth in the present tense. IT IS TRUE NOW, should be the soul of every affirmation, and this "soul" should be deeply felt in every fiber of our being. When you think or say that you are going to get certain things you desire, you impress the subconscious with the idea that those things can be secured in the future but do not exist for you in the present. The result is that the subconscious will not produce those things for you at the present time. When you impress the subconscious with the idea that any particular condition or quality does not exist in the present, or that it is expected to appear only in the future, the subconscious can only respond with nothing for the present. When you think or affirm that you are now sick but hope to get well, you impress the subconscious with the idea that you are now sick, and the subconscious will accordingly respond by producing more sickness for the present. This fact will be a new thought to many, but it is a thought of extreme importance. Whatever we impress upon the subconscious that we are now, that the subconscious will create for us now; and everything that we affirm with deep feeling will be impressed upon the subconscious. When we make the statement, "I AM well," we impress the subconscious with the idea that we have health now, and the subconscious will respond by giving us more health now. Many minds, however, do not think it consistent to say they are well when they really feel sick, but this seeming contradiction disappears when you know that the real man is well, and that you are the real man. When you impress the subconscious with the truth about the real man the subconscious will respond by giving the personal man those very qualities that are possessed by the real man.

How to Stay Well

When you impress the subconscious with your opinions about the personal man you are sowing inferior seeds, many of which may become obnoxious weeds; and the subconscious will accordingly produce more of those personal imperfections, ills, troubles, weaknesses, etc., that were previously impressed in this manner. This is what a great many people do, and therefore never succeed in making the person as strong or as healthy as nature has the power to cause it to be. On the other hand, when you impress the subconscious with the truth about the real man you are sowing superior seeds in the garden of life and good fruits will appear in the personal man the fruits of health, harmony, peace, freedom, power, purity, righteousness, wisdom, joy, spirituality and scores of others that are in the likeness of the perfect man. Whatever you sow in the subconscious will bear fruit without fail. Therefore it is absolutely necessary to sow good seeds only; and to impress upon the subconscious the truth about the real man is to sow good seeds. This is done by affirming absolute truth in the present tense.

Since the real man is well and since you are the real man, you would simply be speaking the truth about yourself when you say, "I AM well." At the same time you are impressing health upon the subconscious, and the subconscious will respond by expressing health into every part of mind and body.

The use of affirmations and positive suggestions is practically the A, B, Cs of metaphysics and like all A, B, Cs will be needed constantly. Never give up your affirmations, but aim to make the act of affirming the true, the ideal and the wholesome so perfect that you become a living affirmation of your own sublime ideals. Aim to give your affirmations more life, more spirit, more soul, and before long every thought you think and every word you speak will contain soul. Then you will actually think and speak with power; your words will carry weights; they will attract attention and produce lasting impressions; and your thought will produce any conditions in the body that you may clearly picture in the mind.

The use of affirmations along the lines of constructive thinking will gradually correct all wrong habits of thinking. In fact, to affirm constantly the ideal is to train the mind to think the ideal, and to think the ideal is to make real the ideal. To think that you are well is to train the mind in wholesome thinking, and such thinking leads to wholesome living in mind and body. The result will be perfect health through and through the entire human system.

There are a number of metaphysical systems that have been based upon the idea that we should deny the evil and affirm the good, and at first sight this idea seems right and good, but when we examine this subject more closely we come to a different conclusion.

In the first place we may ask why we should deny evil, why should we devote time and energy in trying to destroy something that has no actual existence. It is a well known fact, and is admitted by the best thinkers in the world that evil in its last analysis is simply a condition that implies the absence of something that nature requires to be there. It is therefore simply emptiness, and emptiness cannot be said to have existence; nor can the condition we call emptiness be changed by acting upon that condition itself. We must act upon something if we wish to fill a place where there is nothing, but we cannot act upon something while our attention is centered upon nothing. That person, however, who makes it a practice of denying evil is mentally acting upon nothing, and is thereby using his mental energy in trying to drive away an empty condition.

We have been told that when we deny evil we remove false belief from the mind, and that false belief must be removed before right belief or truth can find a place; but this idea has no place whatever in exact scientific thinking. We do not have to drive the darkness out before the light can come in. We do not have to remove the emptiness from the pail before we can pour in the water. We do not have to remove that which is nothing before we can introduce that which is something. We conclude, therefore, that it is simply a waste of time to employ denials; and besides, it can be readily demonstrated that any system of denials may become a serious obstacle to the attainment of health, freedom and the higher development of mind and soul.

Denials, however, are said to be effective, and that is true in some instances; but they affect the mind in the same way that opiates affect the body. That is, they deaden the mind to the existence of conditions and this is an effect that we do not desire.

In this connection we must remember that it is not the denial itself that produces this effect but the force of mind that goes with it. We might continue denials for ages and have no results whatever if no mental force were employed in the process; but mental force employed for the purpose of impressing denials upon the mind is a misuse both of force and mind. Those impressions that are forced upon the mind during the process will establish in the mind the very nothingness that we are trying to deny. The result will be another harvest of empty conditions in the mind. That the mental force employed in these denials is misdirected is readily understood when we realize that all mental force is misdirected that is not turned into constructive channels; and no constructive process can possibly follow the use of mental force in denying the existence of nothing. It is the misdirection of energy that causes all the trouble in the world; therefore to avoid it absolutely must be our purpose, and this is accomplished by training the entire mind to become constructive.

Constructive thinking is based upon the principle that everything that is real is good; that every force, every element, every personality, every individuality, every law, every quality, every attribute, every principle everything that has independent or permanent existence is good. When the good is misdirected we produce a condition that we call evil, and this condition is an empty state, the result of the absence of the good. And here we should remember that no place can be filled by anything but reality, and also that all reality is in itself good. When the good is misdirected it fails to go where it should go. It will therefore be absent temporarily from its true sphere, and it is this temporary absence of the good that causes evil conditions, or what might be termed states of emptiness. It is the fullness of life that makes for a perfect life. Therefore, empty conditions are contrary to the natural order of things, and for this reason produce pain; but the pain is a good friend provided by nature to inform us that we are not living the full life. The misdirection of the good, or the wrong use of reality, comes from an incomplete mental conception of life. This condition forms in mind a wrong idea which serves while it lasts as a pattern for thinking. "As a man thinketh, so is he." Therefore if his thoughts are wrong, wrongs will be formed in his system, and he forms wrong thoughts by conceiving false ideas about life, and those things that exist in any sphere of life. It is evident therefore that the secret of overcoming evil lies in removing false ideas, and this is accomplished by creating true ideas. To try to remove false ideas by denying them away is not to remove them at all, but to so blind our mental eyes that we do not see them and also to so deaden our sensibilities that we do not feel their effects. False ideas will not disappear until true ideas are formed. So long as we think about certain things we will have ideas about those things and we will continue to have false ideas until we find the true ideas. When the true ideas are formed the false ones will be no more, because no mind can think the false after it has begun to think the true.

In the face of these facts the idea of driving out false ideas by some fixed system of denials becomes utterly absurd. We know that ignorance will remain until knowledge comes, but when knowledge comes, ignorance will of itself entirely disappear. The secret, therefore, is to know the truth; to grow in the truth; to keep the eye single upon the absolute truth, and to perpetually enlarge the mind in a more and more perfect understanding of the truth. When light and truth enter the mind, wrong will disappear, and sickness will vanish, poverty will disappear, and troubles will be no more. Bring in the light, waste no time in fighting the darkness either in the body or in the mind. To bring in the light and to work exclusively for the increase of that light is to enter the path of the life we all desire to live. Never deny evil. Never think of evil. Forget it entirely; and the best way to forget evil is to think only about the good in yourself, about the good in others, about the good in the universe.

To train the mind to think of the good, and the good only, affirmations should be used daily and continually. The purpose of an affirmation is to help the mind to keep the eye single upon the ideal that we desire to realize, and as we wish to direct the mental eye upon higher and higher ideals constantly, we may use affirmations to advantage for an indefinite period. We should avoid the ordinary use of affirmations, however, as it becomes too frequently a system of valueless and mechanical suggestions. An affirmation properly used culminates in realization; and in the proper use of an affirmation the first principle to be observed is that it is true. An affirmation is the truth about some principle,

How to Stay Well

quality or attribute in life expressed in such a way as to convey to the mind the essence of that truth. Since an affirmation is a truth, the mind must express that affirmation as a truth, and must inwardly feels that it is the truth. It is when the mind feels the soul of an affirmation that the truth is realized. When an affirmation is expressed it should be expressed because we know it is true and should therefore be used constantly, because it is our desire to constantly express that which is true.

Do not use an affirmation as you would some ordinary remedy to be taken when in pain and at other times put away. There are thousands of metaphysical students who employ affirmations in this fashion. They affirm the truth when they desire to secure certain results, but at other times they think whatever may happen along. Accordingly the results they secure are neither remarkable nor numerous. An affirmation should be lived, and should be expressed, not for temporary results but for a permanent realization of a larger life. When the larger life is realized all other results that we may desire will surely follow.

The formation or wording of an affirmation should be left to the individual, and in each instance that affirmation should give expression to the highest conception of truth that has been attained. An affirmation should not deal with relative truth, but with absolute truth; and the difference can be illustrated by the two statements, "I AM better," and "I AM well." The statement, "I AM better," is a relative truth, it deals with a changing state and no changing state can serve as a permanent ideal for right thinking. Therefore, such affirmations are of very little value. The statement, "I AM well," is an absolute truth, because in the absolute or in the perfect all is well; and we can conceive of no higher ideal in the world of wholeness than that of being absolutely well. Such a statement therefore gives expression to the real truth as it is, and will also inspire the mind to produce thought and mental states in the exact likeness of that truth.

When sickness appears in the body affirm, "I AM well," and know that it is the truth, because you, the real you, the individuality, the real "I AM," always is well. As you affirm this statement think of the absolute wholeness that permeates your being, and keep the mental eye single upon this absolutely perfect state. In this way perfect health becomes your ideal, and all your thinking will become healthful. Every thought you think will accordingly contain the power of health, and as your thought is so will also be the states and conditions of your personality.

The statement, "I AM well," however, should not simply be used when sickness appears in the body. It is a statement that every mind should think at all times, because it is the truth about the true being; and the person who always thinks the truth about the true being, will always be as well in body and mind as he is in the perfections of his true being. Live and think constantly the statement, "I AM well" and you always will be well.

Every quality or state of being should be affirmed in the absolute truth and not in the form of a changing ideal. Learn to see the whole of yourself from the standpoint of the perfect and think of every quality, talent or power in your possession as you know it is in the perfect. Affirmations of absolute truth should never be expressed audibly unless you are teaching the use of affirmations to another. There are many reasons for this, though the principal reason is that the thoughts we hold sacred have the greatest power. Every affirmation should be a strong, and quiet aspiration that draws the entire mind into a higher state. With this attitude of mind there should be a perfect faith that the soul's desire will be realized now, that it is even now realized, which is true in the absolute; and we should always base our affirmations and faith upon what is true in the absolute. Affirm the positive and the true of all things in your life, and whenever you express an affirmation think of the inner truth that the statement contains. Concentrate upon the spirit of the thoughts you think, and the truth you know those thoughts to contain will become a power in your life. While affirming the absolute truth about any quality or power that exists within you it is well, though not absolutely necessary, to desire the outward expression of that quality or power, because what is realized in the within will of itself, express itself in the without. Everything in the personal life will gradually change for the better as the mind grows in the understanding of absolute truth. The first and greatest essential, therefore, is to change the within, and to attain an ever growing understanding of that which is true of the real man.

Chapter 22

Statements of Truth and Selected Affirmations

Wrong thought is the root of all evil. Right thought is the cause of all good. The art of right thinking, therefore, becomes one of the highest arts in existence, and its attainment one of the noblest aims of the human soul. To think right is to think the truth. Accordingly, the art of right thinking is cultivated by training the mind to think the truth. The average mind has been thinking wrong thoughts so long that wrong thinking has become a habit, and a very undesirable habit, as we all know. This habit we must overcome if we would have perfect health; and the only way to overcome bad habits is to cultivate good ones. Therefore, if we would overcome the habit of wrong thinking, we must cultivate the habit of right thinking; and for this purpose there is no method that is superior to that of concentrating the mind upon positive affirmations and constructive statements of truth. Everybody is advised to use this method extensively, whether in perfect health or not, and if used properly no one can fail to obtain most excellent results. We shall present herewith a number of these statements which may be employed with great profit whenever the elimination of the wrong and the attainment of the right is desired. To proceed, concentrate the mind upon each statement for a brief period of time, say several minutes if possible, and during this concentration repeat the statement mentally over and over again for a number of times. These repetitions or affirmations should be made slowly, quietly and with deeply-felt conviction. You will find it profitable to spend from fifteen to thirty minutes two or three times a day at this practice, but do not permit the practice to become merely mechanical. No results will be secured unless the whole heart, the whole mind and the whole soul are in the work; and while affirming these statements realize by all means that they are absolutely true absolutely true about the soul, the true self, the real man, which is you yourself. A few of these statements are as follows. You can form and employ others as you desire:

> I AM strong and well.
> I AM a soul. I have a body.
> I AM master over myself.
> I can be what I will to be.
> I will be what I will to be.
> All good things are within me.
> I AM one with the Infinite.
> I AM pure spirit, and spirit is perfect.
> I AM filled with the fullness of life.
> I AM filled with the spirit of health.
> I AM perfectly free and always shall be.
> I have perfect health in abundance.
> I have life and power in abundance.
> I AM well, I AM well, I AM well.
> I AM strong, I AM strong, I AM strong.
> I AM perfect in being, through and through.
> I AM peace, I AM joy, I AM harmony.
> Nothing but the good shall come to me.
> I desire nothing but that which is good.
> I AM pure and clean in thought and speech.
> I shall seek only the right in every action.
> My life is filled with the beautiful and the true.
> I love everybody and desire everybody to love me.
> I AM in harmony with every creature in existence.
> Spirit is in perfect health, and I AM a spiritual being.
> I AM always happy, for I AM living the life beautiful.
> Peace, power and plenty are my constant companions.
> My body is real and good, and all its functions are good.

The blessings of health, happiness and harmony are forever mine.

> I AM the real man, and the real man is always well.

How to Stay Well

I know the truth and the truth has made me free.

I AM strong in the spirit, for invincible power is mine.

Infinite power is in me, for I AM one with the Supreme.

I can do what I will to do, for my life is my own.

I AM living the life of the spirit, the life of infinite good.

Every thought that I think, I think in oneness with divine wisdom.

Every word that I speak, I speak in oneness with divine truth.

I live and move and have my being in the infinite sea of divine spirit.

The future is mine. I have the power to determine what it shall be.

I have faith in God, I have faith in man, I have faith in myself.

My whole life is in my own hands, I can do with it whatsoever I will.

Within me dwell infinite possibilities. My future is wonderful.

I rejoice eternally that I AM blessed with the precious gift of existence.

I AM filled with the fullness of health and shall always be perfectly well.

I AM living the one life and that life is infinite, perfect, divine.

With God all things are possible, and I AM eternally one with God.

I live and move and have my being in the infinite sea of omnipresent good.

I AM filled and surrounded with infinite power, infinite wisdom, infinite love.

I have found the true life, and I have learned how to live.

I AM able to do whatsoever I will to do, for I AM spirit, and spirit is above limitations.

I AM loving, tender and sympathetic; just, truthful and sincere; patient, gentle and kind.

Whatsoever I will is good, for my will is divine will, and divine will is infinite will.

Whatsoever belongs to God belongs to me, for I AM a child of the Supreme and heir to His Kingdom.

Whatsoever is in God is in me, for I AM created in His image and likeness.

All good is in the spirit, and the spirit is in me; therefore all good is in me.

I now realize the perfect health that is in me, and in that health I shall ever live.

The real substance of my being is always wholesome, always clean, always in health, strength and harmony.

I AM perfectly well through and through, for I AM made of that substance that is always in perfect health.

I AM living forever in the kingdom of good. Therefore I shall always have abundance of everything that is good. Limitless supply is mine.

I AM a spiritual being. The spirit is the everlasting home of joy. Therefore my ways are ways of pleasantness and all my paths are peace.

I AM free from all disease, all misfortune, all sorrow, all want, all ignorance, all evil. I AM living in the truth and am perfectly free.

I forgive everybody to the utmost for what they might have done against me, and ask everybody to forgive me for what I might have done against them.

All the souls of the universe are my brothers and sisters; we are all children of the one God; we are all rays of the one Great Light; and in this spiritual unity I shall ever live.

Peace is mine, freedom is mine, health is mine, power is mine, strength is mine, abundance is mine, wisdom is mine, joy is mine, love is mine all good things are mine.

I think the good, speak the good, act the good. I seek the good and find only the good. I attract the good and radiate the good. I AM surrounded by the good and live the good. Nothing but the good can proceed from me or come to me.

How to Stay Well

I AM created of pure, spiritual substance, and in spiritual substance there can be no evil. Therefore neither disease, poverty, tribulation, weariness, misfortune nor distress can enter my real being; neither can sad or dreary days appear in the luminous pathway of my soul. The violent storms of anguish can never rage upon the crystal sea of spirit, neither can the turbulent billows of passion beat upon its fair, eternal shore. And I AM living in the spirit, now and forevermore. My life is full of beauty and bliss. I AM eternally basking in the celestial sunshine of divine love, and forever surrounded by the balmy atmosphere of peace. The holy book of divine wisdom is ever before me, and the radiant light of truth leads me wherever I may choose to go. The magic wand of divine power is ever in my hand, and at my command all the elements of nature arise with pleasure to fulfill my desire. My life is overflowing with supreme joy, speechless ecstasy and ceaseless delight. I have found the true life. I have learned how to live. All is beautiful, and all is well. The foregoing statements of truth are truths indeed. They are truths about you, the real you, the soul, the spirit, the real man which is always well.

From the standpoint of the body these statements will of course appear to be untrue, but here we should remember that the truth, when viewed from the false standpoint, always seems false. When we affirm these statements, however, we are not speaking of the body. We are speaking of the soul, the spirit, the real you, the "I AM" and if you will analyze the nature of the soul or the "I AM," you will find that the above statements, when applied to the soul, are absolutely true. Always remember that you are the soul. The body is your instrument. The body is therefore dependent upon you, the soul, for all its conditions; and the conditions of the body, be they health or disease, happiness or distress, power or weakness all are results of what you think. As long as you think the untruth, evil and wrong conditions will appear in your body. There will be disease, poverty, distress, misfortune, and the like; but as soon as you learn to think the truth, those conditions will disappear and good conditions will manifest in the body instead. There will be health, happiness, plenty, peace, comfort, harmony, wisdom and power.

The soul, or the "I AM," already has within itself everything that is good, and if you would have all of these good things from within express themselves in your personality, you must think and live right. You must think the truth and think it constantly. Before there can be action in the without there must be thought in the within, and as is the thought within so will be the action without. Most minds in their present state are thinking too much of the untruth; therefore adverse conditions are constantly appearing in their personalities; but when all such minds proceed to train themselves to think the truth, there will soon be a change for the better. To train the mind to think the truth, begin by affirming the above statements of truth as previously indicated. Read them, think them, repeat them with power, earnestness and conviction. Commit them to memory, if possible, and make them a part of your conscious thinking. Say these things to yourself mentally at frequent intervals and deeply believe that they are all true. When you employ these affirmations, or others that convey the same constructive thought, know that you are speaking the truth about your real self, that something within you that is always well, and to speak and think the truth about your real self is to cause those same true conditions that are in the real self to come forth into the personal self. In brief, when you recognize the light of truth and health that is in you, you turn on that light in your entire domain; and when the light of truth and health is turned on in your life, the darkness of weakness, disorder and illness will disappear.

Chapter 23

Chief Essentials in Prevention and Cure

The first essential is to realize that every thought has a definite effect upon the body, that all present conditions in the body can be modified or entirely removed by certain mental states, and that new physical conditions can be formed at any time by simply creating the corresponding states of mind. When this realization becomes clear, the mind gains a deeper hold, so to speak, upon the forces of thought, and can therefore control, direct or change those forces more effectually as the understanding of the metaphysical process develops.

To produce this realization, impress deeply upon the mind the fact that thoughts are things, and that every thought is a power a power that can and does produce tangible effects in the body. Think constantly of the fact that the states of the mind are the causes, and the conditions of the body the effects, and that you can change the effects by changing the causes. Think deeply and with feeling and conviction upon all of these great subjects until you realize that the nature of thought is perfectly clear.

The second essential is to control your thinking, your mental states, your feelings, your desires, your actions and your living, both in the physical and the metaphysical spheres of life. In other words, create only those causes in your life that will naturally produce the effects you desire. To control thinking is not to try to exercise mastery over your present states of mind or modes of thoughts, but to proceed to think exactly what you desire to think, ignoring absolutely every habitual thought that is not in harmony with that desire.

How to Stay Well

The principle of psychotherapy is based upon the fact that undesirable conditions will disappear from the human system just as soon as the opposite states are created and placed in full action, and the secret, therefore, of this mode of cure is not to try to drive out disease, but to proceed to create health. There can be no sickness in the body so long as the mind is constantly creating health, and the mind continues to create health so long as every thought is wholesome and every idea based upon the fact that the principle of health is a part of life itself. Real life is health, therefore everything that lives has within itself the power of health, and where the power of health is fully expressed in the body there can be no disease.

To create health in the system is to awaken and express that power of health that is latent in the system, and this is accomplished through wholesome thinking, and the thinking of health as a real, permanent factor in the system. In other words, keep your mind concentrated upon the great fact that you have the power of health in every part of your system. Then train all your thinking to act in harmony with that fact. To concentrate your attention upon the fact that your system is filled with the full power of health is to impress the subconscious with the idea of health, and the subconscious will accordingly proceed to express the full power of health.

The subconscious mind always does what it is impressed to do, and whatever we think deeply with feeling and conviction will impress itself upon the subconscious. To mentally picture perfect health in every part of the body will also impress the idea of health upon the subconscious, and health will in consequence be created and expressed in every part of the body. To give the subconscious mind full freedom, however, to workout the health-producing process, all thinking must be wholesome. When thinking in general is unwholesome, conditions of disease will be formed in the system, and these will interfere with the expression of those conditions of health that the mind is trying to create. At such times a part of the mind will be working for health, while the other part will be working against health. This accounts for the fact that the average human being is seldom entirely well.

To promote wholesome thinking, the first essential is to cultivate the calm attitude. The second essential is to eliminate wrong thinking by cultivating right thinking; and the third essential is to mentally live in the reality of the ideal, or what may be termed sublime realism. The calm attitude is necessary first, because it stores up energy, thus giving greater strength to mind and body, and second, because it gives self-possession, one of the great essentials in the control of mind and thought. To turn the energies of mind into wholesome and healthful channels of thought, a certain amount of self-control is absolutely necessary, but no one can develop self-control or self-possession until the calm attitude is attained.

There are many causes for the failures that are sometimes found among those who attempt to apply the principles of right thinking and ideal living, but there is nothing that produces more of such failures than the absence of the calm attitude. When the mind is not calm, it cannot act without scattering its forces to a considerable degree, and forces that are scattered are misdirected. The result, therefore, will be mistakes, abnormal states, unwholesome conditions, weakness, and possibly ill health. Perfect concentration is not possible unless the mind is calm, and without concentration the mind cannot think or do effectually what it is determined to think and do, and therefore cannot create those conditions of health and harmony that alone can remove adversity and disease.

How to Stay Well

To remove wrong thinking, it is necessary to cease all anger, all worry, and all fear, and to eliminate every state of mind and action of thought that is more or less similar to these wrong states; but these wrong states of mind cannot be driven out; they will disappear only as their opposite good states are cultivated. The opposite of anger is love, kindness, sympathy, forgiveness, humaneness, mercy and justice. The opposite of worry, faith, self-confidence, self-reliance, trust, mental sunshine, and a keen insight into the greater possibilities of life. The opposite of fear is the understanding of life, changeless law and principle, and the discernment of that finer consciousness that knows that we live, and move, and have our being in the spirit of the Supreme. To cultivate these most desirable qualities is very simple, because we naturally grow into those states, qualities, characteristics and realizations that we constantly think about with deep and undivided attention.

The third essential to wholesome thinking is to live in the reality of the ideal, that is, to mentally live in the understanding of sublime realism. This will give the mind the true understanding of everything with which it may come in contact. In other words, the mind will see the true side and the upper side of everything, and will consequently create all thought in the image of the whole the wholesome instead of in the image of the partial, the imperfect, and the incomplete. The realism that is passing is temporary. It appears real to the senses, but it is only a passing condition, imperfect and incomplete in every way. It serves a purpose, however, because it is the constant coming forth of that which is complete. It is the growing expression of the universal source of all that is, and this source may be defined as sublime realism.

To enter the understanding of sublime realism is to enter the reality of the ideal, and whenever the mind grasps the real that is in the ideal, it will cause that real to be expressed. Through that mode of action the ideal becomes real, that is, the sublime reality of the ideal becomes tangible reality. To live in sublime realism is to be conscious of the reality of the ideal, and what we become conscious of, we express more and more through body, mind and personality; therefore, by living in sublime realism we cause the ideal to become an actual fact in tangible realism.

To live in sublime realism may seem difficult to the beginner, but it is very simple. All that is necessary is to think of the ideal, live for the ideal, and work for the ideal at all times, knowing that the ideal is real in its own sublime world, and that it can be made real in the tangible world. In addition to this, view all things from the upper side; that is, do not think of the faults or the defects that may exist in anyone, but think only of the strength, the health, the wholeness, the power, the worth and the superiority that exists in everyone. When we view all things from the upper side, we develop the upper, the stronger and the more worthy side in ourselves. We thereby grow out of weakness into strength, and as sickness can exist only in weakness, we soon may become permanently well.

The great secret of metaphysical methods of healing is found in clean, wholesome thinking, combined with the constant creation of health in the subconscious mind. As the mind is, so is also the body, therefore when the entire mentality, conscious and subconscious, is clean, strong, wholesome and well, the entire body will also be well.

To keep the physical system brimful of vital energy is one of the great secrets of health, and this is readily made possible through the proper mental attitudes and the proper application of the power of thought. No disease can gain a foothold in the system so long as the vital energy is full and strong, and no disease can long remain in the system after a decided increase in vital energy has begun. Disease thrives only in weakness, never in strength; and strength can be gained to any degree desired and retained for any length of time desired. The first essential is to prevent all waste of energy, and this is accomplished by training the mind to hold the entire physical system in a deep state of interior calm. Begin by forming a mental picture of what you conceive such a calm to be. Then try to feel that calm in your mind. When you are distinctly conscious of that calm state, you can hold your mind in that state by simply proceeding to do so, and in whatever state you can hold your mind, you can hold your physical system also. Train your mind to hold itself, as well as the physical system, in the deepest calm that you can possibly realize, and train yourself to live in such a calm perpetually. To increase the supply of vital energy in the system, learn to draw upon the subconscious for a continuous increase of life and power. Remember there are layers upon layers and layers beneath layers of unused energy in the subconscious world, and we can awaken and develop as much of that dormant energy as we may require. To awaken more of this energy, turn your attention upon the subconscious at frequent intervals, and deeply but calmly desire more vital strength. As soon as your desire for more power and energy enters the vast subconscious field of power, you will awaken more power, and added power will begin to come forth and fill your system through and through.

The subconscious field is that deeper, or interior field of life and consciousness that permeates the physical personality within what may be called a finer state of life and action; therefore, by deeply and constantly thinking of that finer state that fills us through and through, we naturally enter into that state more and more; that is, the actions of the mind will come in contact with and enter into the life and the power of the subconscious, and whatever we strongly desire at such times will be impressed upon the subconscious. Accordingly, if we desire more vital energy at the time, we impress the subconscious to give us more vital energy; and the subconscious never fails to do what it is actually impressed to do.

Through this method anyone can build up the strength and the vitality of his system until his physical as well as his mental capacity becomes remarkable; and the principal reason why so many who have learned to draw upon the subconscious for more power fail to permanently increase their strength is found in the fact that they do not retain the added strength and power gained. When the added power is received, they lose it almost immediately, because their conscious mind has not been trained to hold all of its power within its own personal domain.

If you wish to retain your power, and consequently build up greater capacity and vital strength, you must hold yourself constantly in the deep, interior calm, and live, think and act in perfect poise. Another essential in this connection is to remove the cause of weariness, and to eliminate the habit of getting tired. To feel tired is just as unnatural as it is to feel sick. Weariness is a twin sister of sickness. The two come directly or indirectly from the same cause, barring a few exceptions, and this cause is due to insufficient life force in the human system.

When the system is full of life and energy, there can be no sickness, any more than there can be darkness in a room that is full of light, Neither can there be weariness in such a system; and since it is natural for the human system to be always full of life and energy, we must conclude that both sickness and weariness are unnatural. Both come from false conditions, or the wrong use of what is in us; therefore, neither belongs to the true order of things. When a person feels tired, it proves that he has used up energy, and has either failed to generate a new supply or has lost, through lack of poise, the new supply that has been generated. Neither of these two conditions, however, is natural.

When the system is in a natural condition, it generates strength just as rapidly as the most active personality could use it up; and a natural condition of the system always prevents the loss of every form of energy that that system may possess. Frequently the human system generates more energy, the more active we are or the more energy we apply, so that it is possible to establish a condition whereof we can say of ourselves, the more energy we use in our system, the more energy we generate in our system. This condition is the natural outcome of the principle that much develops more, and that increase tends to promote greater increase. Under such a condition, work, if properly performed, will increase strength and capacity; and this condition is always present when nature is at her best.

When a man is at his best, and all things in his system are working together in harmony, he never tires from his work. He is just as full of life and spirit in the evening as in the morning; and this is natural. The fact that work under natural conditions will increase strength and capacity does not indicate, however, that it is wise to work continuously in order to secure a continuous increase of strength and capacity. It is only under natural conditions that work will increase strength and capacity; but natural conditions demand plenty of sleep and a reasonable amount of recreation. The man who secures seven or eight hours of sleep every night, and two or three hours of recreation every day, can work fourteen hours a day, six days in the week, and fifty-two weeks in the year, without ever feeling tired, that is, if he is living a natural life and has eliminated the inherited habit of getting tired. The fact that nature generates energy in the human system just as rapidly as it is used up when conditions are natural, proves that no man has a legitimate reason for ever feeling tired. Weariness cannot possibly come from the right use of nature. When it does come, it always comes from the misuse of nature. This misuse may be one or more of various things. It may be overeating, breathing impure air, irregularity in living, dissipation, anger, worry, excitement, nervousness, lack of poise, destructive mental states, nervous rush, indolence, any habit, and especially the habit of getting tired. It has been found, however, that a man may live a wholesome, constructive life and still feel tired at frequent intervals. His system may be in natural condition, and all his functions may be in harmony and expressed in useful action, still weariness comes at times, and if it does there can only be one reason, his system has the habit of getting tired. Weariness in his case does not come from any other cause whatever than simply the habit of feeling weary or getting tired after a certain amount of work has been done.

We have believed so long that it is natural to get tired, that action used up energy, that the supply would necessarily be exhausted, and that we could not help feeling weariness, as the result, that it has become a habit both to expect to get tired and to feel tired; in fact we have believed for ages that a certain amount of action would inevitably bring weariness, and that it was a credit to feel tired because it indicated that we had not been idle. In consequence, we have through generations and generations of this belief gradually trained our systems to become tired whenever a certain amount of work has been done, regardless of the fact that our systems might be brimful of energy at the close of the day's work.

How to Stay Well

In this manner we have formed the habit of getting tired, and it is a habit that has become a part of human life, so that every child is born with it to a certain extent. In some people the habit is not deeply seated, so that they seldom feel tired unless they misuse mind or body, while in others the habit is so deeply seated that it is second nature for them to feel tired at the close of every day. They are the people who are born tired, so to speak, and many of them usually continue to be too tired to shake off their adverse inheritance. But every inherited weakness or tendency can be absolutely removed; and the simplest way to remove the habit of getting tired is to impress the mind many times every day with the great fact that nature generates energy in your system just as fast as you use it up, and usually much faster. Under natural conditions your system is always full and running over with vital energy, so that whether or not you are working at the highest speed, resting or in the midst of pleasure, physical or mental, your system will always be brimful of life, vitality and power, provided, of course, that you are living a natural life.

There is, therefore, no reason whatever under such conditions why you should ever feel tired in the least. The feeling of weariness is a false condition which should be removed completely, and it can be removed by becoming so interested in the fact that nature is generating more and more life force in your system the more you work, that you will forget to expect to become tired. In consequence, you can do a full day's work without feeling tired in the least when evening comes, and you can thoroughly enjoy your evenings, or devote the evening hours to study for self-improvement, because you will feel just as full of life and spirit during the evening as you did at any time during the day. You will always be full of life and spirit, and always ready to do whatever may add to your own improvement, or to the joy, the comfort and the welfare of those who may have the privilege to live in your world.

The fact that the natural man never gets tired may cause many people to undertake more than they have the present capacity to carry through, but these should remember that the vast amount of life and energy that we receive from nature while we are living a natural life is not intended for work alone. Useful work is a part of life, but the same is true of pleasure; it is also a part of life. In fact, an abundance of good wholesome pleasure is just as necessary to good health, and to the development of man, as sunshine is to the growth of the flowers and trees. Work while you work, but take plenty of time for pleasure. This is the method that counts in the long run; and we are living for a greater future, as well as for a larger and more enjoyable present.

To remove the habit of getting tired is absolutely necessary if perfect and continuous health is to be enjoyed, and the reason is that the moment you permit yourself to feel tired, you lower your vitality and thereby decrease the amount of your physical energy and strength. In addition, you cause your physical and mental system to enter into a negative condition whenever you feel tired or give up to the attitude of weariness; and here it, is important to remember that it is only when the vitality of the system is low, or when the system is in a negative condition, that disease can gain a foothold.

To remove the habit of getting tired, realize that it is nothing more than a habit. It is thoroughly unnatural; and you do not have to feel the condition of weariness at any time. Remember that nature generates new energy in your system just as fast as you use it, and that so long as you continue in harmonious action you give nature the power to generate more energy the more energy you apply. In other words, impress upon your mind the great fact that the more energy I use in my system, the more energy I generate in my system. Realize that fact so deeply that you are positively conscious of it at all times. Then continue in a positive attitude under all circumstances, and keep your system in perfect poise so that you will always be brimful of vitality; and to this add the living of a natural life, physically and mentally, and you will always be well and strong.

Another essential is that of the control of the circulation; and that the circulation can be completely controlled, or at least greatly influenced by the power of thought in any mind, has been demonstrated conclusively, not only in personal experience but also by a number of scientifically directed psychological experiments. Imagine that you are running a footrace and the circulation will be increased in your feet. Imagine that you are taking a hot footbath and your feet will actually become fiery red; and even though they were icy cold before you began your experiment, they will, in a few minutes become "as warm as toast." Concentrate subjectively upon your hand, and you can make the veins on the back of your hand swell to full capacity in less than five minutes. You can produce the same results anywhere in your body with the same method.

Think of something very serious and the blood will rush to the brain; and if you continue this thought for several minutes the circulation will become too strong in the interior part of your cranium. In consequence, you will feel an uncomfortable pressure in various parts of the brain, while your face will look pale and tired. When thought becomes too serious and takes the form of anxious thought, the circulation will be withdrawn from the surface of the face and brain, and the results are most detrimental both to thought and to personal appearance.

You can think best with that part of the brain that lies close to the surface, in fact, it is those brain cells that come in contact with the bones of the skull that constitute the most important channels for the mind. Therefore, what may be termed the outer layers of the brain must receive an abundance of vitality and nourishment if the mind is to do its work properly; and this may be accomplished by keeping the circulation full and strong at the surface of the brain. It must never be forced, however; but no forced conditions will ever appear so long as all the states of mind are normal and wholesome.

Anxious thought takes the blood away from the surface of the brain and thus makes thinking heavy and difficult; but joyous thoughts cause the blood to flow freely into the surface of the brain; and therefore, the bright and happy mind produces the clearest thought, the strongest thought, the richest thought. The circulation can also be increased in any part of the brain through subjective concentration; and in this connection it is well to remember that to moderately and harmoniously increase the circulation in any part of the brain is to cause that part to develop, both in working capacity and in the power of actual, practical ability.

When the circulation is more or less withdrawn from the surface of the face, the skin will not be properly nourished, and the result is wrinkles, a poor complexion and an old-looking, dried-up appearance. Anxious thoughts and worry invariably cause the blood to be withdrawn from the surface of the face; therefore, people who worry much grow old, haggard looking and unattractive in a very short time. Cause the circulation to be full and strong at the surface of your face and your complexion will be good, your cheeks will be rosy, you will have no wrinkles, and you will look young as long as you live. In addition to happy and wholesome states of mind, subjective concentration will enable you to do this, both readily and perfectly.

The cause of gray hair is found almost entirely in a lack of circulation at the roots of the hair. For this condition worry, fear and anxious thought are almost wholly responsible. If the circulation was full and strong through the roots of your hair, the color of your hair would never change, no matter how long you might live. The same is true in regard to baldness. Even when the tendency to baldness is hereditary, which is frequently the case, such a condition can be entirely prevented by increasing the circulation in every part of the scalp. The same method has, in a number of instances, caused hair to reappear after baldness had been in evidence for many years, and there is no reason why it may not be applied successfully in every case.

When the circulation is increased in any part of the body, that part is not only more thoroughly nourished, but its natural function is greatly promoted. This means that all waste material will be eliminated completely and the process of repair will perform its work most perfectly. When there is a diseased condition in any part of the body, that part is usually burdened and clogged with waste material; and as a rule, all that is necessary to remove the disease is to remove the waste material. When that part is made clean, nature will be able to restore normal conditions; and you can make any part of the body clean by increasing the circulation throughout that region.

Whenever there is anything wrong in any organ, one of the first things to do is to increase the circulation in that organ, and this you can readily do through the power of thought. To increase the circulation in an organ is to increase the life and vital power of that organ; obstructions and waste will be removed; the broken-down tissues will be replaced with new, healthy tissues; the process of repair will be promoted; and every element or condition that is not in harmony with wholeness and health will be eliminated. In brief, there is no one thing that will do so much toward the restoring of health in any part of the body as to increase the circulation in that part; and this is especially true when the increase of the circulation is produced directly through the conscious use of the power of thought. Any change in the system that is produced by the power of wholesome thought is almost certain to be permanent, because the real power of thought is deep in its action, and therefore produces its effect, not only on the surface, but all the way through.

To use the power of thought for the purpose of increasing the circulation in any part of the body, all that is necessary is to concentrate attention, with deep feeling, upon that part. But do not concentrate directly upon the physical side of that part, and do not make your concentration a forced mental action. If you wish to increase the circulation in your hand, begin to think deeply of the finer elements that permeate your hand; then desire deeply to express more and more energy through your hand. Do not give any special thought to the circulation of the blood, because that will cause your attention to come to the surface into the purely physical. Wherever there is an increase of energy, and especially the finer energy, there will be an increase of the circulation.

You cannot increase the circulation anywhere until you first cause finer energy to accumulate in that place; and where you have caused an increase of energy, there an increased circulation will come of itself. Whenever an organ in your body is not performing its function properly, proceed at once to increase the circulation in that organ, and further trouble will be avoided. Any threatening ill can be "nipped in the bud" in this manner, especially if it has its origin in the digestive organs. Three-fourths of the ills that appear in the human personality come directly or indirectly from an imperfect digestion; but every condition that may tend to interfere with the process of digestion can be removed at once, provided the circulation is increased throughout the digestive organs the very moment we feel that something is not right.

The power of thought should be used whenever necessary to maintain a full, strong circulation throughout the system. When the circulation is full and strong in every part of the body and the mind is alive with positive, wholesome thought in every part of the body, it is practically impossible for disease of any kind to gain a foothold in the system; that is, so long as the laws of mind and body are observed with special care. The principal laws of the human system are very easily observed, however; all that is necessary is to be temperate in all things, to use good sense in all things and to aim to be wholesome in every thought and deed.

When you do not feel as vigorous, as strong or as well as you ought to feel, give yourself a general treatment at once; and proceed as follows:

Be perfectly quiet in mind and body. Relax perfectly into a deep, interior calm. Think of nothing external. Give your entire thought to the peace, the calmness and the soul-serenity that you now feel in every atom of your being. Hold your entire system in poise. Do not try to be quiet, but just let yourself be quiet, and let every fiber in your being be perfectly still. When you feel this calm, restful condition through and through, begin to think peacefully about the power there is in peace. Look, with the eye of the mind, down through your entire body, and mentally see the accumulation of power in the deep calm throughout your system. In a few moments you will begin to feel life and power accumulating from within, and a calm feeling of great strength will begin to permeate every part of your personality. But do not become aroused by the presence of this power. Continue to be calm, peaceful and deeply serene in mind and body.

When you begin to feel more and more power accumulating in your system, turn your attention upon the abdominal region and begin to affirm that you are strong and well. To concentrate upon the abdominal region at this time will cause all the extra energy that you have gained to accumulate in the organs of that region. The result will be that those organs will be aroused to greater activity, and will throw off those undesirable conditions that are on the verge of gaining a foothold in your system. Almost any threatening ill will disappear at once if the abdominal region is made more alive, and the reason why is found in the fact that the entire system is cleaned and purified when the activity of the abdominal region is increased.

The deep calmness that is gained in every part of the system through this general treatment will tend to harmonize all the forces of mind and body, and when the harmony of the system is deep and strong, nature can work to the best advantage in restoring normal conditions. Harmony removes discord and produces health. When all the forces of the system are placed in harmony they begin at once to work together for health. Everything in human life that is harmonious tends to produce health, while discord, be it physical or mental, tends to produce disease. The power of thought, therefore, should be trained to be harmonious at all times and in all of its phases. Impress harmony upon everything you think, do, or say, and aim to hold yourself in harmony perpetually, no matter what your circumstances or conditions may be.

How to Stay Well

To establish perfect harmony in mind and body is frequently all that is necessary to regain perfect health. Chronic ills always begin to lose their hold when harmony begins to permeate every fiber in the system, and all threatening ills can be "nipped in the bud" by placing the system in a calm, quiet, deeply harmonious state. This general treatment, therefore, may be employed as a sure preventive of every ill; and if applied in time will never fail to place the body in that condition where it may continue to stay well. While giving yourself this general treatment, hold yourself as much as you can in the consciousness of the subconscious and deeply feel that you are gaining more and more power from within. Also give some attention to the increase of the circulation all through the surface of the body and in the feet.

When you increase the circulation through the surface of the body, you open the pores of the skin, and thus give nature a chance to throw off impurities, foreign materials, poisonous elements and false gaseous formations that interfere with the true order of things. To remove colds, fevers, grippe and similar conditions, all that is necessary is to open the pores of the skin all over the body, and at the same time increase the activity of the abdominal region; though these things should be done as soon as possible after you feel the ills coming on. All wrong conditions should be put out the very moment they threaten to enter your door; and a few moments of scientific application on your part will do it.

To increase the circulation all through the surface of the body and thus open the pores of the skin, be perfectly quiet in mind and body and concentrate attention down through the body. In a few moments you will be perfectly still, and the power that always develops in peace will begin to well up from within. When you feel this calm, interior strength, deeply desire the force of this strength to accumulate all over the surface of your body; and while in the attitude of this desire, cause the deeply serene power of your strong thought to move down, from head to foot, over your body and through the surface of your body. If your thought is deep, strong and harmonious, your skin will glow all over your body, and your purpose has been accomplished.

When you feel deeply quiet in mind and body and your thought is full and strong with the finer forces, all that is necessary is to desire the circulation to increase through the surface of your body, and your skin will glow in a few minutes. That "stuffy feeling" that precedes a cold will at once disappear and all will be well again. In like manner, you can cause any unpleasant or sickly feeling to vanish completely; though do not give up simply because you do not feel all right the first time you try the treatment. It usually produces immediate results, but if not, repeat the process at frequent intervals until you feel that air threatening ills have lost their hold. Then forget all about it and leave nature to finish the work. After you have, with the power of your thought, aided nature in overcoming the enemy, nature can so much better restore full normal conditions if you will then drop all thought of disease from your mind.

To increase the circulation through the feet is extremely important whether the treatment be general or for the elimination of some special condition. When the vital forces move toward the feet, all the vital organs are stimulated to greater action, and nature is given added power in its efforts to restore or maintain perfect health. But there is also another reason, equally important. We have all demonstrated through personal experience that any disease that may exist in the system has a tendency to come down and away from the vital organs whenever the circulation is drawn toward the feet. On the other hand, when the circulation is too strong in the upper part of the body, causing the lower extremities to become cold, diseased or abnormal conditions will gain a firmer foothold in the vital organs. We therefore realize why it is so important "to keep the feet warm and the head cool;" but we need not employ external methods in order to realize this ideal state. Through the power of well balanced and harmonious thought we can cause the circulation to become full and strong wherever desired, and this power is always with us.

There are a number of ills that come from wet feet, but all of these ills can easily be prevented if the circulation is increased through the feet while you are waiting for the opportunity to change your shoes and stockings. And when exposed to excessive cold or damp weather you can avoid becoming chilled by simply keeping your circulation full and strong all over the surface of the body. When trying to control the circulation in this manner, however, do not use any forced will power. Such a will power is superficial and will not only prevent results, but will also waste energy. All forced action of mind or body is wasteful and weakening, while all deeply-felt, calm action is constructive, strengthening and accumulative.

The use of the will should always be combined with deep desire, and both should be given soul; that is, when you use the will, try to enter into the spirit of the will, and when you feel the action of desire try to feel the interior life of that desire.

All thought, all feeling, and all mental action should be made deeper and more serene the further you advance in the mastery of your life. You thus gain more and more power and greater interior capacity both in mind and body; in addition you gain control of those deeper forces of your being the finer forces that are at the foundation of all the organs and functions in your system. And to control the finer forces of the system is to control all the organs and functions of the system, because it is the finer forces also termed the subconscious forces that govern everything in the human system, and that determine every change of improvement that is to take place in your personal life.

Chapter 24

Practical Helps to Good Health

It is the belief of many that no one can expect to be perfectly and permanently well unless he has a very high understanding of truth and life, and that such an understanding is very difficult to secure; but this is all a mistake. The path to health is not difficult; neither must one be a spiritual giant to remain permanently well. Anyone can keep himself free from disease by simply giving his system a reasonable opportunity to do its work right.

Before proceeding to apply the metaphysical process in the cure of disease, place yourself in a state of perfect peace, and the more deeply this peace is felt, the better. The deep, silent forces are the most powerful, therefore we should not begin this important work without placing ourselves in what may be termed the deep soul calm. Simply being quiet is a powerful treatment in itself; and there are a great many ailments that require nothing else. The daily practice of being perfectly still in mind and body while the silent forces from within are given free expression through every part of the system, is one of the best preservers of health that can be found. Ten or fifteen minutes of this practice two or three times a day will, under commonsense living, keep any person in perpetual health.

When undesirable symptoms are felt in the system, they should be attended to at once. No one would ever be sick if this were done, because it is not difficult to nip a disease in the bud. The first thing, of course, is to have no fear. Know that you are master of the situation; then proceed to exercise your mastership. Live in the strong mental attitude of supremacy. Have faith in yourself and turn attention upon that inner, higher power that never fails. Awaken your consciousness of the perfect being, and try to feel the fullness of life that is always in health and wholeness. Know that the physical discord you have noticed is as nothing in the presence of real life, and that discord will at once be transformed into health and harmony.

When symptoms of weakness appear, give the entire system, especially the mind, a complete rest for a few hours. Enter a deeply-felt, silent attitude, breathe deeply and quietly, and think only of peace. It is remarkable how easily and quickly strength can be regained and the system recuperated by this simple method, and if practiced whenever necessary you will never lose any time from your work. When weakness is felt, however, we should not give up to it nor permit ourselves to feel weak. This will make the mind negative and make matters worse. Simply rest the body, and hold the mind easily and quietly in the consciousness of unbounded life and power, and what you become conscious of will immediately begin to express itself in mind and body.

Get rid of the idea that you have to take something when you do not feel well. This is simply a bad habit, and tends to give your mind the tendency to depend upon the limitations of things instead of upon the boundless power that is within you. You do not have to take anything if you give nature a chance to remedy the wrong in the beginning. Nature can do this, provided physical nature and metaphysical nature are taught to work together. There are no objections to taking medicine. Medicines are frequently required, and what people require they ought to have; but to burden the system with indigestible and poisonous drugs simply because you think you need those things is to take a path that leads directly away from health.

How to Stay Well

To secure health and preserve health it is absolutely necessary to be in harmony with everything. Discord breeds sickness and trouble every time, therefore avoid it at any cost. Be in harmony with your work and with your environments, even though you may have to blind yourself to certain things that are not as they ought to be. Be in harmony with the people with whom you associate, even though you have to let them all have their way about most things. Go their way when necessary to secure peace, and if you are living an ideal life at the same time you will gradually reach that higher scale in life that will give you a superiority which everybody will recognize. Then you will find that by living in harmony at all times you have increased your power and worth to such a degree that instead of being compelled to follow others for the sake of peace, others will be more than happy to follow you. Superiority and worth will invariably secure leadership in time; and to live always in harmony is to place your system in a condition where it can readily build itself up until greater worth is obtained.

When we are dealing with our own ills, or with those of others, it is necessary to pay as little attention as possible to the appearance of things. No matter how serious things may look from the standpoint of the person, the fact remains that the real man is well, and the perfect health of the real man can be brought out into the personal man if he will continue to give the real man full and constant recognition. What we fully recognize we become conscious of, and what we become conscious of we tend to express in mind and body.

The habit of magnifying a symptom with the mind should never be permitted, because the most insignificant trouble may in this way become intense and even overpowering. The mind gives added life to whatever we think about deeply, and whatever the mind magnifies in imagination will grow and develop. For this reason, when threatening symptoms appear we should think as little of them as possible, and we should train ourselves to look upon them as mere nothings that will soon pass away. The fact that we give life to whatever we think about, reveals a law that can be used to great advantage in building ourselves up physically and mentally; and that everything in mind or body develops when magnified in the imagination is another law that contains remarkable possibilities. We have, however, employed these laws to our disadvantage most of the time. We have magnified our fears, while our faith has been pictured upon the smallest possible scale. This process, however, must be reversed. It is our faith in the good that must be enlarged, while our fears of ills and troubles should be made as small and as insignificant as nothingness itself.

There is a current belief among many that when you have a fair understanding of metaphysics you can do as you please; that is, that you may violate the laws of life without feeling any ill effects there from; but few fallacies could be greater than this, and among a certain class of metaphysical students than this, there is no greater obstacle to freedom and growth. Our object in seeking truth, and a greater understanding of all things, physical and metaphysical, is that we may know how to live in harmony with all the laws of life, because it is from such living alone that we can secure emancipation and perpetual ascension into the greater and the greater good.

When you violate the laws of life you will reap the consequences, no matter how learned you may be in any or all of the higher wisdoms. You may rise above the laws of man, and as you advance into a higher state of being you may cease to be subject to the laws of the lower states, but the new sphere of action also has its laws, and these laws must be lived or there will be pain and death as before. We never get away from law, nor do we desire to do so. On the contrary, our desire is to learn how to use law.

The belief that laws are heartless taskmasters is also without foundation. A law is simply a path that leads to greater things; therefore to follow a law is to rise in the scale, to pass from the lesser to the greater. Every law is so constituted that when we move forward in harmony with that law we find greater freedom and greater increase, but when we go contrary to that law we invariably meet bondage and failure. The great secret of life is, therefore, to follow all the laws of life, and thus move forward at all times and in all things.

In many instances disease is simply the result of inharmonious conditions in the body, and all that is necessary to remove both the disease and its cause, is to restore harmony. It can be truthfully said that fully twenty per cent of the ordinary ailments of life would entirely disappear if perfect harmony was restored to mind and body. Realizing this, we must not permit ourselves to develop any fear of discord. The fear of discord is worse than the discord itself; and the fear of fear is worse than the fear itself. We should therefore ignore all those conditions completely.

We all know that grief may change the color of the hair, and we also know that a change of color means a chemical change, which proves that a state of mind can produce a chemical change in the body; but this particular chemical change is not the only change that can be produced by grief. Experiments have proved that grief frequently changes the very nature of the vital forces, making the positive forces negative, and thereby placing the system in a condition that is entirely helpless. Nothing wastes life and vitality like grief; and there is nothing that produces so much disease as lack of vital energy. We therefore cannot afford to grieve, nor is there any reason why we ever should grieve. We grieve simply because we do not understand things. To understand all things is to know that all things are well and that there is no occasion for worry. To permit tears at any time or under any circumstances is to ignore the higher light of life and replace the greater love by the lesser love. There is a better way to show your love and respect than to grieve and we can all find that better way.

All depressing states of mind, such as regrets, despondency, gloom, despair, and the like, must also be avoided completely. They invariably produce weakness in mind or body, and frequently are the direct causes of serious ills. We should train ourselves to be stronger than appearances, and we will not feel depressed. If we fail today, we shall succeed tomorrow, provided we look upon the failure as an opportunity and count everything joy. When we understand life we shall always be happy, no matter what comes. We shall then realize that all things are working together for greater good, if greater good is our purpose, and that unpleasant experiences come simply to shake us out of the old ruts. The best of us will get into grooves at times and feel it our religious duty to stay there; but man was not made for grooves; neither were grooves made for man.

Thousands of people think they have heart disease; and are living in constant fear of death; but there is no cause for alarm. What is usually thought to be heart disease is simply the result of a poor digestion disturbing that part of your body. The remedy, therefore, is to begin to live in poise and to correct your digestion. You will then find that your heart disease will mysteriously disappear. To attain poise, learn to live the serene life, and combine the serene life with the strong, positive life. When we live constantly in the attitude of poise we shall never feel weak nor tired. The system will always be full of life, and the fullness of life is the very best preventive of disease that has ever been discovered.

When threatening symptoms appear, eat less, drink more water, breathe more, move to the sunny side of life, have abundance of faith in the supremacy of the good, and give yourself a substantial metaphysical treatment every hour or two. You will soon restore perfect order in every part of your system. When there is anything wrong with the digestive system divide your meals in two. This will not do any harm, because all of us could live and flourish on one fourth of what we usually eat. Give the digestive system less work to do for a few days, and with the power of your thought cause the circulation to increase all through the abdominal region. You will soon feel entirely well, and feel much stronger than you ever felt before.

In the cure of any disease, the subconscious mind is a very important factor, for in many instances the body is ailing simply because adverse impressions have been given to the subconscious. You may have an idea that you cannot eat certain things. That idea may be correct, though the probabilities are that it is not. It may simply be a subconscious impression that makes you believe that you cannot eat that particular thing, and the subconscious responds by causing your system to revolt whenever that particular thing is taken. The moment, however, that you impress the subconscious with the fact that you can eat that particular thing, the subconscious will place the physical system in a condition where that particular thing will be accepted and digested without any trouble whatever. The subconscious mind can do practically anything along these lines, and it always obeys every idea that you deeply or intensely feel, or that you positively believe to be true. Impress the subconscious with the firm conviction that you can eat anything, that you can digest and assimilate perfectly every nutritious element that is taken into the system, and that you can properly eliminate all indigestible elements without discomfort to the body. Impress the subconscious with the conviction that you will never require medicine any more, and that sickness will never again enter your body. Then impress health, strength, power, peace, poise and harmony upon the subconscious, and continue to impress those states and qualities until you actually feel that they have become a permanent part of yourself. The subconscious will not fail to bring forth according to the seed you have sown.

Whether you are trying to remove threatening symptoms or chronic ailments of long standing, there is nothing that will prove more helpful than the conscious directions of the finer forces of the system in the creating of perfect health. To simply feel the finer vibrations of life force that are back of, and within any part of the body where there may be pain will cause that pain to disappear. A sickly feeling throughout the system will take flight instantly if we cause the finer vibrations to become active in every part of the body, and old chronic troubles will become airy nothings under the influence of these powerful forces. The reason why is very simple. These finer forces when placed in action can undermine the very foundation of disease and cut it loose, so to speak, from its foothold in the system. Besides, the ordinary malady is not one-tenth as serious as it appears to be. It is at best founded upon sand, and can easily be removed if we go about it properly. The average disease would be practically harmless if it were not for the life and the power that it receives from the patient. We magnify our ills, and thus make them worse, and we increase their life and power by living for them and placing ourselves at their mercy. If we would look upon an ailment as insignificant, and then proceed to arouse the finer elements and forces of mind and body, those elements that can undermine and remove any conditions, we would soon restore perfect health and order. To be able to prevent ourselves from giving life and thought to adverse conditions is a great secret, and it is accomplished by turning attention to. the inner, finer side of being. It is here that faith becomes such a remarkable power, because through the attitude of faith the mind goes beyond the things that are in the seeming, and enters into that sublime state where everything is always well. In this connection we should remember to give our thought and our life to the higher, and the higher will give its wisdom and its power to us in return.

Never begin any thought or action without recognizing the presence of higher power. We are all living in a great sea of limitless power, and we may consciously draw upon that power whenever we recognize it sufficiently to feel its presence. The more power we possess, the more we can accomplish and the sooner we shall gain complete emancipation, if that is our purpose in view. It is very unwise, therefore, to proceed with a small amount when we can, through the proper conscious effort, appropriate a much greater measure.

One of the greatest essentials in the application of the metaphysical process, whether our desire is better health or more life, is to depend absolutely upon the power of the spiritual elements in human existence. Material elements and material means have their place and value. If not for all, they do for the majority; but the power of the spiritual is infinitely greater than that of the tangible. It is therefore unwise to fritter away our time with the small when we are prepared to receive and apply that which is so very large. Let those who are unable to understand the spiritual have the material for the present, but let those who can understand the spiritual go to the spiritual for all things and at all times.

The reason why a number of aspiring souls fail to reach the heights is simply this: that they give too much thought to things, thereby limiting consciousness according to the measure of things. So long as we depend upon small things we shall remain small, but when we look to the larger life that is within us, we shall become larger and larger in proportion to our understanding of that life. Our capacity is no larger than our consciousness, and consciousness is only as large as our understanding of that upon which we depend. Therefore the sooner we can learn to depend absolutely upon the limitless the better; and this is especially true in the application of metaphysical and spiritual means to the attainment of health.

Resolve to gain your power, your freedom, your health, your peace, your wisdom, your everything from the infinite source, and do not change your mind for a moment. Whatever comes or not, be in the perfect faith that the infinite source cannot fail, no matter how great your deeds or demands may be, and you shall have the joy to witness another great victory.

Where faith in the boundlessness and the power of the spiritual is absolute, failure becomes impossible. It is the trembling faith that fails; it is the anxious mind that falls down; and it is material thought that obstructs the way to complete emancipation. On the other hand, when good judgment declares that physical remedies are required, we should not hesitate to employ them. We should, however, continue to impress our minds more and more deeply with the great truth that the greater life within us is sufficient. When a person trains himself to depend absolutely upon spiritual means, he steadily enters more deeply into spiritual life and consciousness, and therefore gains possession of higher spiritual powers; and to possess such powers is to possess the greatest remedy in the world. Experience has demonstrated in thousands of the most difficult cases that when the spiritualizing process began in the system, disease simply was compelled to take its departure. No disease can possibly exist where the spiritual forces are acting with full expression. Those forces invariably bring health, strength, wholeness and vigor wherever they may go; and we should always bear in mind the great truth that the powers of those forces have no limitation whatever.

How to Stay Young

How to Stay Young

Table of Contents

Introduction: Conclusive Reasons Why Man Should Learn to Stay Young 309

Chapter 1 - According to Exact Science Man Can Do Whatever He Learns to Do, and He Can Learn Anything 317

Chapter 2 - When Man Learns To Be Himself He Will Stay Young Without Trying 325

Chapter 3 - Why Man Looks Old Though Nature Gives Him A New Body Every Year 335

Chapter 4 - Growing Old Is A Race Habit That Can Be Removed 345

Chapter 5 - Eliminate The Consciousness Of Age By Living In The Great Eternal Now 355

Chapter 6 - Training The Subconscious To Produce Perpetually The Elements Of Youth 364

Chapter 7 - Conscious Harmony With The Law Of Perpetual Renewal 374

Chapter 8 - Why Experience Produces Age When Its Real Purpose Is To Perpetuate Youth 382

Chapter 9 - All Thinking Should Animate The Mind and Invigorate The Body 391

Chapter 10 - Mental States That Produce Conditions Of Age, And How To Remove Them 398

Chapter 11 - Mental States That Perpetuate Youth 408

Chapter 12 - Live For The Purpose Of Advancement, Attainment And Achievement 416

Chapter 13 - Love Your Work. And Know That You Can Work As Long As You Can Love 423

Chapter 14 - Perpetual Enjoyment Goes Hand In Hand With Perpetual Youth 431

Chapter 15 - Live In The Upper Story, And On The Sunny Side 439

Chapter 16 - The Ideal, The Beautiful, The Worthy And The Great Should Be The Constant Companions Of The Soul 447

Chapter 17 - To Love Always Is To Be Young Always . 453

Chapter 18 - How To Live A Life That Will Perpetuate Youth 458

Chapter 19 - Regularity In All Things, Moderation In All 464

Chapter 20 - The Rejuvenating Power Of Sleep When Properly Slept 470

Chapter 21 - The Necessity Of Perfect Health, And How To Secure It 476

Chapter 22 - Live In The Conviction That It Is Natural To Stay Young 483

Chapter 23 - What To Do With Birthdays 488

Chapter 24 - How Long We May Live Upon Earth 494

Chapter 25 - A New Picture Of The Coming Years ... 500

Introduction

Conclusive Reasons Why Man Should Learn to Stay Young

The world is changing its thought; in the past, those who believed in the perpetuation of youth were among the isolated few, and were looked upon with suspicion by the many; in the present, the great majority desire to perpetuate their youth, and most of these believe it is possible.

This change of thought is due to two great causes: first, we are fast eliminating the term "impossible" from our vocabulary, and second, we have made several important discoveries in the chemical life — both physical and metaphysical — of the human system.

We are living in an age of wonders, and have come to the conclusion that almost anything is possible, especially if it can add to the welfare, the beauty, the joy and the advancement of human existence.

We are convinced that life is not made for sorrow; we now believe that sorrow is but a temporary creation of man gone astray. We do not believe that this world is a "vale of tears," nor that we must suffer in the present in order that we may gain bliss in the future. We do not gather figs from thistles, neither can a life of pain be the direct cause of a life of pleasure. It is an immutable law that like causes produce like effects, and we are beginning to intelligently use this law in shaping our life and destiny.

The thinking world today is convinced that life is intended by the creator of life to be "a thing of beauty and a joy forever"; we therefore conclude that anything that can add to the joy and the beauty of life must be possible.

How to Stay Young

That the perpetuation of youth can add to the joy and the beauty of human life is a self-evident fact; and to be consistent in our thinking we must conclude that the perpetuation of youth is possible. An ideal life — the life we picture as the real life — is unthinkable in a world where the age producing process is constantly at work. To live life as we believe the Creator of life intended life to be lived, this process, therefore, must be removed.

To live as he should live, man must learn to stay young; this is becoming a worldwide conviction, and in consequence thereof, many minds of many modes of research are diligently at work trying to find the great secret of eternal youth.

Many of these are working in the belief that the secret is to be found in the world of material elements, while a constantly growing number are working in the belief that the power of mind alone can perpetuate the youth of the body.

The great facts in nature, however, are never one-sided; they are invariably both physical and metaphysical; they have soul as well as form, spirit as well as substance, and act through physical as well as mental laws.

The secret of eternal youth cannot be found through a study of the body alone, nor the mind alone; it does not have its sole existence in the elements of the earth, nor does it exercise its power exclusively through those forces of nature that cannot be seen.

That something that produces youth, can, under natural conditions, perpetuate youth; and as this something is an inseparable part of life itself, it can be found only through a study of the process of life as expressed through the whole man. For the same reason, the law through which the perpetuation of youth may be promoted, can be applied only through the living of life as life is intended to be lived.

That something that produces youth, and perpetuates youth, has been discovered; and like all great facts in nature, it is not only very simple, but abides at our very feet. We did not see it, however, because there is a tendency in man to look afar off whenever he is in search of the great and the wonderful. The wonders at his own feet and in his own immediate world are therefore overlooked, at least for a time; but for that something that produces youth the time of enforced seclusion is at an end; it has been found, and is being incorporated as a part of exact science.

The fundamental law through which the perpetuation of youth may be promoted is one of the basic laws in nature, and being basic, it is a law that man will not be required to apply; nature already applies this law in the life of man; all that is required of man is to conform the living of his life to this law.

This can readily be accomplished by any person whether he be highly educated, or not; it is therefore evident that anyone can learn to stay young, and there are many conclusive reasons why everybody should learn this most wonderful art.

When we learn to perpetuate youth, we shall add immeasurably to the joy of living, and since man is made for happiness, everything that can increase his happiness should be made a part of his life.

The consciousness of youth will not only deepen and enlarge the consciousness of joy, but the perpetuation of the consciousness of youth will eliminate completely all those ills that come directly from old age conditions. These ills are almost too numerous to mention, but we can realize at a single moment's thought what a burden will be lifted from the life of the race when complete emancipation from these ills has been secured.

Man would also gain freedom from all these adverse conditions that come indirectly from the aging process; and as these are likewise too numerous to mention, we have another most powerful reason why everybody should learn to stay young.

When great minds come to a place where they have sufficient knowledge and experience to turn their talents to some use that is really worthwhile, they usually take their departure. But if they knew how to perpetuate their youth, they would not leave this planet just when we needed them the most, and when they could serve us to the greatest advantage.

The great majority of the great minds leave their work upon earth unfinished — not because they have to, but because it is a habit they have inherited from the race; and the loss that the race must annually sustain through the perpetuation of this habit is almost incomprehensible.

The gain that the world will realize when great minds learn to stay young until they have finished their work will be extraordinary, to say the least.

It requires great ideas and great deeds to advance the world; but great ideas spring only from great minds, therefore, great minds should remain upon earth as long as they have something great to do.

It is a self-evident fact that no great mind can be just to himself, to the race, or to the great gifts in his possession, unless he continues to serve the race as long as the race may need him; but to this end he must learn to stay young, and this alone is sufficient reason why he should stay young.

The same is true of lesser minds; when they begin to know enough to live a life worthwhile on this planet they pass away. While they are mere amateurs on the stage of life they are with us; when they begin to become artists they are with us no more. But it is not right; it means a great loss every day, both to the race in general, and to each individual in particular.

The perpetuation of youth would prevent this loss, and herein we find another conclusive reason why everybody should learn to stay young.

When the average person has gained sufficient knowledge and experience to appreciate the real value of those things that give quality, worth and real joy to life he is too old, too weak or too tired to enjoy them. When his mind is sufficiently developed to partake of the rich feast that the art of man is placing before him, he is too infirm to partake of anything. When he has gained sufficient insight to understand the marvels of nature his senses are dimmed, and the gorgeous splendor of the universe can charm him no more. His loss is great, but if he knew how to stay young his gain could hardly be measured.

If youth could be retained and life prolonged, we should find more time to Live, and every moment would be one of contentment and joy. The nervous rush of the strenuous life would cease, because we would realize that there was sufficient time to do everything we wanted to do, and that we could take time to give quality, worth and superiority to every product that was shaped by our hands.

We would not only work for quantity, but also for quality; everything in life would consequently become far richer, and we should also have the time to enjoy this greater richness.

The habit of passing through life in a nervous rush comes originally from the belief that life is so short; we wish to accomplish as much as possible before age and infirmity begin, and rush becomes the order of the day. It is a habit, however, that produces nothing but loss. More mistakes, troubles and ills come from nervous rush than from all other adverse causes combined. The same habit is responsible for a great deal of inferior work, as well as for broken down human systems.

It is the verdict of exact science that work can harm no one; that it is the nervous rush so frequently associated with work that wrecks the mind and body of man. But this habit will immediately cease when we learn to stay young.

When we realize that youth can be retained for an indefinite period, we shall undertake more, and consequently accomplish more. We shall never fear failure because there will be sufficient time to try again and again until the goal in view has been reached. We shall not, however, become negligent or indifferent, because the life and the vigor of youth will give us ambitions without bounds.

The majority of those who fail, fail because they fear failure, and they fear failure principally because they subconsciously believe the time of action to be limited.

There are very few who undertake as much as they are competent to carry through; and the reason is, they think life is too short in which to complete the greater undertaking.

How to Stay Young

It is therefore evident that everybody would proceed to do what they were fully competent to do if they knew that they could stay young until their work was finished.

To be just to himself, man must be and do all that he can be and do; but before he will naturally undertake everything that he feels competent to carry through, he must be convinced that he will have sufficient time to complete his work; and this conviction he will gain when he learns to stay young.

To those who desire to develop the greater possibilities that are latent within them, the perpetuation of youth becomes actually indispensable.

To unfold the greatness of mind and soul, the personality must become a more and more perfect instrument of expression; but that personality that is growing older every year is becoming less and less efficient as an instrument of mind and soul. Therefore, those who desire to promote their higher development must learn to stay young.

The most important reason why man should learn to stay young is found in the fact that the perpetuation of youth is in perfect harmony with the purpose of life.

Continuous advancement is the purpose of life; but only those elements in life that stay young can advance. The age producing process is a deteriorating process, directly opposed to the advancing process. The two, therefore, cannot abide in the same person. If the age producing process continues, advancement will cease, retrogression will begin, and it has been conclusively demonstrated that retrogression, or retarded progress, is the original cause of all the ills in the world.

How to Stay Young

To promote continuous advancement is to emancipate the individual from the ills that may exist in his system; but to promote continuous advancement it is necessary also to promote the perpetuation of youth; therefore, to secure complete emancipation, man must learn to stay young.

The further development of the faculties and talents of the mind, as well as the functions of the personality, demand the perpetuation of youth. It is not possible to improve that which is growing old, because the age producing process ossifies, deadens, weakens and deteriorates everything in which it has gained a foothold.

The power of genius demands a young, vigorous personality if it is to give full expression to the highest order of mental brilliancy. It is only a fine instrument that can respond to a fine mind, but to be fine, the instrument must contain the qualities of youth.

The greatest obstacle to extraordinary talent and rare genius is the tendency of the brain to ossify with the passing of the years; and the cause of this tendency is found wholly in the age producing process. This process, however, will disappear when we learn to stay young.

When we learn to stay young the passing of the years will not decrease the brilliancy of the mind, nor cause the power of genius to wane; instead, every active faculty will become greater and greater the longer we may continue to live.

Chapter 1

According to Exact Science Man Can Do Whatever He Learns to Do, And He Can Learn Anything

The nature of man is metaphysical as well as physical; and these two natures are so intertwined that it is not possible to understand the one without understanding the other.

What transpires in the mind will also transpire in the body; and every physical action is both preceded and succeeded by a metaphysical action.

What affects the body affects the mind; what affects the mind affects the body; therefore no final conclusion can be gained concerning any force, action, element or condition in human life unless the factor under consideration is analyzed from the metaphysical as well as the physical point of view.

The facts gained from this mode of analysis constitute exact science, and it is evident, even at a casual glance, that no other mode of analysis can evolve exact science.

Those who have studied only the body do not understand man; and the same is true of those who aim to study only the mind; their conclusions are not scientific, because incomplete; therefore those who act upon such conclusions will fail to secure the desired results.

The principal reason why the secret of eternal youth was not hitherto discovered, is found in the fact that the law through which youth may be perpetuated is metaphysical as well as physical; therefore, neither physical research alone, nor mental research alone could find it.

Another reason is found in the fact that physical science proclaims the limitations of man, and that mental science, by ignoring the true nature of the body, produces limitations in man.

The old thought, whether it be wholly physical or wholly mental, is incapable of giving man the power to do what has not been generally done before; and as the perpetuation of youth is not, as yet, a general accomplishment, a new mode of thought becomes necessary before man can learn to stay young.

This new mode of thought is otherwise termed exact science, and through this science man can learn to stay young, because according to exact science, he can learn anything.

Exact science not only proclaims this as a demonstrated fact, but presents the principles and the laws through which the demonstration becomes possible, no matter by whom these principles and laws may be employed.

The statement that man can do whatever he learns to do, need not be confined to the narrow interpretation of mere objective knowledge coupled with tangible action; it is a statement that will hold true in every form of interpretation, even when considered in connection with the possibility of realizing in the real everything that can be idealized in the ideal.

What man can learn to idealize in the ideal he can learn to realize in the real; this is the conclusion of exact science, and since any desired attainment can be idealized in the ideal, any desired achievement can be realized in the real, because attainments and achievements follow each other invariably as causes and effects.

How to Stay Young

The fact that the perpetuation of youth can be thought of as an ideal proves that it can be worked out in the real; according to exact science it is not possible to have an ideal until we have the power to make that ideal real.

The reason, however, why the majority who have ideals fail to make them real, is found in the fact that they do not employ the principles of exact science; they depend either solely upon physical laws or solely upon mental laws, not knowing that the nature of man is both physical and metaphysical, and that no change or advancement can be made in human life unless both physical laws and metaphysical laws are employed cooperatively and simultaneously.

The statement that man can learn anything is the logical conclusion of that analysis in exact science that explores the metaphysical as well as the physical. To analyze the mind in its relation to the external world is to find that no limit to the powers of discernment, perception, conception, insight, understanding or comprehension can be found.

A study of the fundamental actions of mind reveal the fact that the more the mind proceeds to learn, the greater becomes its capacity to learn; and as the mind may proceed to learn more and more indefinitely, it may continue to increase its capacity to learn during the same indefinite, or rather, endless period.

To be logical, we must therefore conclude that the mind may learn an3rthing that it proceeds to learn, and that that mind that proceeds to learn everything will constantly be learning everything.

This mode of reasoning, not only proves conclusively that man can learn to stay young, but also that while he is staying young, he can learn everything that may be necessary to make his life as large, as beautiful and as ideal as his soul inspired heart may desire.

To learn to stay young, and to enjoy in greater and greater measure all the privileges of youth, are therefore possibilities according to exact scientific thinking; but these things are more than possibilities.

A clear understanding of mind reveals the fact that man can learn to do what he has never done before, thus eliminating completely the term "impossibility" from the human domain; the perpetuation of youth, however, has already been done; for that reason it is more than a possibility.

That which has been done once, can be done again, and done better. Every human being has been young, and has stayed young for a time; the law that perpetuates youth is therefore inherent in human nature. What is inherent in human nature can be aroused and employed at any time, and for any length of time; this is natural law, and it proves conclusively that any person, no matter how long he may have lived upon earth, or what his physical condition may be now, can become young now, and can stay young as long as he may desire.

This statement may appear to be too strong, too sweeping, and even unfounded, but no person can analyze the whole nature of man without coming to the same conclusion. It is therefore an indisputable fact, and the truth must be accepted, no matter how much stranger than fiction it may appear to be.

The first essential in learning to stay young is to place the mind in the proper attitude towards the goal in view.

How to Stay Young

To enter into this attitude it is necessary to establish all thinking upon the conviction that there is no limit to anything in the nature of man; and all thinking must recognize the supremacy of the conscious mind in the life and destiny of the personal man.

It is not possible to become as proficient in any action as one may have the present capacity to become, so long as any form of limitation in human nature is recognized; nor can the individual advance to any considerable degree until all thought of personal limitation is eliminated completely.

The art of staying young is a very high art, and though it is simple when learned, yet it cannot be learned so long as the mind has not entered that attitude where it is always at its best. To enter this attitude, and continue in this attitude, all that is necessary is to live in the conviction that the possibilities of human nature have no limitations.

The fact that there are no actual limitations in human nature is conclusively demonstrated by exact science; therefore, any person who will employ the principles of exact science may prove to himself that there are no limitations in his nature. He will thereby become convinced, and will naturally enter the necessary attitude.

To employ the principles of exact science is to analyze everything in human life from the two points of view — the physical and the metaphysical; and those who are not familiar with this mode of analysis will find methods, as well as the detailed application of those methods, in the pages that follow.

The necessity of proper mental attitudes in the perpetuation of youth is clearly evinced by the fact that the personal man is the tangible expression of the mind's subconscious thought, and that subconscious thinking is determined fundamentally by the attitudes of mind.

The personal man is the direct, or indirect result of subconscious thought; subconscious thought is determined by mental attitudes; and man can enter into any mental attitude desired; therefore, any change, modification or condition decided upon may be produced in the personality.

In the last analysis, subconscious thought is fundamental cause of everything that exists or transpires in the personal nature of man; and as man may subconsciously think whatever he desires to think, the nature, the life and the destiny of his personality are in his own hands. That man has the power to perpetuate his youth is therefore a foregone conclusion.

All thinking, however, to produce the desired results, must be consistent with natural law, and must act in harmony with the expression of this law, both in mind and body. To comply with natural law in its physical actions and ignore its metaphysical actions or vice versa is to neutralize results. The necessity of exact science — the science of the whole man, is therefore evident.

To be consistent with natural law, man must aim to do only that which the laws of his nature make possible now; though all things are possible, still it is the proper application of specific laws that makes them possible.

It would not be possible for man to perpetuate his youth for an indefinite period, if natural law made old age inevitable; nor could man learn to stay young through the application of any other law than the one that produces youth in the domains of nature herself.

Natural law, however, makes no personal condition inevitable; the personality is an instrument, not a final product, and can be changed, modified or perfected to suit the advancing requirements of man.

It is the purpose of natural law to supply man with those essentials that he may require to promote the object of his existence; and as this object is advancement, nature is prepared to supply everything that may be necessary to promote advancement.

The perpetuation of youth is one of these necessities; continuous advancement without continuous youth is unthinkable, a contradiction to every law in human life; nature must therefore have made provisions for the perpetuation of youth. The pages that follow will prove that she has.

To examine man through the principles of exact science is to find that law in his being that can, will and does perpetuate youth; and since this law is a permanent part of human nature, the finer consciousness of man instinctively feels that youth can be retained.

In every mind where this finer consciousness is recognized and developed, a desire for the perpetuation of youth will arise; whatever we inwardly feel that we can do, we will begin to desire to do, and the more keenly we feel what we can do, the stronger will this desire become.

To discover the purpose of life will also produce a strong desire for the perpetuation of youth, because the finer consciousness in man discerns most clearly that continuous advancement and continuous youth are inseparable factors on the path to the greater life.

How to Stay Young

It is therefore evident that if man is to do what he is here to do, he must perpetuate his youth; to be true to himself and the life he is here to live, he must learn to stay young.

The coming of man upon earth is not an accident; he is here to fulfill a certain definite purpose, and since continuous advancement in the great eternal now is necessary to promote that purpose, nothing must be permitted in his life that retards advancement.

The age producing process, however, does retard advancement; to grow old is to go down, to deteriorate, to tail; therefore it is a violation of the laws of life, an obstacle to the purpose of life that must be removed if man is to do what he is created to do.

To be just to himself, man must be now all that he can be now; he must attain and accomplish all that his present capacity will permit; he must secure from life now all that life can give now; his nature must manifest the highest worth of his conscious being; his world must be filled with the richness of his present sphere of existence; his joy must be complete, and he must live.

However, before he can live such a life he must learn to stay young, and exact science declares that he can.

Chapter 2

When Man Learns To Be Himself He Will Stay Young Without Trying

A perpetual renewing process is constantly in action throughout the entire being of man; every cell in the human body is removed after a certain period, and a new one built in its place; this period varies from a few weeks to eight or nine months, at times eleven or twelve months; no part of the human body therefore can be said to be more than a year old at any time.

This fact is one of the most startling as well as one of the most important facts in the science of human life, and it proves conclusively that the age producing process is an artificial product, placed in action, not by nature, but by the mistakes of man.

To stay young is natural; to grow old is unnatural; therefore, all that man is required to do to stay young is to be natural — to be himself — to be what nature hourly makes him to be.

It is not necessary for man to produce youth in his own system; this is already done by nature; but it is necessary to learn to cease to make the system look old and feel old when it always is young.

To learn to stay young is simply to learn to be what you are; it is therefore one of the simplest arts in the world; there is nothing new to learn, nothing special to do; simply stop doing what you are doing, and leave that which is be what it is.

How to Stay Young

The fact that the body always is young should cause the body to always look young and feel young; no matter how long the person may have lived upon this planet, his physical form is never more than eight or nine months old, while the greater part of his system has been built up from new material within the last few weeks.

The body of the octogenarian is just as young as the body of the twelvemonths old babe; this is a fact in nature — a most astounding fact in the presence of human conditions as we find them.

There is no reason to be found in the domains of nature why the octogenarian should look any older than the twelvemonths old child; the fact, however, that the longer people live on earth the older they look and feel proves that some great law in nature is being violated constantly, absolutely and universally.

This great law is the law of perpetual renewal; the law that is constantly rebuilding the human system, removing every fiber in the system after it has been in use for a few weeks or a few months, and causing a new one to be formed in its place.

The new fibers and the new cells are actually new, just as new as the green leaves in the springtime, and when first formed, they are just as new in the body of the octogenarian as in the body of the child. But why are these new cells transformed almost at once into old looking, weary looking cells in the body of the octogenarian? This is a question that science must answer, and it is far too important for any form of science to ignore.

The new cells that are formed in the body of the child continue to look new until they are replaced by other new cells; then why should not the new cells in the body of the octogenarian do the same?

In the body of the child the new cells continue young and vigorous so long as they remain in the body, which is but a few months at most; in the body of the octogenarian the new cells wither up, becoming weak and practically useless almost immediately after they have been created; but why? There must be a reason; there is a reason, and exact science has found it.

The law of perpetual renewal does not simply aim to renew the human body; its fundamental aim is to repair and reconstruct the body, and in promoting its process of reconstruction, the process of renewal is promoted through the same action.

The cells and the fibers of the human body are created to perform definite functions, and during the period of their creation are given a certain amount of latent energy; when this energy has all been placed in action, the purpose of the cell has been fulfilled; but instead of recharging that cell, nature removes it as waste matter, and builds a new one, full of youth and vigor, in its place.

This process of reconstruction is constantly in action throughout the human system; the very moment a cell becomes useless, it is removed and a new one built in its place; in a normal human system there is no opportunity therefore, to retain in the system a single cell that is weak, withered or useless.

In a normal human system only young, vigorous cells can remain; when they cease to have life and vigor, they are removed as waste; the fact, therefore, that people who have lived upon earth for a period exceeding thirty or forty years, have withered, useless, empty, old looking cells in their systems, proves that they are not normal; the law of reconstruction is not permitted to perform its function completely; natural law is being violated and the individual is consequently untrue to himself.

It would not be possible for any person to look old or feel old so long as he was true to himself — so long as he was himself. When man is himself he is young because nature makes him that way; therefore, when man learns to be himself, he will stay young without trying to stay young.

To try to stay young is to fail to stay young. To try to be what you already are is to proceed in the belief that you are not what you are; you will thereby misdirect your energies, and consequently fail to reach your goal.

When man discovers himself, and learns to be himself, he will discern the modus operandi of his real nature; he will discern that his entire system is constantly being renewed, and will cease to interfere with the renewing process; instead, he will feel that he always is young, and his desire to express what he is will perpetually increase.

The more perfectly the mind discerns its own true nature, and the more keenly the individual becomes conscious of his complete self, the stronger becomes the desire to perpetuate the qualities of youth. The reason why is found in the fact that the more perfect conscious realization of self will place the mind in more perfect contact with the fundamental law of self, and will consequently desire more and more to act in harmony with this law.

To act in harmony with the fundamental law of self is to be oneself, and to be oneself is to be young because nature is perpetually making the self young.

That nature is ever making the self young through the law of repair and reconstruction can be demonstrated conclusively by any chemist; and every close student of human life knows that the very moment the process of reconstruction should cease, all conscious life would depart from the personality.

When the cells of the body have served their purpose they become mere waste matter, and as no cell in the body can continue in action more than a few months, the entire body would, in a few months be a mass of waste matter if the process of reconstruction were suspended.

The process of reconstruction, however, in order to perpetuate the life of the body, removes every cell after it has remained in the body for a few months, and forms a new one in its place. The entire system, therefore, is being perpetually renewed; in fact the human personality must continue absolutely in the hands of the law of reconstruction and perpetual renewal to live a single day.

The human personality has been placed permanently in the hands of this law, and will remain permanently in the hands of this law, or until man so completely violates this law that he severs his connection with personal existence.

The fact, therefore, that the human personality is completely governed, and perpetuated in its existence by the law of perpetual renewal, proves that it is being perpetually renewed, and is always young.

The very moment the personality ceases to be renewed, it will cease to exist as an organized form; the continuation of organized life demands the continuation of reconstruction, and reconstruction means renewal — the perpetuation of youth.

A closer study of the law of reconstruction reveals the fact that nearly ninety percent of the cells in the average human body are replaced by new cells in less than four months. Those muscles that are exercised to a considerable degree every day are completely renewed every three, four or five weeks, depending upon the nature of the exercise and the health and vigor of the body.

To promote the orderly renewal of the muscles, the best exercise is that which never goes beyond moderation and that is never mechanical. Mere mechanical exercise will weaken the muscles, while violent and too constant exercise will destroy many of the cells that are still new and vigorous.

The purpose of physical exercise is to place in constructive action all the energy generated in the system; and when all of this energy is in constructive action, the entire personality will renew itself orderly, rapidly, completely and perfectly. It is therefore evident that forced action or retarded action will interfere with the work of the reconstructive process.

The average athlete grows old rapidly and dies young; the reason being that his exercise has been too violent, or too mechanical, or both.

Those muscles that are called into play during work that is thoroughly interesting, receive the best exercise, and therefore will renew themselves most thoroughly in the least time.

All muscles, however, are renewed, whether they are fully exercised or not, but where the exercise is very slight, the old cells may remain nearly a year before they are replaced with new ones.

How to Stay Young

The vital organs, such as the heart, stomach, lungs, etc., renew themselves rapidly, providing the health of the body is reasonably good.

The average person who breathes properly and breathes only pure air, will receive three pair of new lungs every year.

When the stomach is never overloaded nor abused, it will renew itself from two to three times every year; the same is true of the other organs in the abdominal region.

The heart, the arterial system, the brain and the nervous system will, under normal conditions, renew themselves every sixty or ninety days, while the skin is renewed completely every week or ten days.

The bony structure of the human body requires the longest time to complete the renewal process, the time required, varying from seven months to a year, at rare intervals, fourteen months.

When the health of the body is not perfect, the renewal process is somewhat retarded, but even chronic invalids will renew their bodies completely in less than a year and a half.

In the face of these facts, where does old age have an opportunity to present itself? This process of renewal is constant, and will continue, with but slight variations, so long as the personality continues to live. The entire human body is therefore always young, and for that reason should always continue to look young and feel young.

The fact that the body, after leaving the teens, does not look as young as it actually is, proves, as stated before, that some natural law has been violated.

How to Stay Young

To cease to violate this law, and to learn to live in perfect harmony with this law, is all that is necessary in order to stay young; mere simplicity itself when accomplished, but before it can be accomplished, the ordinary mode of living and thinking will have to be reversed.

To begin, the individual must learn to be himself; he must learn, not only to think of himself as young, but to Be young, because he is young. The actions of thought, feeling and consciousness must reproduce in the mental life, as well as the personal life» the same qualities of youth that nature is producing in the chemical life.

The movements of man himself must produce youth, and reproduce youth, thus cooperating with the renewing process everywhere in action among the movements of nature.

The real life of man is young at all times, and everything that lives in the being of man, is, for the same reason, young at all times. Therefore, to be young, man must live his real life; he must not live an artificial life, nor live in an artificial mental state.

He must be himself, and live in the conscious realization of what he is in the reality of himself.

Youth is not merely skin deep; it is the result of an interior life process that penetrates every atom in the being of man, and gives eternal youth to every atom in the being of man. No external lotion will therefore produce the qualities of youth, neither will chemicals, externally or internally applied, count for anything whatever.

The secret is to enter into the consciousness of this interior life process; and it is in this consciousness that man enters when he is himself.

How to Stay Young

Youth comes from within; it already exists within the life of every fiber in the human system, but man, through the violation of certain laws, prevents the youth within from coming forth into full and natural expression.

To promote the full and natural expression of youth, man must be himself; he must be young in thought, life and consciousness because he is young in himself; and to train the mind to be young, the fact that the entire human system is being renewed perpetually should be constantly impressed upon the mind.

The individual should train himself to live in the constant recognition of the great fact that his body is always young; that every fiber in his being is now as new as the leaves and the flowers of the springtime; and that every fiber will, in a few short weeks, be replaced by another, fresh from the hands of creative power.

To train the mind to constantly recognize the perpetual youth of the body will cause consciousness to enter more and more deeply into that interior life process that always is young, and that causes every atom in the being of man to always stay young.

To live in this consciousness is to discern the actions of the law of perpetual renewal; and to discern this law is to discard everything in thought or action that violates this law.

When the law of perpetual renewal is no longer violated, the body will always look and feel as young as it is; and as the body always is young, the individual will continue to look young and feel young, no matter how long he may continue to live upon this planet.

How to Stay Young

This may appear to be a far-reaching statement, but it is the conclusion of exact science, and as exact science is based upon absolute facts as they stand in the complete nature of man — physical and metaphysical, to be true to the truth, there is no other alternative than to accept the statement, and act accordingly.

It is the truth that the personality of man is always young; therefore when man permits himself to be himself he will always stay young without trying to stay young.

Chapter 3

Why Man Looks Old Though Nature Gives Him A New Body Every Year

There are two reasons why the personal man, after reaching what is termed middle life, begins to look older and older in appearance every year. The one is ossification and the other is old age conditions.

The tendency of the human body to ossify is produced by various causes, some physical and some mental, though all of these causes, in their last analysis, have their origin in certain abnormal modes of mental life.

When the cells and the fibers of the body begin to ossify, the muscles will harden, the bones will become stiff, the various organs will become heavy and sluggish, and a shriveling up process will pervade, more and more, the entire system. Reconstruction and repair will be retarded, waste matter will increase in the system and will soon begin to clog the system because the various organs are too sluggish to perform their functions properly.

When the cells of the brain begin to ossify, they will respond less and less to the actions of the mind; the intellect will become less and less lucid, and memory will gradually wane. New impressions are formed in mind with difficulty, usually not at all; the acquisition of new knowledge becomes almost impossible as the brain is no longer a perfect, responsive instrument upon which the mental faculties may act.

The fact that "old people" remember more readily what occurred in their childhood than what occurred in recent years, is in this connection, simply explained. The impressions formed upon the mind in childhood were deep and penetrating because the brain was then in a plastic condition; later impressions, however, scarcely produced any impression because the brain had become too hard; that the impressions gained in childhood should be vivid while the impressions of recent years are hardly perceptible is therefore evident.

The same phenomena explains why a number of "old people" who have left the beliefs of childhood, return to those beliefs in their "declining" years.

When the brain becomes so ossified that clear, penetrating, comprehensive thinking becomes difficult, or impossible, the mind can discern only those ideas that are deeply impressed, and naturally can believe only that which it can discern. And as the deepest impressions are always those impressions that are formed in childhood, that is, in the minds of those who permit ossification to take place, the beliefs of childhood are the only beliefs that "old" ossified brains can understand.

The fact that "old people" frequently return to their earlier ideas proves nothing for or against those ideas; it only proves that ossified brains are too dull to discern other than the deepest impressions in the mind; and those impressions are usually the ones gained in childhood.

When the "old people" become childish, the cause is the same; their brains are too dull to be influenced by the wiser ideas of later years; such brains discern only the deep impressions of childhood, and are influenced by the nature of those impressions, and consequently become childish both in thought and action.

How to Stay Young

The impressions of childhood are not always the deepest and most vivid impressions, however; if the brain is just as plastic at sixty as at ten, the impressions formed at the one period may be just as deep as at the other; but in the average person the brain begins to ossify at fifty, sometimes at forty or thirty five.

Minds that are highly developed will form their deepest impressions after the half century mark has been passed, providing the ossifying process does not enter the brain. It is therefore evident that those minds that are constantly being developed, and that never permit the brain to ossify will do their best work later in life; in fact, the nearer they approach the century mark the more remarkable will their work become.

The fact that ossification can be prevented, not only in the brain, but in the entire human system, is therefore tidings of great joy, especially to those who wish to live a life worthwhile and accomplish something worthwhile.

The second reason why man looks old though nature gives him a new body every year, is found in old age conditions. These conditions are purely mental and are produced principally by the conscious or subconscious belief in age.

To believe that you are growing older and older every year, and to positively expect to look older and older every year, is to produce old age conditions in the system; these conditions will cause the new cells that have just been formed, to take on an old age appearance, and thus the new body will look as old as you think you are, regardless of the fact that the new body has been in existence less than a year.

The old age conditions will bear the stamp of your thought of yourself, because they are the product of your thought of yourself; therefore, if you have lived upon this planet for fifty years and think that you ought to look just as fifty-year old people are supposed to look, you will create old age conditions that have the fifty-year old stamp, and your new body will be stamped by this old stamp.

The new body will be so permeated with fifty-year old conditions that it will feel like fifty and look like fifty. It is all false, however; there is not a cell or a fiber in your system that is over a year old; the majority are less than three months old, therefore, could not look as if they were fifty unless they were changed artificially by some false mental process.

The fact that the actions of the mind can change the appearance of the body is thoroughly demonstrated whenever a person worries or indulges in similar mental states. A few hours of worry will cause the person to look ten, and even twenty years older than he did before the worry began. Then what may we not expect from a lifetime of constant old age producing thought?

The power of thought is creative, and the conditions that are produced by thought are similar to the nature of the thought itself; therefore, to constantly think, year after year, that you are growing older and older, is to fill the system with conditions that will impress the appearance of more and more age upon every fiber and cell in the system.

The new cells that are formed in your body today will be caused, by these old age conditions, to look as old as you think you are today; next year you will think you are a year older, and the old age conditions that are constantly being evolved from your mentality, will cause you to feel a year older, and the entire body to look a year older.

To think that you are growing older, or to expect to grow old sometime in the future, is to form old age conditions in the mentality; therefore, no thought whatever must be given to old age, or the age producing process in any of its forms.

The chemical processes of the body, the vital processes of the functional system, the conscious processes of the brain and nervous system — in brief, all the processes of the personality, obey the ruling tendency of the mind absolutely; the mind can, either through direct or indirect action, modify all the natural processes in the human system; the process that perpetuates youth can be neutralized by the adverse actions of the mind, and this is what the average mind is doing; to learn to stay young, therefore, it is necessary to change the mind completely on this most important subject.

The color of the hair changes with the passing of the years because it is a race habit to grow gray as you are growing old. It is a tendency that every person inherits from the race, but the time of its action varies among different persons to a considerable degree. This variation is produced principally by personal habits and environments, and occasionally by exceptional conditions in mind or body.

The tendency to change the color of the hair was originally produced by adverse mental states, the result of which was intensified by repetition. The longer the person lived, the more he worried, the more he grieved, and the more he misdirected the efforts of mind, thought or action; and as these continued to change the color of the hair more and more, man came to look upon the change as the result of age. Finally it became a race habit, but it is well to remember that all habits can be removed.

To dwell a great deal in wrong mental states will tend to change the color of the hair before the race tendency we have inherited begins to produce the change; and to continue to dwell in wrong mental states after this tendency has begun to act, will increase the power of this tendency. This is why some people grow gray early in life, and why others grow gray very rapidly when they once begin.

In the presence of the fact that the entire body is constantly renewed, it seems difficult for some minds to understand why scars, tumors, artificial growths, etc., continue to appear in the same place and frequently in the same form, year after year; but this is a matter that is simply explained.

Every cell in the human body is produced by an individual chemical action, and this action has its root in the subconscious life of the body; to change the form or the nature of the cell this chemical action must first be changed, and this is possible through the use of any method that will affect the subconscious root, or cause of that action.

It is possible, however, not only to change the subconscious cause of any chemical action along the line of orderly development, but it is also possible to produce unnatural chemical actions. This frequently occurs both through external agencies and through conditions that arise wholly within the system itself.

When any part of the body is cut, the chemical actions within the cells that are affected, are so shocked that they become unnatural actions. These unnatural actions will tend to produce cell structures similar to the cut through which they had their origin; that is, they will tend to produce and perpetuate a scar.

Nature, however, always aims to remove unnatural chemical actions, and when it succeeds the scar finally disappears. Sometimes it succeeds only in modifying the false action, while at other times it fails, the reason being that the unnatural chemical action has become so thoroughly individualized and so firmly established that nature cannot remove it without assistance.

Artificial growths in the body are produced by unnatural chemical actions that have become individualized. These particular actions usually have their origin in diseased conditions within the system, and they will continue to produce the artificial growth until nature can remove them. If nature fails, other agencies, either physical or metaphysical, will be required to reestablish normal conditions.

The fact that every chemical action, both natural and unnatural, has its origin in the subconscious life, gives extreme importance to that phase of metaphysics through which the subconscious may be changed and reconstructed in any manner desired. Since the subconscious can do whatever it is properly directed to do, any false chemical action, and in consequence, any artificial growth in the system, can be removed by those who know how to direct the subconscious.

The law of perpetual renewal will renew all the cells in the system, whether these cells are the expressions of natural chemical actions or not; but the new cells will, in each case, have the same form and nature as the old ones, because the same causes always produce the same effects.

An artificial growth in the system will renew itself just as rapidly as any organ in the system, but the new cells in the artificial growth will be similar to the old ones because they were all produced by the same unnatural chemical action.

How to Stay Young

An artificial growth that is growing will multiply cell structures through the same law that multiplies cell structures in a growing muscle, but each individual cell will be similar to the cell that preceded so long as the individual chemical actions remain unchanged. When these actions change, the efforts of nature, singly or in cooperation with external assistance, are responsible.

To those who understand the nature of the human organism, it is evident that the law of perpetual renewal is ceaselessly at work rebuilding everything, both the natural and the unnatural, in the personality of man; everything in the human system is always new, therefore should never look old, and never would look old if ossification and old age conditions were not produced in the being of man.

Nature, however, does not produce these two causes of the aging process; they are both produced by the mistakes of man, and he himself can completely remove them.

When man removes the process of ossification from his physical system, and removes every age producing thought from his mental system, he will have mastered the art of staying young.

Great minds have for some time realized that the perpetuation of youth would be possible if ossification could be overcome, and have searched diligently for that strange chemical action that, seemingly without reason, hardens the cells of the system with the passing of the years.

Their failure to find it, however, is due wholly to the fact that we cannot understand the secret processes of life until chemistry is combined with metaphysics.

How to Stay Young

The cause of ossification is partly physical, partly mental and partly hereditary, and these various phases of the subject will be analyzed thoroughly in succeeding chapters; but in our effort to remove the process of ossification, we must not forget to hold the mind in that attitude where old age conditions of thought are eliminated completely.

It will not be possible for man to perpetuate his youth, no matter what methods he may employ, so long as he believes in the reality and the inevitableness of age. To live in the belief that age must come is to mentally create the age producing process, or to perpetuate the age producing process that we have inherited from the race. And to create or perpetuate that process is to fill the system with old age conditions, and we will look as old as we think we are, regardless of the fact that our present body has been in existence but a few short months.

To fix a future time for the coming of age, is to impress the idea of age upon the mind, and to impress the idea of age upon the mind is to impress conditions of age upon the cells of the body.

We are receiving from nature perpetual youth now; to live in that youth now is to retain that youth now; and as there is no end to the eternal now there can be no end to the youth of the eternal now.

The future will care for itself if we care well for the present, and to be true to the present we must be true to ourselves in the present; we must be what we are now, and we are young now.

To think, at any time, of the possibility of future age is to create age producing thought; it is to create that thought now that has no place in life now; it is to bring age into the present when there is no age in the present.

The present body is young; it is this year's product; it is new and ought to look new; but man thinks he is old because he has lived upon earth sixty or more years; he therefore feels as old as people are supposed to feel at sixty, and the body always looks as old as the mind feels.

The body always is young, and will look young as long as the mind feels young; this is the great secret.

Chapter 4

Growing Old Is A Race Habit That Can Be Removed

The scientific analysis of the subconscious mentality of the human race proves conclusively that the tendency to grow old is a mere habit. It is a habit, however, that has been acquired by the race as a whole, and is therefore transmitted to every child coming into the world.

Through the force of this habit we all think subconsciously that we are growing old, that age is inevitable, and that nothing can prevent the final culmination of age. We think these thoughts without knowing what we are doing, because that mode of thinking has become a part of the subconscious life. But by this mode of thinking we constantly direct the subconscious mind to produce the conditions of age, and whatever the subconscious is constantly directed to do, that it constantly will do.

The cause of every habit is found in some subconscious action, and whenever any subconscious action becomes fully individualized it acts automatically when prompted to do so, either by its own inherent tendency or by the influence of corresponding suggestions from without.

To individualize a subconscious action is to form a habit, and every conscious action that is frequently repeated will become an individualized subconscious action.

There are a number of conscious actions that tend to produce age, and many of these have been repeated so constantly, and for so many ages, by the individuals of the race, that they have become individualized subconscious actions, that is, race habits.

The habit of growing old was therefore originally produced by the repetition of those conscious actions that tend to produce age; in like manner, the habit of staying young may be produced by frequent repetitions of those conscious actions that tend to promote the perpetuation of youth; and as every habit may be removed by establishing an opposite subconscious tendency in its place, the possibility of removing the growing old habit is positively assured.

The subconscious mind can be entirely changed and completely reconstructed in all its phases, and since every habit is subconscious it is evident that every habit can be removed.

The fact that the tendency to grow old is a race habit proves that no person can stay young simply by accepting the idea that he naturally is young. Though nature gives him a new body every year, the growing old habit causes that new body to look old and feel old; therefore, if the new body is to look young and feel young, the growing old habit must be completely removed from the subconscious mind.

To remove this habit it is necessary not only to change the subconscious mind in this respect, but also necessary to change the conscious ideas of everything we see in tangible life.

The entire human race is growing old because every child was born with the habit; therefore the idea of age is constantly being suggested to our minds, and this idea is constantly adding life to the growing old habit. To prevent this we must constantly impress upon our minds the fact that the tendency to stay young is alone natural.

How to Stay Young

The tendency to imitate the false must be counteracted by training our minds to think and act in perfect harmony with the law that produces perpetual youth.

The conscious conception of life must be formed in the exact likeness of the absolute truth about life, and according to absolute truth, that is, exact science, man never grows old. He may change his youth into age through the violation of natural law, just as he may change the conditions of his physical system from health to disease through the violation of natural law, but it is only through the violation of natural law that age and disease can come. While man continues to be true to himself he is always well and always young.

To remove any race habit, it is necessary to act upon the fact that it is only subconscious tendencies that are inherited. Man does not inherit disease, or weakness, or adverse characteristics; but he may inherit the subconscious causes of these conditions.

Therefore, to prevent the mistakes of the race from being reproduced in ourselves, it is necessary to eliminate from our subconscious minds those adverse tendencies that we may have inherited from the race. The tendency to grow old is one of these, and it may be removed by training the subconscious mind to work in harmony with the natural renewing process.

It is not possible, however, for the conscious mind to direct the subconscious to work in harmony with the natural renewing process, so long as the idea of old age is believed to be real.

What we think of as real we impress upon the subconscious, and what we impress upon the subconscious, is seed sown in the garden of life; it will invariably bear fruit after its kind.

How to Stay Young

The idea of the three score and ten must be forgotten, and the idea that life can perpetuate youth so long as you may desire youth, must be impressed upon the subconscious instead.

The fact that the mistakes of man made the three score and ten practically the limit of his physical existence, originated the belief that the three score and ten was the natural limit, and that a longer life was merely accidental. But that which is produced by the mistakes of man does not corroborate what is produced by the laws of nature.

The laws of nature declare that there is no limit to the possibilities of life; neither is life confined to certain special actions. It is just as easy for the forces of being to perpetuate youth as to produce age; it requires no more energy to do the one than the other, but what these forces are to do man himself must determine.

It requires no more life-force to live a thousand years than to live one day; the living of life does not exhaust life, but rather develops the power of life.

It is the misuse of life that alone will exhaust life; therefore, when man learns to live life he will no longer be limited in any form whatever, by those conditions that have sprung from the mistakes of man.

To continue to believe that certain things must be because they have been, is to place the mind in complete bondage to the habits of the race, regardless of the nature of those habits, whether they be detrimental or not.

We are not required to believe anything but the truth, we are not required to do anything but that which promotes the highest welfare of each and all; and it is the understanding of

How to Stay Young

life itself that reveals what thought to think and what action to pursue.

To continue to grow old simply because the whole race is growing old, is not scientific; the free mind refuses to grow old unless nature says he must. And to the mind that is free, free from race thought, free to think the truth as it is, nature declares that to be true to himself he must stay young.

The average mind is practically filled with adverse tendencies and habits that have been inherited from the race; these tendencies are implicitly obeyed by the forces of the system, because these forces are controlled by the subconscious, and the subconscious always does what it has been directed to do.

It is therefore evident that the average person is doing a great many things, not because they are right and natural, but because he has inherited the habit from the race. And since the majority of the race habits originated in the prehistoric mistakes of man, the present man to be just to himself, must examine his life anew. He must no longer continue to do things because they have been done; his purpose, henceforth, must be to learn what his life actually is, and act accordingly.

What a man thinks is of extreme importance, because what he thinks or believes with conviction will impress the subconscious, and what the subconscious is impressed to do it invariably will do.

To believe that you will finally grow old is a habit; every child is born with the cause of that belief in its mind; but that belief will daily impress the subconscious to produce age, and age will be produced.

How to Stay Young

To believe that you are young now, and that nature is giving you a new body now, may be simple if your present body looks young and feels young; but in the midst of the realization of present youth, nearly every mind will persist in believing that age will come sometime. This belief, however, must be eliminated completely, and the subconscious mind must be trained to think the truth about life as it is.

To believe the truth about yourself is to believe that you are always young, because the law that perpetuates youth cannot cease to perpetuate youth so long as life has personal existence.

To believe with conviction that you are always young is to impress the subconscious with the idea of perpetual youth, and accordingly, the subconscious will begin to produce the elements of youth. The habit of growing old will cease and the habit of staying young will be established in its place.

The fact is that however long you may live in your present organized form, you will have a new body every eight or ten months. This body ought to look new and would look new if the subconscious system had not inherited the habit of growing old.

The personal man should look young and feel young, at all times, regardless of the years.

It is not the truth that years produce the feeling of age or the appearance of age; years produce experience, and experience, if not misapplied, will develop both mind and body. Development, however, means improvement, but it is not possible for that to improve, that is growing old and useless, neither is it possible for that to grow old and useless that is constantly being improved.

It is the truth that not a single cell in the human system ever becomes old; the belief in old eyes, therefore, is a false belief.

The belief that the eyes need glasses when they become "old" is a race habit, and it is contrary to every fact in exact science. The eyes do not become old; there is not a human eye on the face of this planet that has been in existence more than six or seven months; the same is true of all the other senses, and the fact proves conclusively that the only reason why the eyes become weak and dim after a certain number of years, is because the subconscious system has formed that habit.

To think that your eyes are growing old and dim is to impress age and weakness upon the subconscious life of the eyes, and according to subconscious law, conditions of age and weakness will be formed in the eyes. The eyes will consequently feel old and weak not because they are old and weak, but because they are filled with weak, old age conditions Where the eyes are defective in shape, glasses may be used to advantage for the purpose of correcting the defect, but this use should be temporary only, and should be taken up with that thought in mind.

No person should ever begin to wear glasses in the belief that he will have to use them all his life, nor should anyone ever think that his eyes will need glasses when they become old, because the eyes do not become old.

To live in the belief, however, that the eyes will grow old is to fill the eyes with old age conditions, and as such conditions interfere with natural functions they are invariably weakening in their effect.

The eyes of the octogenarian are no older than the eyes of the seven year old child; the eyes of both persons have been formed within the last six or eight months, and, therefore, the one pair is no more in need of glasses than the other.

The belief that the bones must become stiff, the physical organs weakened, the memory impaired, etc., when "advanced age" has been reached, is likewise contrary to exact science. There is not a single cell in the human system that will have to ossify, no matter how long the person may live.

The ossifying tendency is also a race habit, but like all other habits, it can be removed completely.

All the signs of "old age" are abnormal, produced by subconscious tendencies or habits that each individual has inherited from the race; no mind therefore, to be truthful, can speak of age as being natural and inevitable, nor can any person be true to himself unless he removes all age producing tendencies from hit system absolutely.

To try to demonstrate, in detail, that the tendency to grow old is a mere race habit will not be necessary, because the fact proves itself so completely the very moment the true relationship between physical conditions and subconscious actions is discerned. It is the removing of this habit, however, that demands our best and most thorough attention.

To proceed, the first essential is to remove the age producing tendency from the subconscious, and the second is to train the conscious mind to think the exact truth concerning the appearance of old age conditions.

When conditions of age are in evidence anywhere in our environments, the conscious mind should impress upon itself the fact that there is only eternal youth in the true state of life. All conditions of old age should be looked upon as unnatural, and every idea of old age should be contradicted at once.

The conscious mind should think of old age as contrary to nature, as a mere race habit, for which no individual is directly to blame, and should think of the age producing process as something that any person can eliminate from his system at will.

What enters the mind through the senses will impress Itself upon the mind, and will tend to reproduce itself in the life of the individual; for this reason, the idea of age must never enter the mind, and all thought of age should be immediately dismissed as unreal, the very moment it is suggested to consciousness.

The conscious mind must look upon old age conditions as foreign, as wholly false, and as things apart from the real life of man. No attempt, however, should be' made to resist these conditions, because they have neither power nor existence of their own; they simply are creations of our own minds, and will cease to be when we create them no more.

To remove those subconscious tendencies that cause the creation of old age conditions, it is necessary to form mental tendencies that are directly opposite in nature and purpose; the principle being that no mental state or tendency can be removed unless it is displaced by its exact opposite. The darkness disappears only when displaced by the light.

The habit of growing old will disappear when we form the habit of staying young, and to the art of forming this habit a separate chapter will be devoted.

When the tendency to grow old is recognized as a race habit having its origin in the prehistoric mistakes of man, we may be tempted to think that the habit is too well established to be removed in our own lifetime; we may argue that what is a race habit can only be removed by centuries of training in the formation of the opposite tendency, and that that training will have to be applied to the entire race.

Such conclusions, however, are not scientific; it is not necessary for the entire race to learn to stay young before individuals may acquire that art, any more than it is necessary for the entire race to develop genius before we may have genius in the individual. Besides, man will not be required to produce youth; he already is young; he will simply have to remove the habit of growing old, and this any individual can do now.

All habits are subconscious, and anything can be removed from the subconscious by anyone at any time.

The subconscious can do and will do whatever it is directed to do, and it begins to act the very moment the directions are being made. It is therefore in the power of every individual to learn to stay young now.

How to Stay Young

Chapter 5

Eliminate The Consciousness Of Age By Living In The Great Eternal Now

The forces of the mind will create and express every quality or condition that is held in consciousness. This is one of the most important of all metaphysical laws, because it is principally through this law that man determines what his personal life is to be.

To live in the consciousness of age is to create in mind the conditions of age, and what is created in mind will invariably be expressed in the personality. Therefore the consciousness of age must be eliminated completely before the perpetuation of youth can be promoted.

The consciousness of age is produced by the belief that time is passing and that the longer man continues to pass with time the older he becomes.

This belief, however, is a direct contradiction to the facts of exact science; first, because time does not pass, time is; and second, because the perpetual renewing process, inherent in man, prevents him from growing old no matter how long he may live.

The true conception of time is extremely important in placing the mind in the proper attitude towards the laws that govern the being of man; and this true conception is based upon the principle that time is. Time neither comes nor goes; it is the movements of nature that come and go, not time.

How to Stay Young

What we call time is but the now of eternity, and this now is eternally in the now; therefore there can be no passing of time.

It is only in the now that man can live; he can live neither in the past nor in the future; he may think of the past or the future, but he can live only in the now. And since the now does not pass, the life of man does not pass.

When man believes that many years constitute age, and that the passing of time produces the many years, he will unconsciously live in the feeling that he is growing older and older with the passing of the years. He will feel older and older every year, and the body always looks as old as the mind feels.

However, when man realizes that many years do not constitute age, and that the years do not pass, he will no longer feel that he is growing old, and consequently will no longer look old.

To train the mind to concentrate the whole of attention upon the great eternal now is to develop the consciousness of the "isness" of the now, and to consciously feel that the now is, is to eliminate the consciousness of age completely.

It is not possible for the mind to feel that it is growing old so long as it feels that it lives in the now, and that the now is.

The now is eternal; that is, the now eternally is now; the now never ceases to be now; therefore to live in the now is to continue to be now what you are now, and you are young now.

How to Stay Young

It is possible for man to grow and develop in the BOW, but he will never pass out of the now, because the now is eternal.

Man should affirm to himself "I AM not passing with time, because time does not pass; time is. I AM living in the now, and the now continues eternally to be the now. I AM living and growing now, but I AM not passing towards age. There is no age, and I do not pass; I AM."

When man develops the "I AM" consciousness, he will attain the realization of what he is now; he will discern that his present nature is limitless in possibility, and that the conscious possession of more and more of the richness of his nature will come, not from more and more years of development, but from more and more present realization.

He will discern that he may accomplish whatever he has in mind by perpetually increasing his present realization of what is latent in his nature now. He will not look to the future for greater attainments, but to the growth of the present, and will consequently concentrate the whole of attention upon the now.

To live in the realization of the now, with no direct thought of the past or the future, is to eliminate from mind the "passing of time" attitude; and when this attitude is removed the consciousness of age will disappear completely.

When man is no longer conscious of age, he will no longer create old age conditions, and therefore, will permit his system to be what nature makes it to be now — young.

To perpetuate the youth that nature is producing now, live in the eternal now, and know that you are young now. Know that the youth producing process in your system is as eternal as the now, and that you therefore will always be young no matter how long you may live.

To live in the great eternal now is to give the whole of attention to the work of the present moment; it is to recognize neither past nor future; it is to think neither of what has been nor what is to be; it is to live, think and act only for what can be lived, thought end attained now.

To live in the great eternal now, is to act upon the principle that it is only what we do now that determines results. The past is gone; it concerns us no more; and since the future will be the natural outcome of the present, the more perfectly we live for the present the greater will the future be.

To live in the great eternal now, is to be so completely absorbed in the now that there is consciousness neither of the past nor the future; the only consciousness is the consciousness of the now.

To live in the great eternal now, is to realize that there is no past, that there is no future; all is now, because the now always is now, always was now, and always shall be now.

There is no time but the now; and the now does not pass away; therefore there is no passing of time; all time is, and in that time man always is.

The heavenly bodies, in their movements, do not record the passing of time, neither do they measure time; they simply record their own speed as they move in the great eternal now; they simply measure the changing distances between their own changing positions as they move about the great center of life during the great eternal now.

How to Stay Young

The universe is not passing away; some parts are only moving around other parts and these parts are moving around still other parts that in turn move around something else; all is motion, but all motion is in circles. The universe is eternally where it is, eternally moving in circles where it is, thoroughly and eternally alive, and all taking place during the great eternal now.

Everything is for the now because the only time that is, is now. Man is conscious only of the now, and to look into the depths of the now is to find that everything is contained in the now.

To give the whole of attention to the now is the secret of gaining in the now all that man may want now. That which is not done for the now is scattered, "It will either be wasted entirely or will produce results that are detrimental to man's welfare now." is only what is done for the now that adds to man's welfare now, and when man lives, thinks and acts exclusively for the now, his life will be complete now.

To live in the great eternal now, is therefore the only scientific mode of living, whatever the individual viewpoint of life may be; and it is one of the fundamental essentials in the art of staying young, To live in the great eternal now, fix no special time for anything in the future. Plan for the future when such plans are necessary to the promotion of what you are doing now, but consciously live in the now.

No thought should be given to what may happen in the future; such thought is wasted because we cannot deal with that which is not here. All the power of life and thought should be used in causing the best things possible to happen now. Such action will not only improve the present, but will also train the mind to eliminate the consciousness of age by giving the whole of consciousness to the now, where age is not.

Learn to be more now, develop yourself now, promote your growth now, and you will become more and more competent to deal with that which may transpire in your life. You will gain the power to make the future far better than the present; you will feel the constant increase of this power and will therefore have no anxiety about the days that are to be.

To make the best of the present is to make the future better, but to make the best of the present all life, all thought and all action must be concentrated absolutely upon the present; no thought must be given to the future; in fact, so completely must attention be concentrated upon the work of the present that we are unconscious of everything but what we are doing now.

To think of the future is to think of how long we may live, and how many years we shall pass through before we reach the expected goal. Such thought will cause the mind to feel that time is passing and that we are passing with time into weakness and age. The consciousness of age will thus be produced, and to be conscious of age is to produce the conditions of age in our own systems.

The great question with man is not how long he may live in any particular sphere of existence, but how well he may live where he is living now; Mid he who lives well where he lives now will live a long time where he lives now; that is, if he so desires.

The man who lives well while upon earth will live a long time upon earth, and retain his youth as long as he lives.

How to Stay Young

To live well, however, it is necessary to live absolutely for the great eternal now; to live now the life of youth now; to be conscious only of the now, and to realize that both the now and the youth that is produced now are eternal.

To realize that man is eternal is to eliminate the subconscious feeling that we are passing towards that condition of age that is supposed to be in store for every person in the future; and to realize that the youth of the now is eternal is to eliminate the consciousness of age, thus removing the principal cause of old age conditions.

The fact that nature is perpetually renewing the entire being of man, proves that there is no condition of age in the future towards which man is supposed to pass; such a belief is a mere illusion, because the only age that appears in the human system is the age that man himself produces through the violation of the laws of life.

To avoid the violation of these laws it becomes absolutely necessary to live, think and act only for the great eternal now. Everything that is done should be done "just for today," and the ruling purpose of life should be to live today the greatest life that is possible today.

The object is to eliminate the consciousness of age, because when man is no longer conscious of growing old he will cease to grow old. The new body that nature is constantly producing in man, will stay new when man ceases to make that which is new look old and feel old; instead, he will look young and feel young; and it is natural that he should, because he is young.

To eliminate the consciousness of age the principal essential is to realize that time is; that time is not passing, and that therefore man is not passing with time.

How to Stay Young

The feeling that we are growing old is produced by the belief that every year adds so much to the age of man; but the facts of exact science prove that the years do not produce age; also, that nothing but the violation of law can produce age.

The consciousness of age is therefore the consciousness of abnormal conditions, conditions that have been produced, not by nature, but by the mistakes of man; and these conditions can be removed only by the development of that consciousness that is absolutely normal, based upon the realization of what is true in the real life of nature.

The first essential in the development of normal consciousness is to place the mind in contact with the present natural processes in the human system. The most important of these are the process of perpetual renewal and the process of present creation.

The first of these rebuilds the entire human system during every period of eight or ten months, thus keeping the body forever young.

The second process creates in the system all those conditions or qualities of which the mind is conscious; but its work is of for by and through the present only.

To place the mind in contact with this second process is to prove to the mind that there is no other time in nature but the now, and that there is no other action in nature but the action of the now. And when this fact is proven to the mind, the whole of attention will naturally be directed absolutely upon the time of the now and the action of the now.

In this manner, natural consciousness will be developed, because the more the mind associates with the true processes of nature, the more keenly will the mind feel that which is natural; and since it is natural to live for the now, the mind will, through the development of natural consciousness, enter absolutely into the life of the now.

To live absolutely in the life of the now is to be conscious only of what is true in nature now; and it is true in nature now that man is young now.

It is therefore evident that man will continue to stay young so long as he continues to live absolutely in the great eternal now.

Chapter 6

Training the Subconscious to Produce Perpetually the Elements of Youth

The subconscious mind has the power to keep the body in health, youth and vigor for any length of time.

The subconscious mind is the source of every quality, condition, characteristic, tendency, desire, element or power that appears in the human personality; and as a source it is inexhaustible; therefore, when man learns to draw upon his subconscious source, he may increase any power, perpetuate any condition, or perfect any quality to the highest imaginable degree.

The subconscious can do and will do whatever it is properly impressed or directed to do; it is therefore evident that any person may, through the proper direction of his subconscious mind, produce youth in his system now, and perpetuate that youth for as long a time as he may desire.

Whatever the present condition of the body may be, the subconscious can remove that condition so that the new body that nature has recently produced may appear as it is — full of health, youth and vigor.

The subconscious mind is the inner side of the whole mind of man; the conscious mind is the outer side. The conscious mind is the wide-awake mind, the subconscious is the interior depths of mentality. The conscious mind is the thinker, the subconscious is the doer. The conscious mind gives directions, the subconscious carries them out. The conscious mind is the sower, the subconscious is the mental soil — inexhaustible in the richness of its productive power.

How to Stay Young

The ideas, the thoughts, the beliefs, the desires and the aims of the conscious mind are mental seeds, and when these are deeply felt they will enter the subconscious, invariably producing fruits after their kind.

To train the subconscious to produce the elements of youth, only those ideas, thoughts, beliefs and desires should be entertained in the conscious mind that are conducive to youth and perpetuation of youth.

It is not possible for any state, condition, element or power to be expressed in the human personality until its cause has been formed in the subconscious.

All causes are held and worked out in the subconscious. The conscious mind originates the cause, the subconscious takes it within itself and evolves the natural effect.

All causes are subconscious, and all subconscious causes bring forth their effects into the outer mind and body. Therefore, the subconscious cause of youth must be established before youth will express itself in the personality.

The subconscious mind of the child contains the active cause of youth, and also the inactive, latent cause of old age. The former cause is produced by the natural renewing process, and so long as this cause is permitted to act youth will appear in the personality. The latter cause is inherited from the race; it is the age producing race habit, and according to the tendencies of its own inherent nature, will begin to produce the old age condition at the expiration of a period of thirty, forty or fifty years.

To perpetuate youth it is therefore necessary to remove the subconscious age producing cause that has been inherited from the race; and to remove this cause the entire subconscious mind must be trained to produce perpetually the elements of youth.

All age producing causes will disappear from the subconscious when the entire subconscious mind is permeated with youth producing causes, and this is our object in view.

To promote this object, the conscious mind must proceed systematically and thoroughly to recreate the subconscious in all its phases; the subconscious must be directed to do everything that is necessary to produce and perpetuate youth, and every subconscious tendency to the contrary, must be displaced by a youth producing tendency.

To proceed, the subconscious should daily be impressed with the fact that you are young now. What you impress upon the subconscious, the subconscious will express in mind and body; therefore, when the subconscious is deeply and thoroughly impressed with the fact that you are young now, it will produce and express throughout your system the elements of youth now. You will consequently feel young and look young, and you should, because you are young.

When the subconscious is impressed with the fact that you are young now it will cease to follow the race tendency to interfere with the natural renewing process, but will instead, work in harmony with this process, thus removing from the system every age producing habit or tendency that has been inherited from the race.

To impress the subconscious with the idea that you are young now is not to present to the inner mind some imaginary idea; you are young now; it is no theory; your entire system has been made new within the last few months; therefore, permeate your mind through and through with the very spirit of that great truth.

To try to impress an idea upon the subconscious that you know to be untrue is to fail; the subconscious will only accept those ideas that you inwardly feel to be absolutely true.

The subconscious will not obey the doubting mind, but the mind of faith and conviction can make the subconscious do anything within its power to do, and To try to impress an idea upon the subconscious there are no limitations, neither is there any end.

To live in the conviction that you are young now is to constantly direct the subconscious to make you look young now, feel young now, and express, through and through your system the vigor of youth now.

The subconscious can; the subconscious can do and will do whatever it is properly directed to do.

What the subconscious has been properly and thoroughly trained to do it will continue to do for an indefinite period, or until the conscious mind gives directions to the contrary. Therefore, when the subconscious has been trained to produce the elements of youth, it will continue to produce these elements perpetually, thus insuring continuous youth for that individual so long as he may live upon this plane.

When the subconscious mind has been trained to produce perpetually the elements of youth, it will not only produce these elements in its own personality, but will transmit the youth producing tendency to the next generation.

When both parents have eliminated from their subconscious minds the age producing race habit, and have permanently established instead the subconscious youth producing process, their children will be born absolutely free from the age producing habit of the race.

Such children will not be born with the habit of growing old, but will be born with a strong subconscious tendency to stay young as long as they may live. Such children will never grow old unless they acquire the habit, later on in life, through the misuse of their own minds.

To transmit to their children the perpetual youth producing tendency, it is necessary for the parents, however, to permanently establish this tendency in their own subconscious minds before the conceptions of those children are to take place.

It is the law that whatever the parents have established in their own subconscious minds, they will transmit to their children; the possibilities of parenthood are therefore immeasurable, and to those who understand the unfoldment of these possibilities, than parenthood there is no greater greatness.

The Subconscious minds of all persons, whether they be octogenarians, or in their teens, contain the age producing tendency; young parents will therefore transmit this growing old race habit to their children just as readily as those parents that have begun to show the signs of age; for this reason, all persons who expect to become parents must completely remove this race habit from their subconscious minds before they can transmit the youth producing tendency to their children.

How to Stay Young

Those parents who succeed only partly in removing the age producing process from their systems, will give their children the power to retain the vigor of youth for a longer period than the average; but all parents can succeed completely in this respect, and all should proceed with that determination in mind.

Every effort to direct the subconscious to do what we desire to have done, should be promoted in the firm conviction that the subconscious can. To have absolute faith in the subconscious is to reach the inexhaustible powers of the subconscious, and when these powers are reached there is no object in view that cannot be accomplished.

To properly impress any idea or desire upon the subconscious, the conscious mind must not only be firmly convinced that the idea is true, but must keenly feel the nature and the purpose of that idea; and there is no attitude of mind that will promote these two essentials as thoroughly as faith. Every effort therefore that is made in the training of the subconscious should be permeated with strong invincible faith.

The fact that the body is being constantly renewed makes it possible for the subconscious, not only to perpetuate the elements of youth in the body, but also to constantly improve everything in the human personality.

Therefore, when the subconscious is being directed to produce the elements of youth, it should also be directed to produce the elements of beauty and physical perfection. Impress upon the subconscious the most perfect idea of physical beauty that the mind can possibly conceive, and desire with deep feeling, that the elements of that beauty be produced and expressed through every atom of the physical form.

How to Stay Young

In like manner, direct the subconscious to build for yourself a finer and a finer personality, a stronger character and a more brilliant mind. And always proceed in the faith that the subconscious can.

Whenever you think of yourself, mentally see yourself as the picture of health, youth and vigor, and introduce into that picture the most perfect idea of physical beauty that you can possibly imagine.

This picture should be daily impressed upon the subconscious; that is, while holding the picture in mind, think of the subconscious with deep feeling, and try to feel that the elements of the picture are being appropriated by the subconscious.

Every mental picture that is properly impressed upon the subconscious will be reproduced in the human system, because whatever is impressed upon the subconscious will be developed and expressed in the personality.

To mentally live in the world of this picture will aid remarkably in bringing the nature of the picture into the subconscious, and this is especially true when the mind pictures itself in the world of health and youth.

To mentally live in a certain state or attitude is to take that state or attitude into the subconscious. That which we live we invariably impress upon the subconscious; therefore to perpetually live in the spirit of youth is to cause the subconscious to perpetually create the elements of youth.

To live in the belief that you are growing older every year is to direct the subconscious to make you feel older and look older every year; and this is what nearly every person is doing, though principally through the force of habit — race habit. He is thereby training his subconscious mind to produce old age; but it is just as easy for the subconscious to produce perpetual youth if properly directed to do so.

When the subconscious is trained to produce youth, and express youth throughout the entire personality, it will cease to produce conditions of old age, and will consequently interfere no more with the perpetual renewing process; instead, it will promote that process.

To remove the tendency of the hair to change its color at those periods when race thought expects it to change, direct the subconscious to perpetuate the natural color of the hair.

The fact that the color of the hair has already begun to turn gray need not cause anyone to hesitate to apply this method. The actions of the mind can produce chemical changes in the physical system; to restore the natural coloring matter of the hair would be no more difficult for nature than the healing of a wound; but changes and modifications in human nature can be produced only through the subconscious, therefore, the subconscious must first be directed to do what we wish to have done.

To direct the subconscious to perpetuate the natural color of the hair, picture this color as clearly as possible in mind; then, with deep feeling, impress the soul of this picture upon the subconscious; that is, place your thought in the very soul, or inner life of that color, and impress that thought upon the depths of subconscious life.

To mentally live in the absolute faith that the subconscious is perpetuating the natural color of the hair is sufficient where the color has not begun to change; but where the change has begun, special attention must be given to the matter daily to restore normal conditions.

How to Stay Young

To retain the natural color of the hair it is also necessary to avoid strenuous mental action, hard thinking, forced thinking, nervousness, worry, fear and similar adverse mental states.

This is also true with regard to the perpetuation of youth throughout the system; all mental states must be harmonious, and all physical conditions wholesome.

To secure harmonious mental states and wholesome physical conditions, all that is necessary is to direct the subconscious to produce them; the subconscious can.

To direct or impress the subconscious with the positive assurance of securing the desired results, there are three fundamental essentials to be closely observed. First, the idea to be impressed should be clearly discerned in mind; second, when concentrating this idea upon the subconscious, the mind should act in the attitude of the deepest possible feeling; and third, the real existence of the subconscious mind itself should be felt in every part of the personality.

The subconscious mind occupies the entire personality and fills every atom with its finer mental life; in fact, it is an immense, inner, mental world that permeates every part of the being of man; therefore, when trying to impress an idea upon the subconscious, attention should be concentrated upon the finer life that permeates the outer life.

When the conscious mind feels the finer life of the subconscious mind, the thought of the conscious mind IS in contact with the power of the subconscious, and whatever the conscious mind, during this contact, may desire to have done, the subconscious will proceed to do.

This contact is always produced when the conscious mind is in an attitude of deep feeling, and this deep feeling will invariably follow the combined action of faith and desire — the desire to impress the subconscious, and the absolute faith that the subconscious can do whatever it is impressed to do.

Chapter 7

Conscious Harmony with the Law of Perpetual Renewal

The entire universe is perpetually passing through a process of renewal; nothing is fixed; all is change, and the purpose of this change is to make all things new at all times. Every action in nature tends to counteract permanency or age, and every movement in life has youth and progress in view.

All things live, move and have their being in the spirit of change, and this change is produced by the law of perpetual renewal, a law that underlies everything, permeates everything and acts through everything.

This law is perpetually at work through the human system, changing everything, renewing everything, but what the results of this change are to be in the life of the individual depends upon how he relates himself to the law that produces the change, and how fully he cooperates with the original purpose of that law.

When the mind acts in conscious harmony with the law of renewal, the results of that law will be expressed through the life, the mentality and the personality of the individual; but when the mind fails to act in harmony with that law these results will be neutralized.

The law of renewal makes all things new at all times in the entire human system, but whether the new system is to express new conditions or continue to express old conditions will depend upon whether or not the results of the law of renewal are neutralized by the human mind.

How to Stay Young

The mind of the individual can permit the new fibers and conditions of its own system to appear new, or it can cause the new to look old and act as if it were old; that is, the mind can give full expression to the results of the law of renewal, or it can completely neutralize these results.

When the mind places itself in harmony with the law of renewal, and recognizes its existence at all times, every action of the mind will become a renewing process, and will cooperate with the law; in consequence, that which is renewed by the law of renewal will be expressed through mind and body in its original newness; it will not be changed, colored or modified by mental interference as it is being expressed, but will come forth as it is — absolutely new.

When the mind does not act in conscious harmony with the law of renewal, and does not recognize the existence of the renewing process, every action of the mind will tend to reproduce the old. As the new is coming forth, fresh from the law of renewal, the mind will cause it to be reproduced in the exact likeness of the old; the results of the renewing process will thereby be neutralized, and though everything in the system continues to be renewed, nothing appears as if it were renewed.

When the mind acts in ignorance of, or at variance with, the law of renewal, it follows the groove of the age producing race habit, and causes what has been renewed in its own system, to be changed so that it looks old, feels old and acts as if it were old.

The mind acts in every atom of the being of man, and has the power to change, color or modify whatever is taking place in the human system; what is changed by the mind becomes more or less similar to the predominating thought, feeling or condition of the mind; therefore, what is renewed by the law of renewal will become old in its nature so long as the mind feels old, acts as if it were old and believes that all things are growing old.

The mental forces are creative but they invariably create in the exact likeness of the predominating ideas, beliefs, feelings or attitudes of mind.

When the mind feels old, the creative forces will cause everything in the system to look as old as the mind feels; and the mind that is ignorant of the law of perpetual renewal will feel older every year because it believes that all things are growing older every year.

The mind that acts in conscious harmony with the law of perpetual renewal will feel that all things are new now, and in consequence, the creative forces of the system will give newness, youth and vigor to everything in mind or body.

To train the mind to act in conscious harmony with the law of perpetual renewal, the existence of this law, in every part of the system, must be recognized in every thought, feeling or attitude. Every trace of belief in age or the aging process must be eliminated completely, and the fact that all things are new now must become a firm conviction.

The mind must aim to perpetually renew itself, and this aim may be promoted by training every process of thinking to form new thought, better thought, greater thought and superior thought about everything that enters consciousness.

The thought of today, on every subject, must be new as compared with the thought of yesterday, and every idea formed in mind must be an improvement upon the corresponding idea that was formed before.

How to Stay Young

Every mental conception that is formed today, on any subject, should be finer, higher and superior to the previous conception formed on the same subject.

To constantly renew its own thinking, and improve its own thinking should be the ruling purpose of mind, and the highest possible point of view should be taken in mind at all times, whatever the subject of thought may be.

The mind that is perpetually renewing itself will think new thought and superior thought on all subjects at all times. Such a mind will comply with one of the greatest of all statements in exact science, "Be ye therefore transformed by the renewal of your mind," and will, in consequence, not only realize perpetual youth in the physical system, but will also transform, advance and perfect the entire world Of mind and character.

To continue the thinking of "old thought" is to perpetuate those hereditary tendencies that produce the aging process, because old thought is thought that does not change or improve. New thought produces new life, more life and greater life, while old thought weakens, deteriorates and ossifies the entire system.

That which is perpetually renewed will never weaken, unless the results of the renewing process are neutralized; but these results can only be neutralized by the mind that lives in the non-progressive attitude of old thought; this attitude will disappear, however, when the mind begins to perpetually renew itself through the thinking of new thought — thought that is always renewing itself by constantly improving upon itself.

When the mind dwells in the old thought attitude, the renewing process will fail to cause the new to be different from the old, but when the mind is constantly breaking bounds, constantly moving forward into the new, the superior and the greater, the renewing process will invariably cause all things in the human system to become, not only new in appearance, but superior in expression and greater in action.

The law of perpetual renewal will cause everything to improve as it is being renewed, providing the mind lives in conscious harmony with the law of renewal by constantly renewing itself.

The perpetual renewal of mind is readily promoted when consciousness is placed in perfect touch with the spirit of change that pervades all things; and that this spirit does pervade all things is clearly discerned when the mind is placed in harmony with the real life of nature.

The entire universe is in perpetual motion, and since motion invariably produces change, everything in the universe is passing through perpetual change.

Change implies renewal, therefore the fact that nature does supply the law of perpetual renewal is demonstrated conclusively.

This law is constantly remaking everything; all things are ever new and ever becoming new; all things therefore should appear new, that is, under normal conditions; but the fact that the new seldom appears new in the being of man, proves that he is not living under normal conditions.

To produce normal conditions man must live a normal life, and to live a normal life is to live in harmony with the fundamental laws of nature. One of the most important of these is the law of perpetual renewal; therefore every mind that does not aim to promote perpetual renewal is not living in harmony with nature.

The mind that is not living in harmony with nature is producing abnormal conditions, and it is such conditions that change or neutralize the results of the renewing process, thereby causing the new to appear as if it were not new.

That which is normal is never old; it is normal or natural to be new and young at all times, because one of the principal laws in nature is ever making all things new.

Those conditions that appear to be old are abnormal; all appearance of age is artificial, and comes from the race habit of mentally interfering with the law of renewal.

The workings of nature do not produce the conditions of age; such conditions are produced by man's failure to work with the renewing process of nature.

All conditions of age, and all the results of what man calls age are unnatural, and must disappear when man becomes natural.

To be natural is to live, think and act in conscious harmony with the purpose of nature, and this purpose is to renew everything and improve everything in the being of man.

The fact that nature has provided the law of perpetual renewal, and based everything upon this law, makes it unnecessary for man to try to change; he already is changing; what man is required to do is to cease to resist that change, and to cease to pervert the results of that change.

How to Stay Young

Man is not required to produce perpetual renewal in his system, but to train himself to live, think and act in conscious harmony with that perpetual renewal that is already taking place.

The law of perpetual renewal is producing perpetual youth in the human system, but the results of this law are modified to such an extent by the false actions of the mind, that the new body does not look new, nor feel new, but looks and feels as old as the mind thinks it now is according to race belief.

To remove these false actions of mind so that the new body may look as new and feel as new as it actually is, this is the object in view; and when this object is fulfilled, man will look young, feel young and stay young as long as he may live upon this planet.

To remove any false action the opposite true action must be established in its place; to prevent the mind from interfering with the process of renewal, all the forces of mind must be trained to promote that renewal, and to train the mental forces in this respect all thinking must become, in itself, a renewing process as well as a developing process.

To perpetually renew itself, the fundamental aim of thinking must be the formation of higher and higher conceptions concerning everything that may be discerned by consciousness.

When the mind begins to think, its aim should be to think better thought, larger thought and greater thought; and the desire to improve constantly upon all previous thought should be made so strong that all the elements of mind are drawn into the very spirit of that desire.

How to Stay Young

To increase the power of this desire is to cause all the forces of mind to work for the purpose of this desire; and when this is accomplished, the tendency to renew itself and improve itself will become so strong in the mind, that every process of thought will become an improvement of thought.

To think is to think better — that will be the condition of such a mind, because every mental action will have formed the inherent tendency to renew itself and improve itself whenever it is placed in action.

When the mind has established this mode of thinking it will renew itself constantly, and will consequently act in conscious harmony with the law of perpetual renewal. Instead of neutralizing the results of this law, the mind will fully express these results.

The new body will look new, feel new, and express all the power and vigor of youth. The personality will continue to stay young, because the new body that nature is giving to man every year, will be burdened no more with old age conditions.

It is the mind that lives in old thought that fills the new body with old age conditions, thus causing the new to look old and feel old; but when the mind begins to renew itself perpetually there will be no more old thought nor old age conditions; old age will vanish like a dream, and man will continue to stay young as long as he remains upon this planet.

Chapter 8

Why Experience Produces Age when Its Real Purpose Is to Perpetuate Youth

To live is to think; to think is to act, and to act is to produce experience; experience must therefore invariably follow the expression of every process in life.

To live is to live more, because living produces experience, and experience opens the mind to the newer, the larger and the greater.

To gain experience is to gain wisdom, power and a larger field of conscious action; and since the enlargement of the field of conscious action is the direct cause of the renewal of mind, the perpetual renewal of mind must invariably follow the perpetual gain of experience.

The gain of experience, however, is continuous, because while life continues, the gain of experience will continue.

The perpetual renewal of mind will perpetuate the youth of the entire personality; and since the inherent tendency of experience is to renew the mind, the real purpose of experience must be to perpetuate youth.

To perpetuate youth in the complete sense, is to promote the growth, the development and the advancement of everything in the being of man, and to gain experience is to gain the elements of advancement; therefore, the tendency of experience is inseparably connected with the tendency of life to advance itself, renew itself and perpetuate its own youth.

To live is to gain experience; to gain experience is to gain the power to live more, and to live more is to perpetuate youth. It is not possible to grow old while life is on the increase.

The gain of experience will produce two opposing tendencies in mind, depending upon the use that is made of the mental elements produced by the experience. The one is a tendency towards the feeling of maturity, the other is a tendency towards the feeling of conscious expansion.

When the mind thinks of development as a process having a definite end in view, the mental elements produced by experience will be used for the purpose of bringing this end into realization; and as this end is being approached the mind feels that it is being matured.

The feeling of maturity tends to retard further advancement, because further advancement is not supposed to be possible where maturity has taken place. Therefore, the mind that permits the feeling of maturity to act in the system will cause a maturing process to be placed in action throughout the system, and as the maturing process is gaining ground, the advancing process is losing ground.

The gradual suspension of growth in one part after the other will be the result, and that which ceases to grow will begin to grow old.

When the mind thinks of development as being perpetual, there will be no thought of any end; every step in advance will be looked upon as a step towards more advancement; the feeling of maturity will therefore be eliminated completely.

To think of every experience as being an open door to a larger mental world is to cause every experience to produce the feeling of conscious expansion, and what the mind feels it is doing it is doing.

The inherent purpose of every experience is to produce conscious expansion, and so long as this expansion is perpetual the renewal of mind will be perpetual; in consequence, youth will be perpetual; but this inherent purpose of experience is interfered with by the process of maturity.

The maturing process, however, is not natural; it is the result of wrong states of mind, being a direct contradiction of the growing process which is natural.

The maturing process has an end in view, and intends to cease action when that end is reached; the growing process has no end in view, and does not intend to cease action at any time. The growing process does not think of the finished product; it simply thinks of growing now, therefore, perpetuates the force of growth now.

In the true order of things, nothing is ever finished; what seems to be finished is but an introduction to something still greater that is to follow, and the process of growth works ceaselessly through all these stages of advancement.

It is therefore evident that to think of maturity and expect maturity, is to introduce a false process in the human system, and as this maturing process does have a tendency to retard natural growth it will prevent the natural renewing process of the system from perpetuating the youth of the body.

The reason why experience tends to produce age in the average person is, according to this analysis, clearly discerned in the fact that the race lives in the belief that experience produces mental maturity; and since the condition of maturity suspends growth, age must follow, because that which ceases to grow begins to grow old.

The condition of age is simply a condition of retarded or suspended growth; it is a condition wherein development has ceased, and wherein retrogression and decay have begun, or are about to begin. But it is not possible, however, for retrogression or decay to take place anywhere in the system so long as growth, development and advancement are in action.

Where progression is in action, retrogression is impossible, and where there is growth, there can be no decay; therefore, the promotion of uninterrupted growth and continuous advancement in the human system will eliminate every condition of age; in consequence, youth will be perpetual.

The law of perpetual renewal provides for continuous growth and advancement in every part of the system, and experience opens the mind to larger fields of action, thereby giving the process of growth the opportunity to promote the development of the human system on an ever-enlarging scale.

In this plan there is no place given to the aging process, therefore, the aging process will never enter the system unless it is produced by man himself through the violation of these fundamental laws in nature.

The inherent purpose of experience is expressed through one of the most important of these laws, and to comply with this law, the mind should be trained to act in harmony with the purpose of experience.

How to Stay Young

This may be accomplished by causing the conscious mind to think of every experience as a path to greater things, and by causing the subconscious mind to feel the expanding, growing, advancing tendency of every experience.

The subconscious mind should be daily impressed with the fact that every experience has an expanding, growing, advancing tendency; ere long this inner purpose of experience will be subconsciously felt, and thereafter the subconscious mind will act in harmony with the tendency of experience.

The conscious mind should expect every experience to open the way to the new, and should confidently live in the very soul of that expectation. In consequence, all the forces and faculties of the conscious mind will move with the tendency of experience — the tendency to enter the new — and will, thereby, constantly enter the new.

When the conscious mind is ever entering the new, and the subconscious mind is constantly acting in harmony with the expanding, advancing tendency, the perpetual renewing process will be promoted throughout the entire personality. The perpetuation of youth must invariably follow, because every condition of maturity and suspended growth will entirely disappear.

When the mind feels the conditions of maturity, these conditions will be expressed in every part of the system, especially in the face, where the expressions of mind are the strongest, and conditions of maturity invariably produce the appearance of age.

It is therefore evident that the unnatural tendency to mature is one of the principal causes of the aging process.

How to Stay Young

The growing mind, however, does not mature; the more the growing mind develops the more it finds to develop, and the stronger becomes its desire to work out the new possibilities that are constantly being discovered. Such a mind never feels matured nor gives expression to maturity; nor can anything come to a standstill and ossify in the personality of such a mind.

The average person, after having passed through a great deal of experience, feels old and worn, because he has looked upon experience as a wearing process instead of as a process of renewal, growth and advancement. In consequence, he looks old and worn, and is gradually placing his entire system under the complete influence of the aging process.

Experience implies action, and action, as ordinarily expressed uses up energy; therefore it is believed that much experience will produce a worn, wearied condition. But the ordinary expression of action does not apply the true purpose of action; results — worn and wearied conditions are for that reason abnormal.

The true purpose of action is to place in action more and more of the stored up energy of the system; and as experience tends to enlarge the sphere of action, it is a foregone conclusion that experience, when not interfered with, will invigorate both mind and body.

When each action in the human system tends to place more stored-up energy in action, the power and the capacity of the system will naturally increase, and such results may be secured from every action when the mind is trained to think of every action, not as a wearing process, but as a building process.

How to Stay Young

To train the mind to use every experience, that is, every group of new actions for the purpose of awakening potential power, is to promote the real purpose of experience, because the perpetual renewal of the entire system demands a constant increase in the expression of life.

To train the mind for this purpose, every experience should be consciously used as a path to the newer, the larger and the greater.

The mind must be trained to think, both consciously and subconsciously, of every experience as an open door to a new world. To enter this door whenever it opens, is to perpetually renew and enlarge the mental world, and while the mental world is being perpetually renewed, old age is impossible.

When the mind thinks of every experience as a developing and enlarging process, there will be no tendency in experience to produce conditions of maturity or age, but every experience will be left free to promote its own inherent purpose, which is to perpetuate the new by ever and ever opening the mind to the new.

The action of every experience tends to produce an impression upon the mind, and the result of this impression will depend upon the mental attitude towards experience while the impression was being made.

To form these impressions with the greatest of care is highly important because these impressions determine the nature of thought, and man is as he thinks.

Those impressions that are fixed in their nature will tend to produce stationary conditions in the system and such conditions invariably become old age conditions. Impressions, however, that are created with an inherent desire to reproduce themselves and enlarge themselves, will originate advancing thought; that is, thought that will work in harmony with the natural renewing process, and thus perpetuate the elements of youth.

To simply "pass through" experience is to impress consciousness with the idea of wear and tear, and this idea, as it forms itself into conditions, will age the personality.

When passing through experience, the mind should aim to "pass out" of the experience that is produced by experience; this effort will impress consciousness with the idea of advancement, and advancing ideas are always rejuvenating.

To pass out of experience while passing through experience is to increase the power of the ascending tendency of thought, and such thought not only perpetuates youth but also develops the faculties of the mind.

To think of every experience as a passing out of the lesser into the greater, is the accurate thought to form concerning the nature, the tendency and the purpose of experience.

There must be no settling down into grooves; nor must anyone think that he is entitled to fixed ideas and final conclusions because he has had an abundance of experience.

There are no final conclusions; every demonstrated fact simply demonstrates the fact that every fact begins to evolve into new and different facts the very moment it has passed through its demonstration.

There are no fixed ideas; an idea to be an idea must be a growing idea. What we call fixed ideas are simply ossified thoughts; they are not alive, therefore, have no truth in them.

The mind that has had an abundance of experience should know that he has just begun to deal with real ideas; that there are universes before him still to be explored and comprehended, and that the experience he has had thus far is mere insignificance compared with what is yet in store for advancing human thought.

To gain these greater ideas man must enter into harmony with the real purpose of experience, and begin to live solely for continuous advancement. While so living he will also perpetuate his youth.

Chapter 9

All Thinking Should Animate the Mind and Invigorate the Body

The forces of thought have the power to affect, not only the personal appearance of man, but also the chemical elements of his system. To retain his youth, man must therefore educate himself to think only those thoughts that have a youth producing tendency.

To think old thought is to give the personality the appearance of age, and all thought is old thought that is not inspired by the spirit of growth and progression.

To think heavy thought is to depress the entire nervous system; and a burdened nervous system tends to produce heavy, depressing conditions in every cell in the body. These conditions, on account of their chemical weight, will tend to harden and ossify the cell structure, and as a result we have conditions of old age.

To think new thought is to give the personality the appearance of youth, and all thought is new thought that is created by the forces of mental expansion and growth.

To think new thought is to cause all thinking to act in harmony with the law of perpetual renewal; to think old thought is to cause all thinking to interfere with this law; it is therefore clearly discerned how old thought tends to produce old age, while new thought tends to perpetuate youth.

To think new thought is to cause all thinking to animate the mind and invigorate the body; but new thought is not a system of ideas; new thought is the latest product of a growing mind.

How to Stay Young

When the mind accepts a system of ideas, it ceases to think new thought, and begins to think old thought. The creation of old age conditions will inevitably follow.

To think new thought at all times, the mind must expand and develop at all times; it must ascend and break bounds, not only once, but constantly. It is only the growing mind that thinks new thought, and it is only the man who is forever thinking new thought who can stay young.

To think new thought, all thinking must be expansive, and every mental action must aim to enter a larger field of action. This will cause the mind to constantly renew itself and enlarge itself, and the conscious possession of more life and power will follow.

To increase the conscious possession of life and power, is to reanimate the mind and reinvigorate the body, and while the mind is being reanimated and the body reinvigorated, the aging process cannot possibly gain a foothold in the system.

In the average mind there is a tendency to think old thought, and to make all thinking hard and heavy. The tendency to think old thought comes from the race habit of permitting every idea that is accepted to remain in the mind unchanged. It becomes a mental fixture, and continues to inspire the same kind of thinking over and over again, year in and year out.

This is the origin of stereotyped thinking; such thinking produces old thought, that is, thought that never changes; and old thought produces old age.

To remove the tendency to think old thought, the mind should aim to develop, enlarge and perfect every idea that may be accepted, and should work in the conviction that every idea does contain unlimited possibilities.

To eliminate hard and heavy thinking, the usual methods of thought, research and mental penetration must be replaced by methods that are in harmony with natural mental expansion.

The cause of hard and heavy thinking comes principally from trying to find the solutions for the larger problems of life by searching in the present limitations, present incompleteness, or present darkness of the mind.

The mind cannot understand the larger while confined in present limitations; to try to do so would result in hard and heavy thinking. Such efforts would weary the mind, and nearly all mental weariness or exhaustion is produced in this way.

When the mind is in a state of clouded or incomplete intelligence, no effort should be made to understand facts, principles or problems that can only be discerned through the light of a brilliant intelligence; such efforts will not only produce hard, heavy thinking, but the mind will be confused and darkened more than it ever has been before.

The proper course to pursue is to increase the brilliancy of the mind; to make the mental light stronger; when this is done the mind can readily see what it desires to see.

There is practically nothing that the mind cannot discern in its present sphere of existence when intelligence is sufficiently brilliant; but when intelligence is not sufficiently brilliant, it cannot fully understand anything it may desire to understand, no matter how hard and persevering its efforts may be.

How to Stay Young

To understand what we desire to understand, the secret is not to try to force the mind into the necessary sphere of comprehension; in fact, we should never "try hard" to understand anything, but should simply proceed to "turn on" more mental light.

To increase the light, the intelligence and the brilliancy of the mind is to give the mind the power to see and understand whatever may be at hand, without the slightest mental effort.

To understand the principles of life, to penetrate the mysterious phases of life, and to solve the everyday problems of existence, the secret is simply to turn on more mental light.

That which seems mysterious, seems so because there is not enough light; mystery and darkness always go hand in hand. Remove the darkness, and the mystery is no more.

The human mind is constituted so that it can clearly understand anything that may enter its mental world, providing there is enough mental light. Therefore, to turn on the necessary mental light is not only to eliminate ignorance and mistakes, but hard and heavy thinking as well.

To increase the light of the mind, the actions of consciousness should break bounds, and place themselves in touch with the universal. No direct effort should be made to understand what may be under consideration until the mind has first illuminated itself.

The mind that is illuminated can understand without trying to understand; such a mind can see more, it can see further, and it can see more clearly.

The illuminated mind can learn easily and rapidly; no strained effort is required, and no hard mental work; it is in the light, therefore can readily see whatever it may desire to see.

The art of learning, not through hard, strenuous, wearisome study, but through the scientific illumination of the mind, is one of the greatest secrets in the new psychology, and should be taught to every child. We should thereby give mental brilliancy and remarkable talents to the great majority, and hard thinking, one of the principal causes of old age, would be removed completely.

The scientific illumination of the mind may be brought about, first, by recognizing the fact that every mind lives and moves and has its being in a universal sea of absolute intelligence, and second, by training the mind to consciously use absolute intelligence in every process of thinking.

There is only one power of intelligence in the universe, and each individual mind employs as much of that one intelligence as its present conscious capacity can appropriate; but that capacity can be constantly increased, and as it is increased, the individual mind gains conscious possession of more intelligence; that is, more light is turned on in the mind.

When the mind places itself in perfect conscious touch with absolute intelligence, it responds to the greater power of that supreme intelligence in which it lives, acts and thinks, and will consequently use as great a degree of absolute intelligence as consciousness can comprehend at the time.

The degree of intelligence that is employed by the mind when it responds to absolute intelligence is always far greater than that which the mind employs when conscious only of its own limited objective mentality; and this is the reason why the mind always outdoes itself when it transcends itself.

To recognize the fact that the individual mind is an expression of the absolute mind, and that the intelligence of the individual mind increases as its conscious unity with the absolute mind is realized, is to place the individual mind in harmony with the power of absolute intelligence; and when this harmony is established, the power of absolute intelligence will begin to work through the individual mind.

The power of absolute intelligence, however, is not a power outside of and distinct from the individual mind; it is the same intelligence that is in action in the individual mind, only in a much lesser degree.

When the individual mind begins to respond to absolute intelligence, it does not receive a different form of intelligence compared with what it now has, neither does it admit an outside power to come in and think in its Stead; the individual mind simply receives more of the same kind of intelligence that is already in its possession, and thus gives greater capacity to its own individual power to think.

When the mind responds perfectly to absolute intelligence it makes conscious use of absolute intelligence in every process of thinking; and this conscious use causes the mind to steadily grow in the consciousness of absolute intelligence. The result is that the intelligence of the individual mind will constantly increase, because we invariably gain possession of those qualities of which we become conscious.

The power of absolute intelligence is unlimited, therefore, when the individual mind begins to open itself more and more to the perpetual influx of this intelligence, the mind will constantly be renewed and enlarged; the intellect will become more and more brilliant, and every action of thought will convey added power to the mind.

To give added power to the mind is to animate the mind, and to animate the mind is to invigorate the body. The youth producing forces in the system will thereby be perpetuated because the aging process cannot possibly gain a foothold so long as mind and body are growing in the power of life.

When the mind begins to consciously use absolute intelligence in every process of thinking, no effort will be required to understand what the mind may desire to understand. The light of the mind will be so clear and so strong that it can see perfectly everything that there is to be seen in its present mental world; and though the world of the growing mind is constantly being enlarged, there will be no difficulty in comprehending the larger, because so long as the mind is consciously using absolute intelligence, its entire world, however large, will always be filled with a brilliant mental light.

It is therefore evident that to keep the mind open to the full light of absolute intelligence, is to give such perfect ease and smoothness to all thinking, that hard and heavy thinking will be eliminated completely; and to remove such thinking is to remove one of the chief causes of old age.

When all thinking animates the mind and invigorates the body, both mental and physical weariness will disappear; the entire personality will ever be full of new life, which is young life. To be full of young life is to feel young, and so long as man continues to feel young he will continue to stay young.

Chapter 10

Mental States that Produce Conditions of Age, and How to Remove Them

To perpetuate the youth of the personality, all conditions of mind and body must be normal. When these conditions are not normal the natural renewing process is interfered with, and to interfere with the renewing process is to produce the aging process.

To insure normal conditions in mind and body, every mental state must be in harmony with the principle and the purpose of life, because every mental state will produce in the system, a condition similar to itself, and every state that is not in harmony with the purpose of life will produce a condition that is adverse.

When adverse conditions enter the system, the natural processes of the system will be disturbed and misdirected, and the forces of nature will produce what the purpose of life does not aim to produce; in consequence, these forces will work against nature instead of promoting the purpose of nature.

It is natural to stay young; every natural process produces youth and perpetuates youth; therefore, every condition that is adverse to any process in nature will produce age. That which is not working with nature is working against nature.

To train the mind to produce only those mental States that work with nature — states that will express only normal conditions in the system — the first essential is to remove adverse mental attitudes, and the second essential is to remove the three original causes of mental adversity.

How to Stay Young

These three causes are anger, fear and worry; and when combined with the four principal adverse states, will produce any and every adverse mental state that can possibly appear in the human system.

The four attitudes referred to are the heavy attitude, the serious attitude, the superficial attitude and the excited attitude.

When the mind is in a heavy or depressed attitude, the states and actions of the mind will become sluggish, and such states will produce conditions in the system that tend to ossify the cell structures.

The reason why is found in the fact that all sluggish actions in the system decrease the power of the life force, and any living thing tends to wither, dry up, harden and grow old when its life force is decreased in power.

Those mental states that are heavy also tend to depress the physical system, and the actions of depression when coming in contact with cell structures, as they invariably do, will harden and ossify those structures.

To prevent ossification is to prevent old age, because nothing can look old or feel old until it begins to ossify. Ossification, however, is not produced by the laws of nature; it comes through the violation of the laws of nature; therefore, when man no longer violates the laws of nature, there will be no ossifying process in his system, and he will continue to stay young as long as he lives.

To remove the heavy mental attitude, the mind should be trained to live constantly in the upper story of consciousness, and should place itself in touch with those superior powers in the greater nature of man that can do whatever he may wish to have done.

To dwell in mental depression is a mere habit, and is produced by the race belief that man is so limited in his powers and possibilities that he can realize only a small fraction of his normal ambition. However, when man learns the truth about himself he will know that he is not limited, but that he has the power to do what he may have the ambition to do.

When this great truth is realized, the present will become better and greater at once, and the future become as bright as the sun. There will be nothing to be depressed about; there will be nothing to worry about; there will be nothing to burden the mind with apprehensions of dangers or misfortunes yet to be, because all ills are passing away; the causes of failure and adversity are being removed by the fuller expression of that greater power from within that can do all things well, and the mind can feel its own complete emancipation.

The mind that dwells in the realization of its own greater power, knows that it can turn all things to good account, and that the closing of one door invariably causes the opening of another — another that opens the way to greater opportunities, greater attainments, greater powers and greater joys.

It is therefore evident that such a mind will never feel depressed, but will ever live upon the mountain top of an illuminated faith, where the richness of all things can be discerned as clearly as the light of day.

The serious attitude of mind will sour the chemical elements of the system, thus producing dissolution and decay among the cells. The system will thereby be clogged

How to Stay Young

with waste matter, and what the system fails to throw off will ossify.

This is the reason why people who take all things so seriously have a hardened, wrinkled up skin. Too much of the matter in their skin is dead matter that has withered up and turned hard. That they should look old and worn is only what could be expected under the circumstances.

To remove the serious attitude, train the mind to live in the conviction that man was made for happiness, and that the man who is filled with the greatest joy now is the greatest power for good in the world now.

The power of the smile is invincible, that is, when it comes from within. A single smile, coming from the depths of soul joy will do more for the welfare of mankind than ten thousand sermons burdened with sadness and gloom.

The mind that learns to realize the full significance of this great truth, will completely change its attitude, and will feel serious no more.

The superficial attitude will prevent the mind from living in touch with the greater depths of life; in consequence, the mind will be unable to draw upon the greater forces of life, and will feel weak and incompetent when the limited superficial supply of power has been exhausted.

To decrease the power of life is to cause the system to go down to weakness and age, because the lifeless cell will wither up, harden and grow old; and when the system is not in touch with the depths of greater life it will soon exhaust its life.

How to Stay Young

To live on the surface, is to use up what you have without being able to secure more; and when the original, limited supply is used up, or nearly so, the system can no longer perform its functions. The result is weakness, disease, age, and the end of personal existence.

To remove the superficial attitude, the simplest method is to daily employ the conscious mind in directing the subconscious. To place the outer mind in conscious touch with the subconscious at frequent intervals, will not only deepen and enlarge the actions of all the mental forces, but will also cause the subconscious to give expression to a larger and a larger measure of life from its own inexhaustible supply.

The excited attitude will produce confusion, discord and misdirected actions throughout the system. The energies of the system will thus be wasted, the force of life will decrease, and conditions of age will follow.

To remove this attitude the entire system should be trained to live in poise, and every thought should be so constructed that it will have an inherent tendency to produce poise.

When these four adverse attitudes are completely removed from the mind, a number of direct causes of old age conditions will disappear, and the mind will be placed in such perfect harmony with the constructive, youth producing forces of the system, that every effort to perpetuate youth can be promoted with the greatest of ease and efficiency.

In addition, a number of adverse mental states will cease to exist, but to eliminate all such states, the mind must emancipate itself from anger, fear and worry.

How to Stay Young

When the mind is in anger, a number of cells are destroyed, especially in the nervous system. For the creative energies to rebuild those cells at once, is practically impossible, but if they are not rebuilt at once and the waste matter removed, the system will be clogged.

However, it is only the clean body that can stay young. Waste matter, when not removed from the system will become dead matter; it will shortly harden and ossify, thus producing conditions of age.

The natural renewing process has the capacity to remove old cells — cells that have existed in the system a few weeks or a few months, and build new ones in their places, but this process does not have the capacity to replace at once new cells that anger has destroyed by the wholesale.

It is therefore evident that anger will overtax the capacity of the renewing process, in fact, completely cripple this process at times, so that its effort to keep the system in a state of youth will fail to a lesser or greater degree.

When the renewing process fails to promote its purpose, the aging process will gain a foothold system, and if not removed will soon cause the entire system to fall into the habit of growing old. This habit, however, can be removed; all habits can be removed, but the prevention is always preferable to the cure.

To emancipate the mind from anger, every thought should be trained to think that all things are working together for good to him who is seeking only the good.

There will be nothing to be angry for when all things are working together for our good; we cannot be angry with those things that are for us, and all things will be for us, ever working together for our good when we seek the good, and the good only with all the power of mind and heart and soul.

When anger is completely removed, every feeling that is antagonistic will also be removed, and this is extremely important, because the antagonistic actions of mind produce resistance to all the natural forces of the system, including the forces of growth.

However, constant growth and development all through the system is absolutely necessary to the perpetuation of youth; therefore, to permit resistance, in any form, to act in the mind is to interfere with those forces that produce youth, and the perpetuation of youth will either be retarded or suppressed completely.

To continue to stay young, the mind must train Itself to resist nothing, and this becomes mere simplicity when every thought is created with a desire to work in harmony with the greater life that is in everything.

When the mind is in a state of fear, the system becomes negative, and all the constructive forces of the system will reverse their actions, thus tearing down what had previously been building. The same results will follow when the mind enters into anxious states, troubled states or states where strength is forgotten and weakness magnified.

The mental actions of grief are wasteful, and will cause decay in the tissues of the physical system. Regret, self-pity, disappointments and similar states, have the same effect, though generally in less degree.

To perpetuate youth, however, everything that is destructive or wasteful must be eliminated completely from the human system.

How to Stay Young

The selfish actions of mind will contract the cells; and all abnormal cell contractions will cause the cells to wither, dry up and ossify.

To be selfish is to be abnormally self-centered, that is, the self attempts to absolutely establish itself within itself, thus producing the contracting tendency, and every tendency that becomes a ruling force in the mind will also become a ruling force in every cell in the personality.

The selfish tendency, however, does not simply contract the cells of the body; it also contracts the faculties of the mind; and this explains why a selfish person always has a small mind, a small character, a small heart and a small soul.

The domineering actions of mind produce hard forceful thinking, and all such thinking produces a hardening effect upon the cell structures. But the greatest enemy to perpetual youth is worry.

When the mind worries it places in action the chief cause of stiff backs, brittle bones, dried-up tissues, ossified cells and wrinkled faces. The reason why is found in the fact that worry is the deepest of all the adverse mental states, and thereby affects the very chemical life of the system.

When the chemical forces of the system are acted upon by worry they produce false chemical elements in the cell structures, and these false elements will harden the cells the same as if they actually were calcareous deposits.

To eliminate calcareous deposits from the system has been looked upon as the secret for perpetuating youth, and many methods have been advocated; among these distilled water has been looked upon with the greatest favor, but so long as a person worries, he will not stay young, no matter how much distilled water he may drink.

When the mind worries it actually produces calcareous elements in the system just as it produces poisons when angry. Therefore, so long as a person worries his bones will become brittle, his skin will become dried up, his cells will wither, the tissues of his system will harden and ossify, his face will wrinkle, and every atom in his body will feel old and look old, regardless of how many methods, physical or metaphysical, he may employ for preserving his youth.

The elimination of worry will not alone insure the perpetuation of youth; there are also other causes of old age; but the elimination of worry is one of the essentials and is made possible through the constant development of a real, living faith.

The man who has real faith in the Supreme, real faith in himself, real faith in everybody and in everything will never worry. He will know that all things are for him, because all things (we for him who has real faith.

To have real faith in all things is to place the mind in touch with the superior life in all things, and that life is not against anything; it is for the advancement of everything.

Therefore, when man is in touch with that superior life — the upper region of existence, nothing is against him; all things are with him; he has nothing to worry about because all things are coming right. When all things are with us the desires of the heart will surely be granted, and we shall reach the very highest goal we may have in view.

When man enters that upper region of thought and consciousness, where he lives in touch with the universal, he actually feels that all elements, all forces, all things and all persons are with him, and to feel, even the slightest degree of worry, is impossible.

The same realization — the realization of the truth about man's real, superior state of being, will also eliminate fear.

To remove selfishness, the mind should cease to live for the personal self, and should live solely for the attainments and the realizations of the superior self. There is a superior something in man; this something is the real man, and to live for this something is to remove everything from human life that is not in accord with real life.

Chapter 11

Mental States That Perpetuate Youth

To perpetuate the youth of the personality, the states of the mind must be in harmony with the law of perpetual renewal; and in order that all mental states may be in harmony with this law, all thinking must aim to produce renewal.

To form only those states that will perpetuate youth, the mind must focus its entire attention upon the fundamental renewing process in nature, and all thinking must be made a renewing process as well as a developing process.

To promote this purpose, the first essential is to train the mind to feel young, because the body will express the same age that is felt in the mind.

Man is as he thinks in his heart, but it is only what he feels that he thinks in his heart; therefore if he mentally feels that he is growing older and older he will steadily change to look older and older; but so long as he continues to feel young he will positively continue to look young.

The average person firmly believes that he is growing old, and this belief is so deeply impressed upon his mind that he mentally feels himself growing old; every thought he thinks is therefore an age producing thought, but it is not in harmony with the living laws of nature.

Man does not feel himself growing old because nature is making him old; nature is not making him old; this feeling is his own creation, and it is thoroughly abnormal, contrary to every law in life.

How to Stay Young

The average person, having artificially produced in himself the feeling that he is growing old, will cause his personality to look older and older every year, regardless of the fact that the perpetual renewal process in nature gives him a new body every year.

To eliminate this artificial feeling of age, the mind must be trained to feel young, and only those states of mental feeling must be permitted that have a natural tendency to perpetuate youth.

To train the mind to feel young, the picture of youth should be constantly impressed upon the mind. What we repeatedly picture in mind we soon shall feel in mind, and it is what we mentally feel that determines what our mental states are to be.

To think of age is to picture upon mind conditions of age; therefore age should never be thought of or mentioned at any time, not even in the attitude of humor.

What we think of during states of humor will impress the mind just as readily as what we think of during states of serious thought; therefore, the idea of age must be eliminated completely from all thinking.

The ideas of age and the mental pictures of age that may have been previously impressed upon the mind should be removed absolutely and at once, with clear, mental pictures of youth.

When you think of yourself, think of yourself as being young, and know that you are thinking the truth. You are young; the laws of nature are constantly it work perpetuating your youth, therefore, to think the truth about yourself, you must think that you are young, and think so with thought that is positive, clear and strong.

To establish this thought about yourself, the power of affirmation may be employed to the greatest advantage, but to affirm a statement of truth, it is necessary to deeply feel that the statement is the truth.

To begin the day with the statement, "I AM young, because my entire being is perpetually renewed," is to place the strong, clear thought of the morning in perfect harmony with the natural process of perpetual renewal, and every state of the mind that is formed during the day will be a youth producing state.

It is well, however, to frequently repeat this statement during the day, though these repetitions should never have the slightest trace of the mechanical.

When you affirm, in thought, "I AM young," make that affirmation so clear, so positive and so strong that you can feel the vibrations of youth and vigor thrill every atom in your being; and try to feel these vibrations so deeply that their actions will penetrate into the very depth of the subconscious.

To train the mind to think the truth about the renewing process that is ever keeping the body young, it is highly important to affirm the statement: "My entire being is ever young and new, because nature permits no cell to remain in my body more than a few months, when it builds a new one in its place." To this may be added, "Nature gives me a new body every year'; "My mind is new every morning," and "My life comes forth from the Creator of life every moment as fresh and as new as the flowers of the springtime."

These statements are statements of truth, and should be affirmed constantly in the whole-souled conviction that they are statements of truth.

To inwardly feel that these statements are true is to purify the mind from all false beliefs and from all ideas of age. The renewal process of nature will thereby be given the freedom to express the newness of the personality; there will be no adverse states of mind to cause the new body to look old, therefore the new body will always look and feel what it is; it will look young and feel young, and will ever continue to stay young.

When the mind undertakes to give deep feeling to its affirmations, a tendency towards emotionalism may be formed, but this must not be permitted.

To be moderately emotional is necessary in order to give deep feeling to thought, but this emotional feeling must not become excited, aroused or overwrought; it must be kept in perfect poise. The most powerful forces of mind are those that are deeply emotional, but that act so quietly that they appear to be perfectly still. When such forces are permeated with a strong desire to perpetuate youth, they will positively do what they desire to do.

In the use of affirmations another essential is not to confound suggestion with statements of truth. To suggest an idea to the mind without giving direct conscious thought to the fact that it is true, is a violation of mental law; and though it may prove beneficial in a superficial and temporary sense, still it is permanently detrimental to the deeper mental life.

When any idea is suggested to the mind, consciousness should be deeply impressed with the fact that this idea is true. If there is doubt as to its being the truth, it should not be suggested to the mind until the fact that it is the truth is fully realized.

The science of affirmation is to affirm only those ideas that the mind feels to be absolutely true, and then to deeply think of them as being true while the affirmation is being made.

The statement, "I AM young," is absolutely true; it simply gives expression to a fact in nature, therefore the mind can affirm "I AM young" with the full conviction that it is the truth. And the more frequently the mind makes this affirmation, in the full conviction that it is the truth, the sooner will the body begin to express what it is — perpetual youth.

The power of affirmation to produce mental states that perpetuate youth is very marked, and it is a power that should be employed daily, regardless of how many other and seemingly superior methods we may find; nevertheless the power of affirmation is insignificant in comparison with clear mental imagery.

To constantly image in mind those qualities that are distinctly the qualities of youth, is to permanently establish those mental states that perpetuate youth; and when those states are established, every action that may proceed from the mind will have youth producing power.

When every mental state is formed in the image and likeness of the state of youth the mind will actually live in a state of youth, and so long as the mind lives in such a state the personality can never grow old. The reason why is found in the fact that the conditions of the body are invariably the exact externalizations of the states of the mind.

How to Stay Young

To establish the mind in a state of mental youth, the most perfect state of youth that the imagination can picture should be constantly held before the mental vision. This picture should be looked upon, not as a mere possibility to be realized in the coming days, but as an actual reality that is at hand to be realized now.

To constantly picture the entire body as being in the life and vigor of youth will aid in producing in the mind a clear picture of absolute personal youth; but in forming this picture of personal youth no thought whatever must be given to those conditions in the body that express age, if such there should be.

To eliminate age, the mind must completely forget age, and give its whole attention to the creation of those conditions that are absolutely in a state of youth.

The imaging faculty can picture the adverse just as easily as it pictures the true, the beautiful and the ideal; and as everything that is pictured in mind will be more or less expressed in the body, no thought whatever should be given to that which is not desired.

The power of the imagination should be used exclusively in taking the mind through the many mansions of the world beautiful; but in the world beautiful old age is inconceivable. There can be no age in an ideal world, therefore there can be no thought of age in an ideal state of mind.

When the imagining faculty is properly employed it will cause the mind to see only the perpetual youth of the personality, because youth is real; old age is artificial, abnormal, wrong. And when the mind sees only youth in the being of man it will create only those states of mind that perpetuate youth.

How to Stay Young

The mind can think only that which it can mentally see, and the person of man is as the mind thinks; therefore, so long as the mind continues to see only those states of being that are young, the personality will continue to stay young.

To give the qualities of youth to every state of mind is the object in view, and to promote this object the mind should daily affirm the truth about the being of man — the truth that the being of man always is young through and through, and should daily give shape to those affirmations in the form of mental pictures of youth.

When the mind begins to realize the permanent reality of youth, the fact that old age conditions are unnatural will become perfectly clear. To refuse to mould life after the likeness of the unnatural will then become second nature, and every creative force in the system, will proceed to imitate the process of perpetual renewal. In consequence, every action of mind or body will tend to perpetuate youth.

The forces of the human system should imitate the fundamental forces of nature, and nature gives perpetual youth to all things at all times. The forces of the human system, however, invariably follow the leading ideas of the mind, and the leading ideas are always those ideas that are pictured upon mind with the greatest clearness, positiveness and strength.

It is therefore evident that if the forces of the human system are to imitate the forces of nature and perpetuate the youth of the system, the imaging faculty must constantly hold before mind the perfect picture of youth — eternal youth.

To try to perpetuate the youth of the personality so long as the imaging faculty pictures in mind the idea of age is useless; and the imaging faculty will continue to picture the idea of age so long as man continues to believe in the reality of age. To train the mind to give the spirit of youth to every single idea or thought that is formed is therefore absolutely necessary.

To train the mind in this respect, consciousness should enter so completely into the life of the renewing process that this process can be actually felt in the system. This feeling should become an established phase of consciousness, and will if given the most prominent recognition possible at all times.

When man can actually feel that his entire system is being constantly renewed all old age beliefs and all old age conditions must disappear absolutely. Even though his system be full of age — artificial age, because there is no natural age — his body will in a year's time change into the full vigor and appearance of youth, after he has begun to feel the process of perpetual renewal.

The personality may have lived for eighty years and may look as old as race thought believes such a personality should look; nevertheless, when the mind that animates that personality begins to feel the process of renewal and begins to live in the mental state of youth, the personality will begin to look young and feel young, and in less than a year will have the vigor and the appearance of one in the prime of life. And why not? Nature gives man a new body every year; this new body is young; then why should not this body look young and feel young?

Chapter 12

Live For The Purpose Of Advancement, Attainment And Achievement

To live the life of continuous advancement is to enter into the conscious possession of more and more life, and the perpetual increase of life is one of the fundamental essentials to the perpetuation of youth.

It is not possible for the aging process to gain a foothold in the human system so long as there is increase of life, because the body begins to grow old only when it begins to lose life.

The losing of life is produced by a multitude of causes; in brief, every violation of the laws of mind or body will decrease the power of human life, but the principal essential to the perpetual increase of life is to live directly for the purpose of continuous advancement.

The continuous advancement of the personality into more and more life will not only perpetuate youth, but will also prolong personal existence; the reason being that the length of personal existence depends directly upon the amount of stored-up life energy with which every cell in the personality is supplied.

To constantly recharge every cell in the human system with life energy is to cause the system to continue to live as an organized form, because it is not possible for death to take place where there is an abundance of life; and this abundance of life will be given to the personality so long as the individual continues to advance into more and more life.

How to Stay Young

To promote continuous advancement into more and more life the first essential is to live directly for the purpose of advancement; every object in view must be larger and greater than what the present has realized, and every action that takes place in the human system must have enlargement, expansion and ascension as the ruling tendencies of its power.

To live for a definite purpose in regard to attainment and achievement is necessary; it is only through higher attainments and greater achievements that the law of continuous advancement can be promoted; therefore the desire to become much and achieve much must inspire the life of every atom in him who has resolved to perpetuate his youth.

The desire to become much and achieve much must be so strong that it is constantly felt in every fiber as an irresistible power, and it must never cease in its action. The mind must picture itself as living perpetually in a life of action, growth, attainment and achievement, and no thought whatever must be given to future retirement from active life.

The future should remain in the hands of the future; to live an active life now and to continue to live an active life now should be the one purpose to engage the whole of attention. To think of retiring from active life is to think of inactivity, and when the mind begins to think of inactivity the life of growth will be suspended.

When man ceases to grow he begins to grow old but he cannot possibly grow old so long as he continues to grow. This growth, however, must be alive throughout the entire personality and must aim to perfect the body and develop the mind.

How to Stay Young

To promote this growth the mind should be alive with interest in all growing life, and should cooperate consciously with all growth, advancement and progress.

When this cooperation becomes a part of personal existence, the spirit of advancement can be felt in every part of the system, and when every atom feels advancement every atom will advance.

The advancement of every atom in the system will promote the improvement of every function, faculty and quality in personal life, providing the mind is working constructively for the attainment of every possible state of improvement, and so long as everything in body, mind and soul is being constantly improved, age will not appear.

The conditions of age are inseparably connected with inaction and retrogression; therefore, so long as the personality is absolutely foil of action and progress it cannot grow old; it will continue to stay young.

To promote eternal progress in the whole of man will perpetuate youth in the whole of man.

The true significance of eternal progress as applied to the individual life of man is that state of being wherein every atom, every active force, every function, every faculty, every talent, every power — in brief, wherein everything that is alive in the personality — is constantly improving upon its own life, action and purpose.

To follow the law of eternal progress everything in the human system must act for the purpose of acting better, and it is evident that nothing can deteriorate, grow old and decay that is constantly improving upon the life, the power and the efficiency of its own action.

How to Stay Young

To act for the purpose of acting better is to become better; it is to promote the very fundamental law of development, and where development is constant, age is impossible.

The development of the mind implies the expansion of consciousness, the enlargement of the intellect, the refinement of the mental qualities, and the increased efficiency of mental action. The development of the body implies the perfecting of the form, the refinement of physical sensation, the increase of the power of personal expression, the improvement of the quality of the cell-structures, the increased efficiency of functional activity, and the improvement of the personality as an instrument of the mind.

These phases of development in mind and body may all be promoted by training the life of the individual to live directly and consciously for the purpose of advancement. The various elements and forces of the human system are governed by the action of consciousness; therefore, when conscious life gives its whole life to the action of continuous advancement, everything in the human system will do the same.

The entire system in general and every part of the system in particular, will advance. And to advance always is to stay young always.

To train the individual life to live for the purpose of continuous advancement the leading essential is to establish the conscious desire to employ all the energy of the system for the promotion of the renewing process and the growing process. It is not sufficient to simply renew the system, the system must be elevated to a more perfect state of being every time that it is renewed.

How to Stay Young

When the growing process and the renewing process are perfectly combined, the personality will continue to stay young, and will continue to express the life of youth upon higher and higher planes of being. The result will be a life that is thoroughly worthwhile. Such a life will continue to enrich itself from every imaginable source, and through the perpetuation of youth will have the power to enjoy those real riches in an ever-increasing measure.

The desire to employ all the energy of the system for the promotion of the growing process and the renewing process, may be established by constantly giving conscious recognition to the existence of those processes, and to the fact that man may, through the promotion of those two processes, reach any worthy goal that he may have in view.

The mind is so constituted that it will naturally develop the desire to do that which is constantly recognized as the real secret to its goal in view; and when this real secret is known to be the law upon which the very purpose of life is based, the desire in question will develop into far greater strength in much less time.

To promote continuous advancement is the purpose of life; therefore, to constantly recognize this purpose as the secret to every worthy goal in view, is to place the mind in harmony with those laws in life that have the power to reach any worthy goal in view; and when the mind is placed in touch with the power that can, it immediately gains the desire to do what this power can do.

It is therefore evident that when the mind is placed in perfect touch with the law of advancement, the law upon which the entire universe is based, a desire to do what this law aims to do will develop, and the ruling desire of the mind will be to advance, to advance eternally, and in every way imaginable.

To employ all the energies of the system for the promotion of advancement will thus become second nature; the individual will live to live more, and will desire to live more in order that higher attainments and greater achievements may be realized.

When the mind gains this desire there will be no satisfaction in the mere gain of that which has previously been held in view; satisfaction does not come to such a mind through the gain of things, but through the continuous advancement of life towards greater and greater things; such a mind gains "the greatest joy of all joys — the joy of going on."

To be satisfied with the present is to cause inactivity in one or all of the phases of mind, and when action and growth are on the wane, age invariably begins.

To perpetuate youth, the mind must find its satisfaction, its contentment and its joy in nothing less than continuous advancement towards the larger, the greater and the superior. The mind must be trained, to be satisfied only when it is moving forward; and every mind that is placed in harmony with the fundamental purpose of life will never cease to move forward.

To gain the greatest good and the greatest joy from that which we have possession of now, it is necessary to advance now. The mind that is inactive enjoys nothing, appropriates nothing, even though it may be surrounded by the greatest riches that the world can produce. It is the growing mind that appropriates the richness of life, and the mind gains enjoyment only from that which it has appropriated.

How to Stay Young

The growing mind is the advancing mind; therefore to be contented and happy now it is necessary to advance now; and to continue to advance is to continue to stay young.

Chapter 13

Love Your Work, and Know That You Can Work as Long as You Can Love

To supply the system with an abundance of life is one of the great essentials in the perpetuation of youth; and there is nothing that awakens more life than the act of giving love to everything that one may do. Love also awakens the finer elements of life, those elements that invariably give newness, freshness, soundness, briskness, sprightliness, vigor and youth to the personality.

To work is to give expression to energy, and to love that work is to give animation to the energy that is being expressed. When this energy is animated, that is, given soul, it is not mechanical, and to prevent physical or mental energy from being mechanical is highly important.

When the energy that is given action in the system has a mechanical action, it soon wears itself out and wearies the system; but when this energy is animated it multiplies its own power while in action, and thereby increases the life, the power and the vigor of the system.

To weary the system is to decrease the normal life of the system, and if this decrease is frequently repeated the normal supply of life will not be sufficient to maintain the action of the natural functions; nor will the renewing process have sufficient power to fully promote its work. The result will be the beginning of age because the aging process always begins when the life force is on the wane.

Those who desire to stay young must never permit themselves to become tired; and they will never feel tired if they never think of being tired, never speak of being tired and never fail to love their work.

It is not natural to become tired; it is an abnormal condition produced by the mechanical action of the energies of the system. This mechanical action, however, is completely eliminated by the presence of a strong love for the work in which the person may be engaged.

The reason why the average person never gets tired from play but always gets tired from work, is because he loves the former but does not love the latter. The work is mechanical, the play is not; therefore the one wearies while the other exhilarates. The work, however, would never be mechanical if it were loved, and it is possible to love work just as much as we love play.

The mechanical action of the system — the grinding action — also has a tendency to take life force out of the cells, and when the cells are deprived of this life force they begin to dry up, to wither, to become hard and ossify. But ossification must be prevented if youth is to be retained; therefore everything that produces ossification must be completely eliminated from the system.

To work in a dull, indifferent, mechanical, lifeless, automatic attitude is to produce conditions in the system that will ossify the cells and thus bring age upon yourself. No person, therefore, can afford to work in such attitudes, nevertheless, it is in these attitudes that the great majority perform their work; and that the aging process should be in action everywhere is only what is to be expected under the circumstances.

To force oneself to do what one thinks is his duty to do, will also produce the same hard, mechanical actions, and such actions invariably grind the life force out of the cells, thereby causing the cells to dry up, ossify and grow old.

The remedy is to love everything that one may do; and when one loves his work he will not have to force himself to do what he has to do; he will want to do it. He will thereby receive the necessary power to do his work with ease, because that which is animated with love is always given additional life and power.

The man who loves his work will gain the power to work as long as he can love, because to love work is to constantly increase the capacity for work. Such a man will never be superannuated, nor placed upon the retired list; he will be so valuable that the world will not permit him to retire, nor will he have any desire to retire. To him who loves his work, work is a pleasure and is one of the great additions to life.

The present demand for young men everywhere in the industrial world has nothing to do with years; it is the men with brains, vigor and life that are wanted; how long they have lived upon earth is of no consequence. The majority of those who have passed the half century mark, however, have permitted their brain cells to ossify; they are therefore no longer competent, and younger men are in demand; but any man who will eliminate ossification from his system will become more brilliant, more powerful and more useful the longer he lives, and the industrial world will continue indefinitely to want his service, even at his own price.

Learn to stay young and the opportunities of the future will be many times as great as those of the present. The longer you live the more you will know, and so long as the system continues in youth and vigor, added knowledge and experience means added capacity and power.

How to Stay Young

To him who has learned to stay young, the coming of more years means the coming of more intelligence, more talent, more power, more capacity, more usefulness, more real life, more real joy and more of everything that is rich and beautiful in the world. He does not dread the coming of more years, because to him it does not mean weakness, age and empty idleness; instead, it means youth combined with experience, vigor combined with opportunity, visions of attainments combined with real attainments, desire combined with realization, the love of the rich and the beautiful combined with the possession of the rich and the beautiful, and the capacity to enjoy combined with the possession of that which can give joy.

The work of the average person seems hard, and the reason is found in the fact that the action he employs at his work uses up energy instead of developing the power of energy. The action of work should have the tendency to arouse more and more of the energy that is latent in the system, and it is evident that work has this tendency the work itself will increase the power of the system instead of decreasing that power as it usually does.

To give work the tendency to call forth the latent energy of the system, the secret is to love that work. The action of love will deepen the action of work, thus placing the action of work in touch with the depths of inexhaustible life. The action of love will also give a constructive tendency to the action of work.

The power of love is always constructive and tends to give to everything with which it may come in contact, a desire to build, expand, enlarge, develop, increase.

The fundamental purpose of work is to build things, but the action of work can also be caused to build the builder; in fact, when the action of work is wholly constructive it will build the builder while the builder is building things, and the action of work will invariably become constructive when the builder loves his work.

It is therefore evident that when a person loves his work that work will become a power of development, and instead of being a cause of wear and tear in the human system it becomes a cause of greater power, greater capacity and greater ability.

When the individual works scientifically his work will make him stronger, more able and more competent. And to work scientifically the first principle is to love the work with all the power of heart and soul; the second principle is to think that all work will build, develop and strengthen the worker. To enter Into all work, thinking that it will act in the capacity of a developing power, is to mentally direct all the energies of the system to build up the system while on their way to be used in the building of things. The energies of the system will do whatever they are directed to do, and we unconsciously direct them to develop our minds and bodies when we love our work and work in the conviction that those energies are wholly constructive in all their normal action.

When an energy is constructive it will necessarily have a constructive effect upon the system wherein it is generated and upon the person by whom it is employed; that is, the person who works with that energy will be constantly developed by the constructive tendency of that energy. And all energy that is employed in the action of work becomes constructive when the worker thoroughly loves his work and lives in the constructive mental attitude.

The person who loves his work will also do his work better, and the reason is that love gives greater building power to all energy. When we love what we are doing we are at our best and will naturally do our best; we call forth the finest elements of life, the finest creative forces and the finest forces of thought; in consequence, the work done will be the best that can be produced in our present state of development.

To thoroughly love the work in hand will therefore become a means to personal advancement, and as the love of the work in hand will also perpetuate youth, we secure from the same cause both youth and advancement — a most happy combination, indeed.

The path to great attainments and great achievements is open only to those who have learned to love their work, and for those who have acquired this art the future has many riches in store; in fact, whenever a person learns to thoroughly love his work, he finds the secret to continuous advancement and perpetual increase; and in addition he will inherit eternal youth.

The fact that the love of the work in hand will completely eliminate the mechanical element from that work, is one of the most important of all facts in human life, because so long as work is mechanical it will be inferior work. Mechanical work will also grind the life force out of the cells, thus causing the cells to wither, dry up, harden, ossify and grow old. Neither youth nor advancement are therefore possible so long as work is mechanical, and all work, whether physical or mental, that we do not love, is mechanical.

The action of every force in the system becomes a mechanical action if that action is not animated by a strong love for the doing of that which called forth the action. To completely eliminate the mechanical from every action in the system we must learn to love everything that we do, or resolve to do only that which we can love with all the power of heart and soul.

To learn to love our work the first essential is to choose that work that we think will prove most congenial; though if such work is not to be had at present, we must remember that we can learn to love anything that we may be called upon to do, and whatever we are called upon to do, before we begin, we should affirm with all the power of heart and soul, "I will love to do it."

To constantly affirm "I love my work" will steadily develop a strong love for that work, providing the statement is made in the depth of subconscious feeling. No affirmation, however, will have any effect upon the system in any way unless it is impressed upon the subconscious, and the same is true of thinking in general.

To think of your work as something that you dearly love is necessary, and if that love becomes a strong passion the gain will be far greater. No person should ever think or say that he does not love his work; to do so is to go down to failure and old age. When we have work to do that does not seem congenial at first, we should make it congenial for the time being by giving it love — strong love, and in the greatest possible abundance. This is not mere sentiment; it is exact scientific thinking, and he who applies it will find that it pays.

To thoroughly love what we are doing now is to enter the path to something that we will love better. He who makes himself as congenial as possible to everything will soon develop such a strong congenial power that he will attract everything that is congenial. By dealing with all things as if they were his own, he will find those things that actually are his own. In other words, the man who loves his work with all the power of his love will develop such a large love for work that he will naturally attract work that is as large as himself.

To find work that corresponds with our capacity, and that is exactly to our liking, the above is the secret. He who always loves his work will always have work that he loves. He will also advance constantly, and in addition will inherit eternal youth.

Chapter 14

Perpetual Enjoyment Goes Hand In Hand With Perpetual Youth

The happy mind alone is normal, and to stay young the mind must be normal, it must be in perfect harmony with nature.

To be happy the mind must have enjoyment; the mind is happy only when something is being enjoyed, be that something tangible or intangible; therefore, if the mind is to continue to be normal and continue to stay young, enjoyment must be continuous.

To secure perpetual youth it is first necessary to secure perpetual enjoyment, that is, every moment of life must be enjoyed, and enjoyment must be gained from everything that enters into life.

To enjoy every moment of life the mind must be trained to enjoy the living of life, and it will be found that when consciousness gains a perfect realization of life itself, simply to be is joy everlasting.

To depend upon things, events or circumstances for happiness, is to find but the shadow; real joy comes only when things, events and circumstances are animated with the living of real life — the soul of tangible existence.

It is the soul of things that gives joy, and it can give joy without being tangibly expressed through things, but the greatest joy comes invariably from the largest expression of soul through the most wholesome condition of things.

How to Stay Young

To seek an abundance of wholesome enjoyment in the world of things is therefore necessary to give richness, fullness and completeness to the expression of that perpetual joy that comes from the living of soul.

To be happy every single moment, must be one of the chief aims of every mind, but happiness should not be sought for the mere purpose of gratifying the desires of the person. Happiness should be sought for its own sake, and for the greater richness of life that is always realized through continued attitudes of joy.

The period of enjoyment should be extended indefinitely, and should not be confined to the earlier periods of personal existence. To be true to himself, every person must be happy as long as he lives, but if he is not happy as long as he lives he is not true to himself.

The world of false belief declares, "Let the young enjoy themselves while they can; they will get old soon enough." Also, "We are young but once, let us enjoy ourselves while we are young; when age comes there is neither desire nor capacity for enjoyment any more. The language of darkness and despair; the language of those who have placed themselves in bondage to false race thought, and do not know that they are others than free men thinking their own original thought.

The belief that the young must enjoy themselves while they can, causes the majority of those who are still young to cram several times as much "enjoyment" into the space of a few years as the consciousness of those years can possibly appropriate.

How to Stay Young

The result is that the greater part of the enjoyment that is sought fails to give joy, but instead wearies the mind and hurries the day of the "settled life."

When the "settled life" begins, the aging process takes a firm foothold in the system, and will soon demonstrate the power of its presence.

When children are taught that they can stay young as long as they may live, and that they may enjoy themselves as long as they continue to stay young, they will not cram a few short years of youth with every pleasure that may present itself; they will know that there is time to enjoy everything, to enjoy everything right, and to seek the most wholesome enjoyment of everything.

When children are taught these great facts they will not only seek enjoyments of quality, but they will also seek to develop greater capacity for enjoyment. The development of greater capacity to enjoy will prove profitable in the light of the fact that enjoyment may continue all through life, and that personal existence may be enjoyed in greater and greater measure.

The belief that we are young but once is true, but that "once" continues as long as we live a normal life; we grow old only through the violation of natural law, but nature has the power to restore youth to any personality that returns to the life that is normal in the full sense of that term.

To live in the belief that youth is for a short period only is to expect age, and to expect age is to produce age.

To live in the belief that we can enjoy ourselves only when we are young is not only to overdo the life of mere pleasure, but pleasure will be sought for the mere gratification of the mind of sense, and pleasures that simply gratify the superficial life are weakening. Besides, such pleasures never have quality, and to seek pleasures of quality is of the highest importance.

We invariably grow into the likeness of that which we enjoy; therefore, to enjoy the superficial, the sensuous and the materialistic is to become materialistic and ordinary; it is to waste the limited energies of the personal life without giving any attention to the appropriation of the limitless energies from the great within.

To promote the perpetuation of youth the race belief about pleasure must be entirely reversed, because pleasure is an inseparable part of life, but that part is not properly played by those who accept the race belief on the subject. The race believes that pleasure is incidental and that happiness is something, the cause of which no man knows; therefore, it comes and goes regardless of what man may think or do. This, however, is not the truth; happiness can be produced by man at will, and to be true to himself he must give happiness to every moment of his personal existence.

To seek enjoyment is just as important as to seek wisdom or virtue, and wholesome pleasures are just as valuable in the moral world as righteous thoughts.

When happiness is absent man has gone astray and when pleasure is sought no more, man has lost his mental grip on the meaning and purpose of life.

The mind that is alive needs pleasure just as much as the body that is alive needs nourishment, and to perpetuate the youth of the personality both mind and body must be thoroughly alive. When the mind is deprived of pleasure it ceases to live the life of youth, it begins to grow old, and an old mind will soon cause the body to look as old as the mind feels. To give the mind enjoyment — perpetual enjoyment — is therefore necessary if the youth of the personality is to be retained.

To provide the mind with perpetual enjoyment is a problem that is easily solved when the fact is recognized that life itself is made for happiness, and that the happy mind alone is normal. When the mind is normal, happiness is a natural consequence; therefore to be happy at all times, all that is necessary is to keep the mind normal at all times.

The normal mind is the mind that is in harmony with the laws of nature, and as the principal laws of nature in the life of man are the laws of growth and renewal, the mind that aims to perpetually renew itself and to promote its own perpetual development, will readily assume the normal mental state.

The normal state, however, can be perfected into higher and higher degrees of realization, and to promote this perfecting process for the purpose of increasing the capacity for enjoyment, the mind should be trained to appreciate the joy of life on all the planes of existence — the physical, the mental and the spiritual.

The reason why happiness in the life of the average person is not constant is found in the fact that enjoyment is sought on one or two planes only, instead of in all three. To give the mind perpetual enjoyment each plane must exercise its power to produce happiness, and the more frequently during each day that these three powers are brought into expression the greater will be the joy secured.

How to Stay Young

To seek pleasure only through the body is to secure only the cheapest kind of pleasure; to seek pleasure only through the mind is to find a degree of intellectual satisfaction but no real happiness; to seek pleasure only through the soul is to find those joys that secret moments alone can receive; they do not touch the personal life of every day unless the life of every day is made to touch the soul.

When the conscious ego undertakes to make body, mind and soul the one complete source of all pleasure, the pleasures of the body will be refined and will, in consequence, produce far greater happiness; the pleasures of the mind will be given warmth from the body and ecstasy from the soul, and will thereby become a continual feast of sublime richness; the pleasures of the soul will be given full expression through mind and body, and will therefore give continual joy t© every moment of personal existence.

The mind should be taught at the earliest possible moment to seek enjoyment from all the three planes of life, and should be taught to combine these three into the most perfect unity of thought imaginable. The result will be perpetual enjoyment, harmony of expression and perfect personal equilibrium.

To combine the three sources of pleasure into one, the first essential is to recognize the fact that happiness is a continuous force in the human system, and that the expression of that force would be continuous if consciousness was always free to receive and transmit that expression. But consciousness is not always free, because the only free consciousness is that consciousness that is conscious of the whole of life — body, mind and soul — all three at all times.

How to Stay Young

When the conscious ego seeks to draw pleasure from the body alone, consciousness is confined in the physical, and a confined consciousness is not a free consciousness. The same is true when the conscious ego seeks pleasure from the mind only or the soul only. To be free, consciousness must not be confined in anyone plane, but must be permitted to encompass all planes. When in that state consciousness is in touch with the force of happiness from every source, and in consequence the individual will always be conscious of happiness — will always feel the real, sublime, immeasurable joy of life.

To live is to create happiness; the living of life gives joy to life, therefore so long as life continues there is a continuous force of happiness in the human system, and this force can be felt at all times when consciousness is free to feel what is in action in the whole of real life. And this freedom of consciousness is secured when consciousness is conscious of body, mind and soul — all three at all times.

The freedom of consciousness to feel the force of happiness from every source at all times will cause the mind to be nourished with that something that is indispensable to the perpetual aliveness of mind.

The mind that is constantly full of joy is always alive, and the mind that is always alive will always stay young.

When the mind gains enjoyment from only one of the three sources it will soon weary of the joy, the reason being that the joy is incomplete, it does not give aliveness to the whole system; but the mind will never weary of joy when it seeks enjoyment from all three sources of joy — body, mind and soul, because such a joy will produce perpetual aliveness throughout the entire being of man, and that which is alive in every part cannot be weary in any part.

To perpetuate the youth of the personality, every part of the human system must be thoroughly alive at all times; to lose life is to grow old and die, and this perpetual aliveness will always continue so long as the mind is supplied with real joy from the three great sources of joy. Therefore, perpetual enjoyment and perpetual youth are one and inseparable.

Chapter 15

Live In The Upper Story, And On The Sunny Side

When we live in the upper story we always look younger, and we always look older when we live in the lower story. In like manner we look older when we live on the shady side and younger when we live on the sunny side. These are facts that have been universally demonstrated, and are therefore highly important to those who have resolved to stay young.

The reason why the appearance of the personality, as to age, is affected by these different attitudes of mind may be readily found through a careful study of the chemistry of life. Conditions of age or conditions of youth are chemical conditions, and chemical conditions in the human system may be directly modified by changing attitudes of mind.

To live in the upper story of mind is to gain consciousness of more life, and the increase of life invariably produces rejuvenation. This same attitude also produces an expanding condition in the mind; the mind feels larger when we live in the upper story, and what we feel in the mind will be expressed in the body. In consequence the expanding actions of mind will affect the chemical actions of the body and will cause the cells to expand to their full capacity. Expanded cells look young and are full of vigor, while withered cells look old and are almost lifeless. To give the cells of the body the expanding tendency will also cause those cells to constantly grow and develop; and where all the cells of the body are growing cells, old age conditions cannot possibly gain a foothold.

Where the mind lives in the lower story, all the actions of mind become depressed and contracted, and according to the same law the cells of the body will contract, wither, feel weak and look old. Such cells will soon begin to ossify, and when ossification sets in the entire system will begin to grow old. Mental depression also has a tendency to check the forces of growth, and the human system always begins to grow old when it ceases to grow.

To live on the dark side of life is to place the mind in a pessimistic attitude, and while in this attitude the mind sees only failure, defeat, the smallness of things and the uselessness of things. Such thoughts and mental states produce retrograding tendencies, and when such tendencies begin to act in the body, the forces of growth will be reversed. The cells of the body will consequently go down to weakness, decay, age and death. Nothing can grow and develop where darkness prevails, and perpetual growth in every part of the system is necessary if youth is to be retained.

To live on the sunny side of life is to place the mind in the attitude of progress and advancement.

It is the law that the mind invariably moves toward that something upon which its attention is directed; therefore, when the mind is facing the sunny states of life it will create within itself a tendency to move towards the light, and to move towards the light is to enter constantly into more and more light. To increase the light of the mind is to promote the advancement of the entire being of man, and continuous advancement invariably means perpetual youth. To live in mental brightness will also polish, refine and spiritualize the entire system, and while the refining or spiritualizing process is in action, retrogression, ossification, decay and age are impossible.

When the mind is living on the sunny side, every action of the mind becomes constructive, everything in the system is purified as it is in the power of sunshine to produce purity everywhere, whether the sunshine be physical or mental; and all the elements and conditions of the personality are made wholesome. It is the tendency of cheerfulness, brightness and mental sunshine to make everything in the system pure and wholesome, and when the mind is in continual sunshine, only that which is wholesome will exist in the human system. Conditions of age, however, are not wholesome, therefore they cannot exist in a system where everything is wholesome, that is, when man is living on the sunny side.

To train the mind to live on the sunny side the greater possibilities that are latent in all life should be constantly analyzed with the deepest of interest. The mind that knows what is possible in the vast domains of the greater human mentality, will never become pessimistic nor depressed. To such a mind life is exceedingly rich, and every moment is not only a promise of greater things but a positive assurance of realizations that far transcend the life of the present. There is nothing but brightness in store for the mind that sees the richest possibilities of life, and that is constantly moving forward into the fuller realization of those riches. The greater good and the greater joy must inevitably develop in such a life.

To hold the greater possibilities of life constantly before the mind is necessary, because the mental eye should be kept single upon all that is rich and promising. When the mind is trained to see only that which has sunshine in it — that which looks bright and promising, it will continue to live in brightness, and to live in brightness is to realize every promise that brightness has in store.

When there seems to be no sunshine in the external world, the mind should turn its attention wholly upon the sunshine that always does exist in the internal world. To look into the deeper life is to find unlimited possibilities ready for man to develop, and to see these riches of real life will give sunshine and joy to any mind. To know what man can attain and accomplish is to give perpetual sunshine to the mind, and this any mind may know by turning attention upon the greatness of the great within. To live in the larger world and to move constantly forward into the fuller realization of the larger world, is to live in the light of the greater life, and to live in this light is to be in real sunshine — the sunshine that makes existence an endless moment of everlasting joy.

To train the mind to live in the upper story of thought and consciousness the first essential is to give clear recognition to the fact that there is an upper region of mental life; and the second essential is to give attention only to those thoughts, ideas, feelings and states of mind that have an ascending tendency. To live in a worried, depressed mental atmosphere and to enter into close sympathy with such mental conditions is to give mind a descending tendency. In consequence, the mind will enter the lower story of consciousness, where everything is clouded, confused and listless. While the mind is in this attitude all work is hard work, and no faculty or mental force is at its best. But when the mind is in the upper story, everything that is done is done well and without the least effort.

When the mind is in the upper story it has more life and power, and intelligence is far more brilliant; the reason why is found in the fact that all the ascending forces of mind are creative, that is, they generate what may be termed a form of mental electricity — a force that produces both power and light. And to live in the upper story is to cause every action of the mind to become an ascending or rising action. To live in the lower story, however, is to cause every action of mind to go down, and to go down is to enter weakness, darkness and nothingness. That it is impossible to do anything of real worthwhile living in the lower story is therefore evident.

To train the mind to live in the upper story, it is necessary to "count everything joy"; the happy actions of mind are invariably rising actions, while those actions that are not animated with joy will move in the opposite direction, thus taking the mind down to the lower story. To count everything joy becomes a matter of ease when the meaning, the purpose and the possibilities of life are understood, because to know life is to live for the purpose of living a greater life, and in the life of him who lives for a greater life all things will work together for the building of the greater life.

The fact that all things work together for good to him who desires only the good, and who desires the good with all the power of heart and soul, is a fact that has been universally demonstrated; therefore the mind that desires only the good can readily count everything joy. To such a mind everything will produce joy, and the more fully he enters into the soul of his expectation of joy from everything, the more joy he will receive from everything. It is also a demonstrated fact that he who counts everything joy will, through that attitude of mind, cause everything to produce joy.

That with which we come in contact in life invariably responds to the actions of our mental attitudes. Man is the master of his environments, his conditions and his circumstances, but he masters these things, not by trying to control them, but by controlling himself, by placing himself in those mental attitudes through which the forces of his own being will be directed, to produce what he desires to produce. And the way the forces of his own being are moving, the forces of his environment will move also. This is one of the great immutable laws of life, and whoever will apply this law in his every action will place his own life absolutely in his own hands.

When the individual mind counts everything joy, and lives in the happy thought that all things work together for good, the forces of that mind are directed to work only for the good, and for the producing of joy in everything that transpires. In consequence, all the forces of environment will also work together for the good of that individual and will cause everything in the world of circumstance to give joy to that individual. Every action in such a life will be an ascending action, and the mind will constantly live in the upper story.

To train the mind to live in the upper story it is also necessary to live in the happy thought that all things can be turned to good account; and it is the truth that you are turning all things to good account when you feel that you are turning everything in yourself to good account. The forces of your own environment will invariably turn the way you turn; it is therefore extremely important that everything in your own being be turned towards the greater goal in view. It is necessary, however, that the actions of your turning be strong and positive. What you decide to do you must do with all the power of mind and soul, and what you desire you must desire with a force that is absolutely irresistible. But this force must not be domineering; the domineering force is the weakest force of all; the strong force is deep and irresistible, but so calm, so gentle and so silent that it conquers without apparently making the slightest effort to do so.

To turn all things to good account, and to continue to turn all things to better and better account, is to perpetually enlarge the individual life, and to perpetually elevate the sphere of action of that life. In consequence, the upper region of mind will be the principal dwelling place, and this region will invariably

face the sunshine of superior existence. Every action of the mind will move upward and onward, and will thereby not only promote advancement, but will also tend to keep the whole of life in the upper world. To live in the upper world of thought is to live in perpetual joy and perpetual sunshine, and according to laws previously mentioned, perpetual youth will be the natural result.

To cause the mind to live perpetually in the upper story and on the sunny side, it is necessary to eliminate dependence upon things, that is, the position of things must not determine the position of the mind, nor must the action of circumstances determine what the mind is to think and feel. Things were made to depend upon the mind, and when the mind depends upon itself, things will arrange themselves to suit the needs and desires of the mind. When the mind determines its own position and attitude regardless of the position of things, things will change their position in accord with the purpose of the mind.

When the mind determines what it is to think and feel regardless of what circumstances may suggest, circumstances will change and will begin to act in accord with that thought and that feeling that the mind has decided to pursue. When the mind ceases to be moved by things, things will place themselves at the disposal of the mind, and may be moved by the mind in any manner desired. In consequence, the mind may continue without any effort whatever to live in any attitude that may be necessary to promote its purpose in view, whether present circumstances favor that attitude or not; but circumstances will soon begin to favor that attitude, and begin to aid the mind in promoting its purpose, if the mind continues in its own favored attitude absolutely unmoved and undisturbed.

To gain this supreme control over its own position will enable the mind to remain constantly in the upper story and on the sunny side, regardless of the fact that many things in the outer world may tend to draw thought and consciousness down into darkness and depression, and by remaining undisturbed in the upper story, and on the sunny side, the mind will cause the forces of adverse circumstances to change, and become friendly the very moment they come in contact with the power of its ascending action.

It is therefore evident that the mind can be so thoroughly trained to live in the upper story and on the sunny side that those attitudes will become second nature. In consequence, many causes of old age conditions will be removed and several of the principal causes of perpetual youth will be promoted to the highest degree. Among these we find growth, progress, advancement and development, and the mind should live firmly in the conviction that old age cannot possibly enter the human system so long as the forces of growth and development are in full, continuous action.

Chapter 16

The Ideal, the Beautiful, the Worthy and the Great Should Be the Constant Companions of the Soul

When the ideal, the great, the worthy and the beautiful are chosen as constant companions, the soul invariably enters a transcending mental atmosphere, and such an atmosphere is indispensable to the perpetuation of youth. The reason being that the mental atmosphere in which the soul lives, determines, to a very great extent, the nature of those conditions that appear in the personality. The transcending atmosphere tends to elevate, expand and develop the mind, thus promoting growth which is inseparable from youth, while mental atmospheres that are not transcending tend to produce the opposite effect, and all the conditions of age will inevitably follow.

The mind that lives in the ideal forgets age, because in the consciousness of the ideal everything partakes of the newness of youth; everything is in a state of youth, being formed in the likeness of that whichever is absolute, and in the absolute the conditions of age cannot possibly exist. The conditions of age are conditions of imperfection, incompleteness and unnaturalness; such conditions therefore cannot exist in the ideal, and to live in the ideal is to eliminate age from consciousness.

To eliminate all thought of age completely from consciousness, that is, to absolutely forget age, is one of the principal essentials to the perpetuation of youth, because when the mind absolutely forgets age it will naturally think of youth and youth only. To constantly think of youth is to constantly impress upon the subconscious the idea of youth; this will cause the subconscious mind to develop and express the conditions of youth; in consequence, the entire personality will feel young, and we always look as young as we feel.

When the mind lives in the ideal and is constantly in touch with that which has quality, superiority and worth, all the elements of mind will tend to give expression to the best that they may contain, and this is another essential to the perpetuation of youth. To continue to stay young it is necessary to promote the perpetual growth of all the qualities of the personality, but it is not possible to promote growth unless everything that is involved in the process of growth, continues to give expression to its very best.

The process of growth is a rising above the conditions of the present; it is the transforming of the largest and the best into something that is larger and better; and to transform and develop the best we must act upon the best; we must be in our best and give expression to our very best.

To perpetuate youth, the entire personality must pass through a continuous process of development; to promote this development, every part of the personality must always be at its best; but nothing can be at its best unless it continues to live in the ideal, and selects for its mental companions, those things that have high quality and worth. It is therefore evident that if the body is to stay young the soul must live in that ideal state where everything always is young; where everything continues to act in such high states of being that conditions of incompleteness are constantly being transcended; and as age is a condition of incompleteness, it cannot possibly exist in such a life.

To live in the transcending atmosphere is to place the mind above the forces of environment, above the influence of the external world; the actions of mind will therefore not be determined by external circumstances but by the superior aims of the inner mentality. And this is extremely important in the perpetuation of youth, because the mind that has resolved to stay young must not permit itself to be influenced by the appearance of age, but must cause all its actions to be governed by the power of its own determination to stay young.

When the actions of the mind are being governed or modified by external circumstances, the states of the mind will be created, more or less, in the likeness of those circumstances; in consequence, the mind will not grow into the likeness of its own ideals, and will therefore fail to realize the objects in view. To prevent the conditions of external circumstances from impressing themselves upon the mind, the mind must place itself in the closest touch possible with the ideal, the great, the worthy and the beautiful. When the mental eye is single Upon the ideal, it will not be impressed by anything that is not ideal.

The mind is impressed only by those things that may enter its atmosphere; therefore, if the mind is to avoid completely those impressions that are not wanted, it must surround itself with an ideal atmosphere — an atmosphere that excludes inferiority in the same manner as light excludes darkness. To produce such an atmosphere the mind must dwell with superiority, because the thoughts of the mind are similar to those things that the mind chooses as its companions, and the atmosphere of the mind is composed of its own thoughts.

The mind has the power to create its own atmosphere, to surround itself with a mental world that corresponds exactly to its own ideals, and it exercises this power by choosing its own subjects Ox thought; in turn, however, the mind grows into the likeness of its own atmosphere; therefore, to promote the perpetuation of youth the mind must live in a mental atmosphere that is animated with a strong growing tendency — a tendency that works ceaselessly for the enlargement, the development and the spiritualization of the entire being of man.

When the mind lives constantly with the elements of greatness, everything in the being of man will awaken its own capacity to produce greatness. The faculties of the mind will expand and develop, and the cells of the body will be aroused from their semi alive condition and be thoroughly charged with life and power. These cells will be transformed from their withered up condition and will begin to give expression to the fullness of their own inherent capacity. In consequence, the entire personality will eliminate the conditions of old age, because such conditions can exist only in cells that are withered, dried up, ossified or depressed.

To place the mind in touch with the power of greatness is to awaken every atom in the human system to new life and new endeavor; every part of the system will proceed to outdo itself, to transcend itself and to outgrow completely its own limited conditions. The entire system will thereby pass through an absolute transformation; the old will pass away, and all things will become new. When the entire system is constantly passing through such a process, every part of the system will constantly renew itself, and the entire system will constantly pass through such a process if the mind continues to live in perfect touch with the power of greatness.

There can be no condition of age while the human system is constantly being renewed, expanded and enlarged; therefore, the man that is constantly growing; in greatness will never grow old. To enter the greater is to enter the new; to enter the new is to give expression to the new, and to continue to give expression to the new is to continue to stay young.

To live in the world of the beautiful is to impress the mind more and more with the idea of the beautiful; this idea will awaken in the human system the power that can beautify the human system, because every idea that gains a foothold m mind will tend to awaken those powers that are similar to itself. To awaken the beautifying power is to cause all the elements, qualities and expressions of the human system to become more beautiful, and everything becomes younger, looks younger and feels younger when it becomes more beautiful. To make the body look beautiful is to make the body look young, and the reason why is found in the fact that the chemical actions of the interior beautifying process tend to produce conditions of youth.

The beautifying process, however, must proceed from the subconscious, and to cause this process to become established in the subconscious the soul should live constantly in the highest realms of the world beautiful.

To think beautiful thoughts is to awaken that power within us that can develop the beautiful in our own minds and bodies, providing those thoughts have soul, and the same power that develops the beautiful will also produce the conditions of youth. To place in action any beautifying process that comes from within is to perpetuate the youth of the personality, and that personality that is ever becoming more beautiful in life, feeling, form and expression, will never grow old. But it is not sufficient to simply preserve that beauty that nature has originally given; to perpetuate the qualities of youth, the qualities of beauty must ever be made more and more beautiful, and this becomes possible when the soul ascends perpetually into higher and higher states of the beautiful.

When the soul grows in the consciousness of the beautiful, higher and higher degrees of the beautifying power of life will be placed in expression, and as the personality always grows into the likeness of these expressions from within, the personality will become more and more beautiful; in consequence, the qualities of youth will be retained. It is not possible, however, for the soul to grow in the consciousness of the beautiful unless the life of the individual is made beautiful, and every thought created in the likeness of that state of the beautiful that we think of as our highest ideal.

Chapter 17

To Love Always is to be Young Always

To perpetuate the youth of the personality, a full expression of life is necessary, and to promote this expression the power of love must be constant and strong. To stay young it is necessary to live, and to live it is necessary to live more.

When the power of life ceases to increase it will begin to decrease, and the decrease of life is one of the chief causes of old age. To prevent this decrease, however, it is only necessary to love always, to permeate the entire human system with the interior actions of a perfect love.

The action of the love principle not only perpetuates the increase of life, but it also tends to bring forth into expression the newness of real life. The reason for this is found in the fact that the actions of love will arouse more creative energy, both in the body and in the mind, than any other action; and to increase the power of creative energy is to promote recreation.

Those creative energies that are awakened by the power of love always tend to create the ideal, because the tendency of love is toward the ideal; therefore when the power of love is strong in the human system, there will be a strong tendency to reproduce the entire system in the likeness of the ideal. To change into the likeness of the ideal is to change from the old to the new; in consequence, the elements of youth will perpetuate their existence.

To dwell in the life of a true marriage will aid remarkably in the perpetuation of youth, not because the action of sex has any power to perpetuate youth, but because a true marriage tends to increase the expression of a higher and a higher quality of love. The expression of love, however, will not by itself, perpetuate the youth of the personality; the other principles of scientific thought and action must also be applied, but a strong, high, ever-growing love nature is one of the fundamental essentials.

Those who have not a companion with whom to unite in a true marriage, should express their love in universal friendship, and all the creative energies that are generated in their systems should be transmuted into forces of ability, talent, genius and forces of personal expression. That is, their energies should be trained to develop extraordinary powers of mind, and a highly organized personality.

To transmute the creative energies of the system, attention should be directed upon the finer forces whenever creative energies are strongly felt in the system. These finer forces permeate every part of the system and act through the finer substance of the personality. To direct attention upon these finer forces and desire to draw all the creative energies of the system into the world of the finer forces will cause the creative energies to change their vibrations and begin to act in the field of the finer forces.

When the creative energies begin to act in the field of the finer forces, the creative power of the personality will begin to express itself in every cell of body and brain, and development will be greatly promoted both in the mentality and the personality. In consequence, those forces that were simply perpetuating creative desire will begin to work for the recreation of everything in the being of man.

To cause the creative energies to recreate the personality, the vibrations of those energies must be refined, because no force can be turned into a new creative channel until it is refined; that is, taken back into its original creative state. All creative energies proceed from the original creative state, therefore it is readily understood why they have to be drawn back to that state before they can proceed with creative work of another nature.

To take active creative energy back to its original state is called transmutation, and is promoted by drawing the active creative energy into the field of the finer forces. When this is done the new energies will follow the directions of desire;, that is, all transmuted energy will immediately proceed to do what the mind at the time may desire to have done, though this desire must be strong, positive and clearly defined.

When the creative energy of the system has been transmuted, the mind, through its positive desire, may cause that energy to rebuild the entire personality; in this manner the creative energies may be trained to work in perfect harmony with the law of perpetual renewal, and as the transmuted energies are always finer than ordinary physical vitality, the personality will not only be constantly renewed but it will become a finer, a more highly developed and more highly organized personality every time that it has been renewed.

The actions of a strong, constant love will awaken all the creative energies that are latent in the system, and through the process of transmutation these energies can be turned into any channel in the human system where a higher development is desired. The desire, however, that is to govern these energies must have great depth of feeling and must invariably have higher attainments as its goal. And so long as these forces are rebuilding, recreating and refining the human system, old age is absolutely impossible.

How to Stay Young

To employ the power of love to the greatest possible advantage, the actions of love should be universal; that is, we should love everything and everybody in the largest, highest and most perfect sense, but in the expression of this complete love, the real alone should receive attention. The attitude of the true love is to ignore deficiencies; it gives thought only to the greatness and the divinity that constitute the real of everything, and to that which it gives thought it also gives love — all the love that can possibly be awakened in the fullness of heart and soul.

The great mind always loves much; in fact, no mind can become great unless it does love much.

It is the power of love that awakens the powers of greatness, and these powers grow in greatness according to the greatness of the love. To increase the power of greatness it is therefore necessary to love more, bat no mind can love more unless it begins to love everything, and no mind can love everything unless it transcends to the love of the soul.

To love everything with the love of the soul is to love the very best that exists in everything, because the soul invariably discerns the best; to love the best in everything is to give expression to the best of everything that exists in our natures, and to express the best that is within us is to outgrow the old and enter into the new. To enter the new always is to continue in the life of youth always, and this is what we do when we love always.

To promote the expression of the transcending soul love, there is no phase of the personal love that need be eliminated. All love is true love in its own sphere, but all love should be given expression, and that expression should be animated with the strongest and most tender feeling that the very soul of life can possibly awaken. The power of love should be expressed in all its fullness through every channel, but its tendency should ever be upward. The eyes of love should always be turned towards the beautiful, the ideal and the divine that we all have discerned in man's transcending nature. When we love persons and things we should love our highest idealizations of those persons and things, and when we love the ideal itself the mind should turn its vision upon the highest heights that our most sublime moments can possibly picture. The best, the truest and the most beautiful — that must be the goal of love.

When love loves as love is created to love, it is evident that youth must ever remain, because when the fires of love are ever at white heat, all the debris of age, weakness, decay, imperfection, disease and impurity will be completely consumed; and the personality of every person will ever be as clean, as young and as vigorous as that of the pure and wholesome child. The power of love will consume everything that is not as pure as love, and the same power will give the limitless life to everything because love is the life of all life.

When the being of man is spotless and clean through and through, and completely filled with the fullness of life, the elements of youth will develop in man in greater and greater measure; therefore, to love always is to be young always.

Chapter 18

How to Live a Life That Will Perpetuate Youth

To live a life that will perpetuate youth, the first essential is to die daily to the old; that is, everything that has served its purpose should be eliminated from the human system. To carry in the system anything that has served its purpose is to produce the aging tendency, because the accumulation of useless elements in the system will retard the renewing tendency.

That which has served its purpose, be it physical elements, mental states or ideas, cannot be used anymore, and that which is of no use to the system will clog the system, thus interfering with every natural process. The accumulation of useless elements in mind or body will also produce ossification, because that which is not in use is not alive; it becomes dead matter, and such matter invariably withers, dries up and hardens every cell with which it comes in contact.

To die daily to the old, the mind must establish a subconscious eliminating process, because it is the subconscious that holds, and it is the subconscious that lets go. To die daily to the old is to live more in the new; therefore, to eliminate the old and the useless from the system, it is only necessary to train the subconscious to enter directly and constantly into the greater life of the new.

The natural way out of everything is to grow out, and to grow out of the old into the new is to eliminate the old without trying to do so. To try to eliminate the old is to practice resistance, and that which we continue to resist will continue to remain with us. We remove the lesser, the inferior, the imperfect by giving the whole of attention to the realization of the greater, the superior and the perfect.

To daily impress upon the subconscious a strong desire to grow into the new, will produce in the system a tendency to pass out of everything that has served its purpose, and enter into that which we can now use in promoting our greater purpose. This subconscious impression must be so deeply felt that every atom in the system is thoroughly animated with the same desire — the desire to retain only that now which can be of actual use now.

To die daily is to pass through a perpetual regenerative process, because to die, in the true sense of the term, is to eliminate the useless and transform to higher states of life and action those things that have permanent value in human advancement; and so long as regeneration is taking place in the system, the elements of youth will be perpetuated. The process of regeneration is a renewing process, a process that causes the human system to recreate itself in the likeness of higher and higher states of being, therefore, it is not possible for the personality to grow old while regeneration is taking place.

To live a life that will perpetuate youth, the first essential is to eliminate that which has served its purpose, and the second essential is to enter into that which can serve our greater purpose. That is; the first step is to die daily to the lesser life, and the second step is to live daily more and more is the greater life. These two essentials must be applied simultaneously and continually, because they are interdependent upon each other.

To enter daily into more and more life it is necessary to increase the inner consciousness of life, and this is accomplished by giving frequent attention to the finest life vibrations that we can possibly picture throughout the system. When we try to realize more life it is the living element in the subconscious field that should receive attention, and as this element is realized to a degree, attention should be directed upon the soul of this living element. This process will take consciousness into the very depth of life itself, and the inner consciousness of life will increase constantly.

To increase the consciousness of life is to increase the power and action of life; the system will consequently become more and more alive, and it is not possible for old age conditions to enter the system so long as the aliveness is on the increase. It is the decrease of life that makes it possible for age and death to take place, therefore, so long as life is on the increase, the youth of the personality will positively be retained.

To live a life that will perpetuate youth, the mental attitude towards life must be in perfect accord with the purpose of life itself; that is, we must think of life as a power that naturally carries him who lives into more and more life. Life is not a burden but a power that removes all burdens and produces absolute emancipation. To think of life as a burden is to produce depressing conditions in the system, and such conditions invariably produce old age. Such thought will also retard the advancement of life into more life — an advancement that is absolutely necessary to the perpetuation of youth.

The proper mental attitude towards life is to approach life as something that lives more the more it lives. To live properly is to live more; to live more is to increase the power, the value and the joy of life, and while these things are on the increase the tendency to stay young will also be on the increase.

How to Stay Young

To live more it is necessary to take an active interest, not only in life itself, but in everything that is alive. To be thoroughly interested in life is to mentally dwell with life, and the more closely we live with life the more life we shall receive. To be thoroughly interested in life is to advance into more and more life because it is the nature of deep interest to advance into the larger domains of that upon which the attention of interest is concentrated; therefore, a thorough interest in life will perpetually increase the power and volume of life, and youth will not depart while such a life is being lived.

To be so deeply interested in life that every atom thrills with the very soul of life, is to perpetually add to the power of life; to increase this power is to prevent all lack of life from ever taking place in any part of die system; there will always be abundance of life, and old age conditions can no more enter where there is abundance of life than darkness can enter where there is abundance of light.

The more we try to live, the more life we shall have to live. Supply is always equal to demand, and to face the limitless life with a strong, irresistible desire for limitless life, is to create a true demand for more life. The necessary supply will invariably follow.

To feel that life is a power that will carry us on and on towards the greater things and the greater heights, is to enter into the soul of this power, and it is when we are in the soul of life that we enter into the inner consciousness of more and more life. Thus we gain possession of an ever-growing abundance of that life that positively will perpetuate youth.

To live the life of youth in practical daily life, regardless of years, the conduct of the individual must be wholly determined by the present conditions of his own system. What a person can do, or what he cannot do, depends not upon how many or how few years he has lived upon this planet; it is never a question of years, but a question of whether or not there are old age conditions in his system.

We must not deny others the privilege of doing what they are able to do, even though they have lived so long that those of similar years have no such ability. The man who can reach the century mark without having old age conditions in his system, has the privilege to do whatever the man of twenty-five has the privilege to do, because so long as there are no old age conditions in the system, the system is young and vigorous, and can do anything that any young and vigorous system can do.

Those who are competent have the privilege to do whatever the competent usually have the privilege to do, and years have no concern in the matter. To think that those who have lived three quarters of a century or more, must not do certain things because they are "old" is to recognize age, and to recognize age in others is to produce old age conditions in ourselves.

What a person is to do, and what he is not to do must be determined wholly by power and ability. If the man of eighty has the same power and the same ability as the man of thirty, the former has the privilege to occupy the same positions as the latter in any sphere of life. If the man of a hundred or more is free from old age conditions, and he can be, he is still a young man, and may live the life of a young man. In fact he will be of far greater service to the world than men of fewer years because he has more experience.

We must deeply and positively impress upon our minds that many years do not produce age, weakness and uselessness. It is old age conditions that render the human system weak and useless, but old age conditions do not come from years; positively not; those conditions come from the violation of natural law, either in the mental or in the physical, or in both.

However, those who have produced in themselves old age conditions, must not think that they can now do what those can do who are free from old age conditions. The proper course to pursue is to first remove these old age conditions, and when this is done the normal vigor of youth will be regained.

We can do the work of youth only when we have the strength of youth, but we have not the strength of youth so long as our systems are full of old age conditions; nor will old age conditions disappear simply by our trying to do what youth alone is competent to do. We do not regain youth by trying to appear young, nor by trying to act as if we were young; we regain our youth by removing old age conditions, and these conditions any person can remove completely from his system.

The elimination of old age conditions, however, is a subconscious process, and will therefore not be affected by attempts to appear young and act as if you were young. When you remove old age conditions from the system you will be young through and through; you will consequently look young and act young without trying to do so. The power of youth comes from within; to enter more and more deeply into the inner consciousness of real life is to awaken this power, and when this power is awakened in the person, old age conditions will absolutely disappear, regardless of how many years that person may have lived.

Chapter 19

Regularity in All Things, Moderation in All Things

To secure normal action among all the functions in the human system, perfect regularity in life, thought and conduct becomes absolutely necessary; and normal action throughout the system is indispensable to the perpetuation of youth. Regularity in all things must therefore become an inseparable part of personal existence, but the mind must not be placed in bondage to the present personal conception of regularity.

When the personal mind becomes so thoroughly impressed with the idea that it is necessary to be regular, even to the second, it becomes practically incapable of acting outside of its own self created groove of regularity, and will consequently prevent its own enlargement and advancement. The mind» however, that goes to the other extreme, disregarding all regularity, will create for itself a mental world that is not only chaotic within itself, but that is also completely out of harmony with the laws and principles of life.

To find the happy mean in connection with the rules of regularity, the mind should be trained to think that you can do anything, but the body should do only what present capacity indicates that it can do, and what it does should be done in moderation.

The mind should be directed to expand constantly, to break bounds completely and to transcend its own laws, but the body should not be called upon to act outside of its regular channels until the mind has established itself in a greater mental world. When the mind is permanently established in a larger mental world, the capacity of the body will begin to increase, and the old rules are no longer necessary, but the capacity of the body will not increase until the mental world has actually been enlarged.

When a person simply thinks that he can do more than he does, and proceeds to use the body in that greater undertaking he fails, and the reason is found in the fact that the capacity of the human system does not increase the very moment we think we can do more. That he can who thinks he can is true, but it is true in this sense that he who continues to think that he can will develop the power that can.

To employ the faculties and the powers of the personality to their full capacity now, and then proceed to enlarge the mind, that is, to think that we can do more, is the proper course to pursue.

To continue to enlarge the mind will cause the capacity of the personality to be enlarged, but the enlargement of the personal capacity is invariably an effect of the enlargement of the mental capacity. The enlargement of the mental capacity, however, is produced by scientific mental development, and does not follow the attempt to do more than we can do simply because we objectively think that we can.

When man thinks that he can, he awakens a great deal of latent energy, but that energy cannot be used in constructive personal action until it is properly trained, and to promote this training, scientific mental development becomes necessary. To practically apply this principle, continue to think that you can do whatever you desire to do, but do not force your personality to do more than you feel that you can do. As the mind is enlarged, you will feel the increase of power and capacity, and will then be prepared to act upon a larger scale.

How to Stay Young

To properly observe the rules of regularity, the same principle should be employed; that is, the personality should be regular in all life and action, and thinking should be systematic, but the mind should aim to steadily transcend rules, methods and habits, and should gradually modify its modes of regularity as the needs of a constantly growing life might demand.

To scientifically apply the law of moderation, each individual must understand his own actual capacity, because to be moderate is to proceed to apply only as much life or power as you now have in actual possession. When a person attempts to do more than he now has the actual capacity to do, he becomes intemperate, and disturbs the normal conditions of the system. Likewise, when he attempts to eat or drink more than he can assimilate, or attempts to enjoy more than he has the present capacity to enjoy, he violates the law of moderation; he overstretches the functions of his system, and in consequence will bring adverse conditions upon himself.

There is nothing in existence that is actually bad; there is nothing that can do us harm unless we take too much of it or do too much of it; therefore, when the law of moderation is observed in all things, everything we do will prove beneficial.

The law of moderation, however, does not apply simply to those things in life that are now in action, but to everything in life that is created to be in action. Nothing should be overdone, neither should anything be underdone. To permit a faculty to lie dormant is a violation of the laws of life, just as much so as the intemperate use of that faculty. Everything in the human system should be placed in use, and in that use moderation should be observed.

When any part of the system is dormant, it merely exists; it is not alive; and that which is not alive will soon wither, dry up, ossify, decay and become "dead matter" in the system. Such matter will also tend to dry up and ossify other parts of the system with which it may come in contact, and age producing tendencies will thus gain a foothold in the entire personality.

Those parts of the human system that are dormant are not growing; and that which is not growing is growing old. To perpetuate the qualities of youth it is therefore necessary to make the entire personality thoroughly alive, and to continue the full expression of the whole of that life. And this purpose may be promoted by causing every faculty, function and force in the system to continue in full normal action.

To place every function in full normal action, the force of every function should be used for some constructive purpose, and this becomes possible through the law of transmutation. When a function cannot be constructively used in its usual line of action, the force of that function should be transmuted and applied in a different but kindred line of action. To place all the forces of the system so completely under the control of the mind that transmutation may take place at any time desired, the mind should frequently concentrate attention upon the subconscious side of every part of the personality, and should, during that concentration, place in the fullest possible action the finest forces at its command.

To give full, normal action to every function in the system, both the mental life and the physical life must be given the best of scientific care. Every impression that enters the mind should be wholesome; in like manner, everything that enters the body should be wholesome, but we should fear nothing. A special system of diet is not necessary, nor do we require extensive systems of physical and mental gymnastics, but we should give all these matters the best attention possible.

To eat anything, drink anything, do anything, and call it all good, is not scientific. Things are what they are whether we call them this or that, nevertheless, our mental attitude towards things will modify, to a great degree, the natural effects that those things have the power to produce. To be scientific, we should select the best of everything in the physical world and combine that best with our best thought; then we shall secure the best effects both from the physical and the mental sides of life, and that is our object in view.

To be reckless in our eating and drinking and living, and then expect to neutralize undesirable effects with the power of thought is to waste energy, but no person who is wasting his energy can stay young. To stay young it is not only necessary to retain the energy we now possess, but it is also necessary to constantly increase the power of that energy. And this is readily accomplished when we live scientifically and aim to so live that we are eternally living more.

To perpetuate the qualities of youth, all the requirements of the human system must be supplied, and to this end both the mind and the body must be well fed, but neither should be over fed. The entire system should be well exercised, but no exercise should become mechanical. To give mental interest and soul to every form of exercise is necessary, because otherwise the exercise becomes mechanical, and mechanical exercise is wearing to the system; it never develops; it never increases power but always uses up power; it is never beneficial but is always detrimental.

The body requires a fresh, physical atmosphere; in like manner, the mind requires a fresh mental atmosphere. To breathe dead air is to weaken the life of the system, and when the power of life begins to decrease the power of youth will begin to decrease also; but to think dead thought is to produce the same effect. To live in a dead, fixed, changeless, motionless, stereotyped mental atmosphere is one of the shortest of paths to uselessness and old age; nevertheless, it is in this sort of mental atmosphere that the great majority live.

To perpetuate the qualities of youth, everything that is appropriated by the human system in any shape or form, must contain the spirit of youth; that is, it must be fresh from the great creative power; it must be new, and it must be wholesome to the highest possible degree. And when the laws of regularity and moderation are applied in the use of all these things, that which contains the elements of youth will invariably give expression to the life of youth. In consequence, man will continue to stay young.

Chapter 20

The Rejuvenating Power of Sleep When Properly Slept

When the conscious ego goes to sleep it enters the subconscious, and in doing so has two objects in view. The first object is to carry into the basic mentality the results of the day's experience, and the second is to receive a new supply of life-force with which to recharge the personality upon awakening.

The nature and the actions of the subconscious mind determine the conditions of the objective mind and the physical body, and since everything that enters the subconscious will affect its nature and actions, it is highly important that the conscious ego, when it is going to sleep, conveys to the subconscious only those things that will promote the purpose that the individual may have in view.

The conditions of old age originate in the subconscious; the same is true of the qualities of youth; but what is to originate in the subconscious is determined principally by what the conscious ego carries into the within when going to sleep, therefore, the art of staying young depends to a very great extent upon the art of going to sleep.

What is taken into the subconscious becomes a part of the nature of the individual, but the conscious ego can, before going to sleep, eliminate those things that will prove detrimental to the health, the youth and the welfare of the individual, and in doing so may determine absolutely the future conditions of the personality. The time of going to sleep is the sowing time; at this time we may sow what we like, and what we sow we shall reap.

How to Stay Young

To sleep properly is to enter the subconscious with those impressions, ideas and desires only that we wish to have reproduced in mind and body.

To sleep well is to reconstruct the entire subconscious mentality according to a higher, larger and more perfect mental conception, and to do so in a state of peace, harmony and sweet repose. To awaken from a refreshing sleep is to awaken in the consciousness of that state of mind that invariably follows the complete renewal of the subconscious mind, and the renewal of the subconscious always takes place during sleep when we go to sleep with mind in the upper story.

To go to sleep with the mind in the upper story is to carry into the subconscious only those impressions that have a constructive tendency; in consequence, the subconscious will in the morning, be superior in comparison to what it was the evening before. It is therefore evident that if the mind is in the upper story every night when it goes to sleep, the subconscious mind will, in the course of months or years, become highly developed through this process alone, and as the subconscious is, so is also the entire personality.

To place the mind in the upper story before going to sleep, the entire attention should be subjectively concentrated, for a few moments, upon the highest conceptions of our ideals that we can possibly form, and during this concentration, consciousness should actually rise into the superior states of the upper region of mentality. In this upper region the mind will find that peace, that harmony, that sweet repose and that unspeakable delight that makes true existence so rich and beautiful; and what the mind finds in this upper region will be taken into the subconscious to be later made a part of the whole man.

When the mind goes to sleep in the lower story, all the worries, disappointments, mistakes, confusions, ill feelings, misconceptions and troubled thoughts that have formed during the day, will be carried into the subconscious; in consequence, the subconscious field will bring forth a harvest of tares, such as sickness, trouble, poverty, adversity, weakness and aging conditions; and if the mind goes to sleep every night, or nearly every night, in this manner, the subconscious will steadily become more and more inferior until its entire power is gone. Then the personality can no longer exist, and the end will speedily follow.

The reason why the average person begins to go down after a period of thirty or forty years have been passed, is due to several causes, all of which have been mentioned except one; and that one is found in the fact that the subconscious is made weaker and more inferior every year because the conscious ego usually goes to sleep in the lower story. In the earlier years of the average person responsibilities are few, but after the age of twenty five or thirty these responsibilities begin to multiply, and to the average mind they feel like burdens. With these burdens the mind goes to sleep and the subconscious is weakened thereby. In consequence, the personality will begin to go down in health, capacity, power, ambition, vigor and life; growth will cease, and when growth ceases, old age begins.

The responsibilities of life should not be looked upon as burdens; they are never burdensome so long as we live for the purpose of turning all things to good account, and we shall gain the power to turn all things to good account when we continue to develop the subconscious. To accomplish this, the difficulties, the obstacles and the adversities we have met during the day must be eliminated from conscious attention before we go to sleep. To build a superior subconscious mentality, the superior only must be taken into the subconscious, and this is done by giving the whole of attention to our highest conceptions of the idea, the worthy and the superior as we are going to sleep. That is, we should enter the upper story of mind for some time, an hour or two if possible, before going to sleep, and we should take that superior state of consciousness with us into the great within.

When we go to sleep in this manner, the quality, the life and the power of the subconscious will be constantly increased and improved; the entire personality will consequently advance, and so long as the personality continues to advance it will continue to stay young. However, to go to sleep in the usual way is to cause the subconscious to go down to weakness and inferiority, and old age will positively follow such conditions. The great majority go to sleep with their minds in the lower story, but it is not possible to stay young unless we habitually go to sleep in the upper story.

To perpetuate the youth of the personality, the subconscious life must be perpetually developed, because youth is inseparable from growth, and all growth originates in a growing subconscious life.

But to go to sleep in the lower story of mind is to take into the subconscious those conditions of thought and experience that will retard growth, while to go to sleep with the mind in the upper story is to impress upon the subconscious the superior only, that which has constructive power, that which tends to build for greater things. It is, therefore, evident that to go to sleep with the mind in the upper story is absolutely necessary if the qualities of youth are to be retained.

How to Stay Young

When we go to sleep properly, we always feel rejuvenated upon awakening; the mind is new, consciousness is refreshed, the body feels thoroughly recuperated, and the entire personality is recharged with life, strength and vigor. We feel young, because we are young; we have been supplied once more with the elements of youth, and should begin the day in the conviction that we do possess the ability, the quality and the power of youth.

When we go to sleep we should enter the subconscious with the idea clearly fixed in mind that we are young; and upon awakening we should impress the same idea upon every atom in the system. To enter the subconscious in the full conviction that we have the life and the vigor of youth, is to cause the subconscious to give forth into the personality a greater measure of that power that does produce youth. In consequence, the personality will feet young, look young and actually be young, regardless of years.

To begin the day with the conviction that we do possess the life and the vigor of youth, is to continue in the youth producing attitude during that day; ere long it will become second nature to spend the waking state in the youth producing attitude, and he who lives every day in the youth producing attitude will perpetually produce youth in his own system, therefore he will continue to stay young.

To secure the best results from sleep, seven or eight hours out of every twenty-four should be taken for sleep; but never less than six nor more than nine; to secure insufficient sleep is to secure insufficient life, because all life-force comes from within, and to take too much sleep is to stupefy the mind. When the energies of the system are not placed in constructive action the very hour the system is fully recharged, their desire for action will express itself in mere desire, and to desire to act without having the opportunity to act is to waste power. Therefore, important work should be undertaken at once in the morning; this method will produce better work, and when night comes again it will be a matter of perfect ease to go to sleep in the upper story.

Chapter 21

The Necessity of Perfect Health and How to Secure It

To perpetuate the youth of the personality, perfect and continuous health becomes an absolute necessity, but this condition is not difficult to secure because the human system has within itself the power to supply itself with a full measure of absolute health so long as it may exist as an organized form.

There is an element of health in every atom in the being of man, and this element when in action has the power to give perfect health to the entire atom; therefore, the secret of perfect health is to give continuous action to all the elements of health throughout the human system, and this may be accomplished in various ways but there is one best way.

Whenever any system of medication succeeds in healing the body, results are due to the fact that the elements of health that are latent in the system were placed in action by the methods employed. There is only one power that can remove disease, and that power is the power of health that is already latent in the life of the human system. To arouse that power is to heal, and any method through which that power may be aroused, may be used successfully in the cure of disease.

To secure the best results, the system of therapeutics that is employed should not be used for the purpose of combating disease, but should be used directly for the purpose of giving greater activity to the power of health that exists in the life of the human personality. When diseased conditions gain a foothold in the body, the normal action of the power of health is interfered with; in fact, a disease is simply something that interferes with the normal action of the power of health, and it has entered the system because the power of health was permitted to run low.

The only scientific method of cure, therefore, is to increase the power of health. To apply this method the first essential is to learn why the power of health was permitted to run low, and the cause will usually be found in an adverse mental attitude. The immediate cause of low vitality in the system is produced by reckless or ignorant waste of energy, and this waste is invariably brought about by the false attitude of the mind towards that something, in connection with which, the energy was applied.

When energy is wasted in connection with work the cause is due to the fact that that work was not properly approached; that is, the work was not taken up in the right attitude. To think of work as wearing and tearing, or as wearisome drudgery, is to work in the wrong attitude; in consequence, energy will be wasted; but when every action applied in work is subjectively recognized as an action of development, every action exercised in work will promote development.

The actions of the personality will do what we direct them to do. When we firmly believe that work uses up energy, every action expressed in work will use up energy, but when we know that every action can place more and more power in action, and work with that object in view, work will become exercise. Such work will not use up energy, but will, instead, increase the supply of energy.

The attitude towards pleasure will, in like manner, increase or decrease the vitality of the system, depending upon the nature of the attitude entered into at the time. To enter pleasure for mere personal gratification is to waste energy and reduce to a minimum the joy expected; but to enter pleasure for the purpose of gaining the soul of enjoyment is to place the mind in touch with the finer elements of life; in consequence, new life will be gained and the maximum of joy secured.

The mental attitudes towards life, action, thought and living in general, will, through the same principle, determine whether life-force is to be decreased or increased; therefore, the first essential in the attainment of health is to place the mind in those attitudes where power is never wasted, but instead, is constantly being accumulated.

The attitudes of accumulation mentally face the limitless at all times, and their object in view is to act in conscious touch with the soul of all things.

When the mind enters into every action with the purpose of unfolding the soul of that action it is in the right attitude providing it subjectively recognizes the soul as the open way to limitless life and power.

To give subjective recognition to any idea, law or principle, is to place the mind in the finer feeling of life and action while that recognition is active in consciousness, and the power to do this is extremely valuable, because subjective action is back of all physical action; therefore, any physical action or change may be secured when the corresponding subjective action can be produced.

To produce any desired subjective change, place the mind in the finer feeling of life, and mentally picture the change as you would wish to see it in reality. Through this simple process, the subconscious mind is directed to do what you desire to have done, and whatever the subconscious is directed to do it positively will do.

The second essential in the attainment of health is to give greater action to the power of health that is latent in every part of the system, and the first step to be taken in this connection is to convince the intellect that the human system has the power to generate its own health. If the system did not have such a power, it would not be possible for the body to regain perfect health through the recuperative powers of the body alone, but the fact that it is nature alone that can heal, proves conclusively that nature has the real secret to health.

The value of systems of therapeutics is to be found only in their power to place in action nature's healing agency, and the best of these systems is the metaphysical system. Chemical systems do not always reach the inner conditions of things that is, the bottom cause, but metaphysics, when intelligently applied, can reach the very foundation of the trouble and remove it.

To actually know and to mentally feel that the human system has the power to generate its own health, opens the way perfectly for the application of metaphysics, and to secure this inner conviction of the reality of health all that is necessary is to reason logically about nature and her recuperative power. Those, however, who already have perfect health can, during their serene moments of thought, actually feel the elements of absolute health permeating every part of the system.

When the power of health is felt in this manner, the consciousness of absolute health has begun, and to steadily develop this consciousness is highly important because whatever we become conscious of we invariably bring forth into tangible expression. To deepen and develop the consciousness of absolute health will therefore cause a larger measure of health and a higher degree of health to find constant expression in the physical form.

When the mind has become convinced, either through logical conclusions or conscious realizations, that the elements of perfect health do exist in every part of the body, and that these elements have the power to give perfect health to the entire physical body so long as it may exist in organized form, steps may be taken to place these elements of health in full, positive action.

To proceed, the mind should first give subjective recognition to the existence of the elements of health in every part of the system. This will place the actions of mind in perfect touch with these elements so that whenever the mind may act upon the elements of health, they will readily respond.

To be able to place the elements of health in greater action when required is to have an infallible remedy constantly at hand.

To give action to the elements of health, the subconscious life of those elements must first be acted upon because every action must proceed from the subconscious. To act upon the subconscious of these elements, the mind should direct attention upon what may be termed the soul of health, and should, at the time, desire, with the deepest soul of desire the full realization of the soul of health. This action of mind will take consciousness into the very depths of the reality of health, and in consequence will produce a larger expression of real health.

The subconscious mind in general, should also be frequently impressed with the idea of perfect health, and the statement, "I AM well," should be made a living power in subconscious thought; In addition, thinking in general should conform absolutely to the principle that the reality of the being of man always is well. Neither word nor thought should ever contradict the great truth that the real man is always well, nor should the individual ever think of himself as being anything else but the real man.

To live perpetually in the consciousness of the reality of life, health and wholeness is to permanently establish the active power of real health in the subconscious, and this is our object in view. There is an abundance of latent health in the system, and what we aim to do is to place that health in action; but this action must be subconscious or it will not be permanent.

When the health of the subconscious life is being placed in action to a greater and a greater degree, the tangible elements of health will begin to express themselves in the body to the same degree; and if this process is continued progressively, the normal health of the body will be increased perpetually, thus providing the greater supply of health that will naturally be demanded by the increasing capacity of an ever advancing life.

To be simply well is not sufficient; continuous advancement is the law of life, and to be in harmony with life everything must advance with life; therefore, both the quality and the power of health must be increased perpetually. To be satisfied with simply having good health, is to begin to lose health, because that which ceases to move forward will begin to move backward. To prevent the losing of health, it is necessary to develop better and better health.

When an ailment appears in any part of the body, the mind should at once concentrate attention upon the elements of health in that part where the ailment has its actual origin; this concentration, however, should be subjective, because subjective concentration invariably gives action to that upon which the concentration is directed.

To give action to the elements of health wherever the ailment may appear, is to cause that ailment to completely disappear. When the ailment is of recent origin a complete cure may be secured almost at once, and chronic ailments may be removed in the course of a few weeks, frequently in much less time. There is no malady, however, that is incurable; the power of health in the system is greater than any disease, because the former is natural, while the latter is unnatural; therefore, perseverance will invariably succeed.

The elements of health should be given greater action, also, in those parts that are in good health; first, because the increase of health in the whole body will make it easier to remove an ailment from any part of the body, and second, because to always have good health we must constantly develop better and better health.

Chapter 22

Live in the Conviction That it is Natural to Stay Young

The purpose of life is continuous advancement; all the principles of life are based upon that purpose and all the laws of life are formed to promote that purpose. Everything in nature is created with an inherent tendency to advance, to move forward, to rise in the scale, therefore anything that retards continuous advancement or that is not in harmony with continuous advancement is unnatural, and that which is unnatural is caused by a violation of natural law.

To promote continuous advancement in the being of man is to cause every element, force, function, faculty and action in the human system to rise perpetually in the scale of life; this means increased activity, a higher order of activity with greater results from every human endeavor; but such results cannot be secured if the system is permitted to go down to weakness and old age. To grow old is to go in the opposite direction; it is to retard all progress and to decrease both the quality and the quantity of those results that naturally follow the actions of life. To grow old, therefore, is unnatural a direct violation of the laws of life.

To act in harmony with the laws of life, the individual must move forward perpetually, but when he permits himself to grow old he does not move forward; instead, he causes everything in his system to go down; it is therefore evident that the aging process is contrary to the purpose of life, and is not a product of nature. Since it is unnatural to grow old it must be natural to stay young; in consequence, every person, to be true to nature, must not only live in the full conviction that it is natural to stay young, but he must so live that he perpetually will stay young.

How to Stay Young

That perpetual youth is a gift of nature is evident to all who will search the real life of nature, but only those who are true to nature can receive the gift. To be true to nature, the individual must not only live in harmony with the laws of nature, but must also aim to become as much as nature has given him the power to become. Nature has given man the power to advance perpetually, and has given him unlimited possibilities through which such advancement may be promoted; therefore, to be true to his nature man must take advantage of the privilege that has been placed in his possession.

To live in the conviction that it is natural to stay young, is to base all life, all thought and all action upon that conviction, and consequently everything that is said or done must be in harmony with the idea of staying young. To be in harmony with this idea a number of usual statements, plans and intentions must be changed completely. We must no longer say, "the older I get," but should say instead, "the longer I live.' To use the first statement is to cause the mind to think that old age is actually coming on, and such thought will invariably produce the aging tendency. To use the second statement is to ignore age and impress upon the mind the idea of a longer and a longer life.

To live in harmony with the idea of youth, we must never think of saving for old age, because such thought will cause the mind to look forward to old age, to expect age, and consequently to produce age. Instead, we should think of accumulating for use in a larger future. To live in the thought of accumulation will cause all the forces of life to produce perpetual increase in our own world, and to constantly look forward to a larger future will cause these same forces to create for us a larger future.

How to Stay Young

To think of saving for a rainy day, is in like manner, thoroughly unscientific. To expect rainy days is to produce hard luck, and to live in the belief that we may be in dire need sometime, is to limit our own powers more and more until their capacity to produce the necessary supply is practically reduced to nothing.

To be scientific we should continue to accumulate in the present in order that we may have abundance in the coming days, and thus be able to take advantage of those greater opportunities that positively will come to him who lives the advancing life. To be natural we must expect to stay young, and to continue to stay young is to continue to live an active, useful, productive life. Such a life will naturally enter into larger and larger fields of endeavor, and to take the best possible advantage of those larger fields we must accumulate the best of everything in the present.

We must not, however, deal penuriously with the present; everything that can be used to advantage now should be placed in use now; nothing should be hoarded in the present that can, if placed in use, produce increase in the present, but we should never try to save and accumulate in the present because we expect want in the future. There will be no want in the future if we make the best possible use of our faculties in the present, but the future will present larger opportunities, and we do not wish to approach those opportunities empty handed.

To live more thoroughly and more completely in the conviction that it is natural to stay young, the statement, "I AM young," should be frequently impressed upon the mind; in fact, the whole life should live and move and have its being in the very spirit of that statement. To live in the real spirit of youth is to absolutely know that we are in the life of youth; that is, we will know the great truth that real life is ever young, and the knowing of that truth will place the entire system in that life. It is this truth that will give us freedom from the falseness of old age and place being in the true state of youth, vigor, health and wholeness.

When we know that real life is ever young, it becomes second nature to live in the conviction that it is natural to stay young, because only that which is real is natural; and what becomes second nature becomes subconscious. To stay young will therefore become an inseparable part of life, due to the fact that as the subconscious is» so is also the entire person of man.

To live in the conviction that it is natural to stay young, it is necessary to train consciousness to enter as deeply as possible into the soul of nature; on the surface, nature may suggest varying ideas, but in the depth of the soul of nature the ideas of continuous advancement and continuous youth are revealed in most positive terms; and it is not appearances, but the real truth, upon which we must base our convictions.

When the mind realizes absolutely that it is natural to stay young, the forces of human nature will begin to produce youth; they will cease to follow unnatural race habits, and will, instead, proceed to do what they were created to do. The entire human system will be emancipated from the false thought of the ages, and will be placed absolutely in the keeping of real life itself. In consequence, the purpose of life — continuous advancement — will be promoted in the life of man; and from continuous advancement, continuous youth must invariably follow.

To move forward is to stay young; and since it is natural to move forward, it is natural to stay young; therefore, there is no old age in store for him who fulfills the natural purpose of life by living the life of continuous advancement. To him, the future is a bright picture of youth, ever becoming larger, more beautiful and more ideal.

To know life — the soul of life, is to know that real life is ever young; and he who lives life grows into the likeness of the life he lives; it is therefore evident that he who continues to live real life will continue to stay young as long as he lives. And real life is eternal.

Chapter 23

What To Do With Birthdays

The number of years that a person has lived upon this planet is not important but it is extremely important to place the mind in the proper attitude towards the idea of years, especially that idea that takes birthdays for its nucleus. To the average person, birthdays and the process of growing old are inseparably united, and for that reason the usual thought about birthdays is an age producing thought; but in reality, birthdays are in no manner connected with the aging process, therefore the entire subject must be viewed under new light.

When a person declares that he is thus or so old, he is not speaking the truth, because age is a false condition, not a product of years. It is a scientific fact that years are wholly incapable of producing any condition of age in the person, therefore birthdays and age can have no connection whatever.

To be scientific, the individual must never think of himself as being so many years old, because such a thought will cause the mind to expect every year to increase the conditions of age; years, however, cannot produce age, but thought can, and the thought that expects age will produce age. The two words "years" and "old", should therefore never be combined in the same sentence. They are contradictions, and will not mix.

To think of age at all is wrong, because in the right there is no age; what we call age is simply a mistake, and should be forgotten. The individual, however, may, with perfect propriety, state how many years he has lived in his present personal life, because it is the truth that he has lived as many years as he has lived, but it is not the truth that those years have produced age.

When the birthdays arrive, the mind should be deeply impressed with the idea that another step in the ascending life has been taken; a birthday should be looked upon as a mark of progress, because in the true, advancing life, that is what it is. When we live the life of continuous advancement, every birthday will indicate that we are, not so much older, but so much higher in the scale of the fife beautiful.

The true birthday is celebrated by the individual proving to himself that he has actually taken another step; that he is more vigorous in body, more youthful in appearance, more perfect in personality, more brilliant in mind and more beautiful in soul.

When you celebrate your birthday, do not think of yourself as being a year older, a year nearer age, uselessness, death and the grave; such ideas should be banished forever; but think of yourself as being a step nearer the greater life, the superior life, the beautiful life, the ideal life — the fair, transcendent goal that you so often have seen during those sublime moments when the soul was revealed to your vision.

There is a great goal that every person has in view; on the path towards this goal there are many ambitions to be perfected, many desires to be fulfilled, many ideals to be realized, many dreams to be made true, and after all of these come the goal itself. To live the true, advancing life is to move forward towards this great goal, realizing one ideal after another, until every wish of the heart has been granted; and every birthday will mark the great good gained during the year that has just been fulfilled.

How to Stay Young

To associate birthdays with the advancement of life is to look forward to every birthday as the realization of a greater measure of the richness of life, and what we constantly expect we invariably produce.

To think of the coming birthday as a realization of more of everything that we have lived for and worked for, is to cause all the forces of life to work together to make all our wishes come true when the next birthday arrives; and to think of every birthday as the beginning of a new life — a life of higher attainments and greater achievements than we have ever realized before, is to cause all the forces of life to proceed to make this greater dream also come true.

When years are considered in connection with birthdays, always state that you are so many years young; and it is the truth; you are not so many years old because you are not old; there is no age in real life; but you are so many years young because you have lived so many years, and during those years you have continued to stay young.

There may be old age conditions in your system, but they do not belong to you; they were not produced by the years you have lived; they are mere mistakes, and will disappear when you take the firm stand that you are young, because nature has placed the gift of youth in the actual possession of every man.

When you desire to learn the number of years that others have lived always ask "how young are you?" or "how many years have you lived?" but do not even think of age; such thought has no place whatever in a scientific mind. Never hesitate to state how young you are; always give the exact number of years when requested to do so; prevarications are not conducive to perpetual youth. To try to hide the number of years you have lived, is to produce a subconscious fear of age, and to fear age is to produce age.

The idea that we can retard the oncoming of age by stating positively that we are eighteen, twenty-two or twenty-seven, when we have lived two or three times as many years, has no foundation in exact science; besides such statements are never true in any sense, and to impress untruth upon the subconscious is to form a tendency in the subconscious to unconsciously accept the untruth; in consequence, we shall be misled in a thousand ways.

To state the exact number of years you have lived, when requested to do so, is scientific, and is in harmony with those laws through which you may perpetuate your youth, but only those who have a personal interest in your life, or who have legal matters to arrange for you, have the privilege to ask how many years you have lived. To ask such a question for mere curiosity is not conducive to youth, because those who ask such questions out of curiosity are thinking of age, not of youth; they therefore bring age upon themselves through their own misdirected inquisitiveness.

The number of years that a person has lived is of secondary importance, and should be thought of as such, nevertheless, no person should try to deceive himself or others in this respect. To be scientific, you should be proud of your years, and you should glory in the fuller life, the larger mentality, the greater power and the more vigorous youth that those years have produced. And these are the results that will invariably follow the coming of more and more years, when we constantly live the advancing life.

When every year is looked upon as an opportunity to add to the power, the richness and the joy of life, and that opportunity is taken advantage of, every year will produce

How to Stay Young

the greater power, the greater richness and the greater joy; the many years will produce a greater measure of the same desirable results, therefore, we may well be proud of the years we have lived; we will have good reason to glory in the fact that we have lived long because we have lived exceedingly well.

To him who lives the true life, the coming of more years will bring more vigorous youth; he will daily pass from the youth of incompleteness to the youth of high development; he will continue to stay young, but every year will give his youth greater power, greater capacity, a more perfect personality, and a superior mind. To him, every year is a rising path, and every birthday the reaching of greater heights than he has ever reached before.

To speak of anything as old is unscientific, because nothing that is of permanent value can grow old, and that which is not of permanent value should not be mentioned. The great products of the race such as music, art, literature, invention, scientific facts, lofty, ideals — these can never grow old; they have the same power now as when they first appeared, and that same power they will continue to possess for countless ages yet to be. They are as young now as when they were born; they are products of real life, therefore theirs is the life of eternal youth.

To speak of the old songs, the old writers, the old composers, the old philosophers, the old masters — all of that is a false conception of life. To think of anything as old because it first existed in the years gone by, is to think of age and years as synonymous, and this is the very idea we positively must eliminate.

To think of time as the great eternal now — beginningless and endless — and to think that everything that was, now is, and evermore shall be — this is the thought of exact science. To him who thinks of life in this manner, all things are eternal, and that which is eternal will never grow old. To such a mind the spirit of youth reigns supremely throughout the universe, and in that spirit he lives; therefore, the life that he lives will be the life of youth — eternal youth. To him, every birthday will be the birth of a new day — a more glorious day than he has ever beheld before.

Chapter 24

How Long We May Live Upon Earth

The greatest thing that man can do is to live the largest life, the best life, the happiest life and the most useful life in the great eternal now. To think of time is unscientific, and to fix any special length of time for existence on this planet is to shorten the period of that existence.

The proper course to pursue is to live so well every moment that that moment is absolutely complete in itself; and he who lives well will live long; in fact, how long we are to live upon earth depends upon how well we live upon earth. So long as the present moment is constructive, the power of life will increase during the present moment, and so long as we can increase the life power of our present state of existence we will continue to live in our present state of existence.

To live well is to live more, and to live more is to live longer. To live well, it is necessary to concentrate the whole of attention upon life, upon the largest life, the best life, the greatest life and the most perfect life that the mind can possibly picture. The thought of death must never enter consciousness, nor must any fixed period of time for living upon earth be formed in mind. To live now must be the purpose, and he who actually lives now, thinks only of the abundance of life and the richness of life that he can give to the life that he lives now.

It is the purpose of life to live, and to fulfill that purpose it is necessary to give our undivided attention to life. To think of death as well as life, is to divide attention; in consequence, the force of life is decreased; life is not lived so well; we fail to receive from life what life has to give; we limit the power of personal existence in every form and manner, and therefore shorten our days upon earth.

To impress upon mind the belief that you will live upon earth for a special period of time, is to place limitations upon the power of life, and the forces of life will consequently work for a temporal personal existence. Such thought will also produce aging conditions in the system, because to expect to get old sometime is to think of old age conditions, and to think of old age conditions now is to create those conditions now.

Whether we expect to live a hundred years or a thousand years, the results will be the same; to fix a time now is to expect age and death, and to expect those things is to give life, power and thought to the producing of those things; therefore to think of future age and death is to produce aging conditions and decaying conditions in the system now. The man who expects to live a thousand years will, subconsciously, think just as much of age and death as the man who expects to live only three score and ten; both will produce old age conditions in their systems now, and both, on account of old age, may be forced to retire from active life at sixty.

To impress any time limit upon mind in regard to how many years we may live upon earth is always a mistake; to limit the mind at all is to weaken the power of life, and to weaken the power of life now is to begin to go down to age and death now. The proper course is never to think of how long we may live upon earth, but to live now in the consciousness of eternal life.

The purpose of life is not how long in any place, but how well in every place. We are here to live until we have fulfilled that purpose for which we came here to live; how many years it may require any individual to fulfill his purpose will depend upon how well he lives while he does live, therefore he can fix no time for himself; he can only proceed to live now the greatest life that he possibly can live now.

To remain upon this planet after we have fulfilled the purpose for which we came, is not according to the laws of eternal life; we will depart sometime; there are other mansions in which the soul is destined to dwell, but when we are to take our departure does not concern us now. We are not here to think of a future life, to live for a future life, or to work for a future life; we are here to think, live and work for this present state of existence — to give all the powers of being to the life we are living now.

When we analyze the purpose and the possibilities of this present existence, we come invariably to the conclusion that the period that the average person lives upon earth is far too short to even fulfill a small fraction of the purpose for which he came; but he must not think, however, that life is too short. To think that life is too short is to make it too short, while to realize that life is eternal, and that we may secure from the boundless, all the life we may desire to live, is to make life as long and as large as we may wish it to be.

The life of the average person is shortened by mistakes, most of which he has inherited from the race, but he can eliminate those mistakes, and when he does, he will find that the capacity of the human personality to extend its organized existence is marvelous indeed. To continue only for one short month to preserve all the energy that is generated in the system is to become so enormously strong, both in personality and mentality, that the mind feels as if the power that moves mountains has actually been gained. It is therefore evident that if the individual continued, not only to preserve his energy, but also to increase his energy, the organized existence of the personality could be perpetuated for an indefinite period, or until the purpose of life in this sphere had been fulfilled.

The power of any organized form to perpetuate its own existence, is far greater than the average mind has heretofore realized; in fact, nature gives every organized form the inherent power to perpetuate its own life until the purpose of that life has been completed; therefore, it is not natural for anything to pass away until it has finished its work in this sphere. When anything leaves its work unfinished, some natural law has been violated. No one in particular may be to blame, and there will be an opportunity to make amends, but there is one great truth to be remembered in this connection; it is this, that if we fail to fulfill the purpose of our present existence now, we will have to work out that purpose in the future. Where that is to happen is not germane to this study, but it must be done before we can rise in the scale. We must take the first step before we can take the second; we must complete the lesser that is at hand before we can inherit the greater that is in store.

This fact will prove conclusively to any mind that nothing is gained by wasting the present moment, and that nothing can give greater gain to any individual than to make the living of life the greatest aim of life. We are not here by chance; there is no chance; we came here because this present life has something in store for us — something that can add to the splendor of eternal existence. And when we have found this something we may rise to greater heights where other treasures are in store — treasures that are richer by far than anything we have ever known before.

The pathway of life is eternal progress, perpetual ascension towards the spiritual heights of the soul's transcendent existence, but the glory of real life is not deferred until some faraway future time. The ascending life is full and complete every moment; all that the present moment can hold, the present moment will receive, so long as life is rising in the scale, and in that all will be found the best of everything that the heart may desire now.

To live the ascending life is to live now for the perpetual ascension of life now, giving no thought whatever to the future; he who lives such a life will continue to live upon earth until the purpose for which he came has been fulfilled; and he will continue in the full vigor of youth as long as he lives. To live the ascending life is to produce a perpetual increase in life, and so long as man continues to increase his life he will not only continue to live in personal form, but that personal form will continue to stay young.

To live upon this planet until our work here IS finished, until we have learned all that is here to be learned, until we have attained all that is here to be attained, until we have received all that is here to be received, until we have done all that is here to be done, until we have given all that is here to be given, until we have reached the highest heights that are here to be found — this is our purpose; and we must live in the conviction that we have sufficient life within us to live in vigor, strength, youth, health and wholeness until that great goal has been reached.

We must never stop, however, to think "how long"; how long we may live upon earth is a question we must never try to answer; if we are true to life we may live here as long as there is anything here to live for; and when we begin to really live we shall find so much here to live for that all thought of taking our departure will have completely disappeared. When we shall have reached the supreme heights of this present life, then, and not until then, shall we turn our spiritual vision upon the path to another world.

How to Stay Young

There is one truth, however, that will soon demonstrate itself conclusively to those who have chosen to be true to life, and it is this, that we may, under present circumstances and conditions, live several times as long as the average person has usually lived; also, that through the advancement of our own circumstances and conditions, we may go beyond that period and prolong life indefinitely, or until we have finished that for which we came; and from that long and beautiful life, neither youth nor happiness will ever depart.

Chapter 25

A New Picture of the Coming Years

The life that is lived exclusively for the great eternal now does not necessarily confine its whole attention to the present moment. Such a life is constantly moving forward, and to move forward is to look forward. To look forward is to form pictures of the coming days, and since the nature of these pictures will determine what the life of the coming days is to be, the entire power of exact science may be applied most profitably in this art of picturing the future.

What is pictured in the mind the life-forces will produce, and every condition that is constantly expected during a lifetime will positively be realized. The average person, however, expects age, physical and mental decline, and everything that inevitably follows such conditions; and he receives what he expects to receive. The picture that he has formed of the coming days contains nearly every undesirable condition that human life has known, and he lives, during his entire personal existence, in the deep subconscious conviction that the details of that picture constitute his future fate. But such thought is wholly adverse to the nature and the purpose of life, therefore, to be true to life we must form a new picture of the coming years.

The new picture will form itself naturally and perfectly in the mind that has accepted the new conception of life, that is, that conception that conceives of life as a path of eternal progress, an existence of continuous advancement and a state of perpetual increase in everything that can add to the worth, the welfare and the happiness of man. This new conception reverses practically ever3rthing that we have believed before, and as man is as he thinks, it is but natural that this new conception should give him a future that is practically the reverse of what has been expected and realized before.

The new picture of the coming years is ideal in the very highest sense of that term, but all ideals that are in harmony with the nature and purpose of life can be realized; and as this picture is such an ideal we may proceed to work it out with the full conviction that every part of it will come to pass.

To gain the realization of an ideal that is in harmony with the nature and the purpose of life, the secret is to live, think and work now for that which, in the tangible world, corresponds with the new picture in the ideal world. That is, while living in the subconscious expectation of a greater future, work for the realization of a greater now.

To constantly expect certain future realization is a part of life; the present is the cause, the future is the effect, and it is natural for the cause to look towards its own effect, but when the cause does not understand itself, it will picture the wrong effect; in consequence, it will misdirect its own forces and produce the wrong effect, because the life-forces will invariably create in the likeness of the pattern or picture that is provided by the mind.

This is the reason why man, through the misunderstanding of himself, has produced a future of age, weakness, decline, uselessness and emptiness, instead of a future of youth, vigor, health, power, attainment, happiness and worth. But by changing the picture of the coming years, he may cease to produce the former, and begin at once to produce the latter. To form the new picture, however, he must understand life as it is, and live, think and work accordingly.

How to Stay Young

The new picture of the coming years is based upon the principle that life, in personal form, can be perpetuated as long as the personal form is required for the advancement of the soul, and that this personal form may retain its youth as long as it continues to be.

To be true to the principle of life, is to picture such a future, and to live in the full subconscious expectation that every detail of that ideal picture will be realized. To live with such a future in view is to think that we are to be young always, that we are to grow in wisdom and power and love always, and that everything that a growing mind may desire will be added in greater and greater measure.

The new picture of the coming years pictures Advancement in everything; health, vigor and youth at all times and under all circumstances; complete emancipation in the fullest and largest sense of that term; perpetual increase in personal capacity, mental power and intellectual brilliancy, constant improvement in all the elements of the personality, both as to form and expression; daily growth in wisdom, understanding, insight and realization; perpetual ascension into the higher realms of peace, harmony and joy; the steady development of a stronger and more beautiful character; the constant refinement of the entire human system; the growing interest in life, and everything that can add to the richness of life; the never ending betterment of friends, associations and environments; the daily advancement into new fields of life, thought, consciousness and action; the eternal ascension of the soul towards the supreme spiritual heights — the peace that passeth understanding, the joy everlasting and the infinite bliss of the cosmic state.

This is the new picture of the coming years — a picture that can be realized — a picture that will be realized by every individual who lives the ascending life, and who lives with this picture constantly in mind. To live for the realization of such a future, with the full subconscious expectation of such a future, is to create such a future. To live with such a future in the making — that, indeed, is Life and he who lives such a life will always stay young.

www.ingramcontent.com/pod-product-compliance
Lightning Source LLC
Chambersburg PA
CBHW031359290426
44110CB00011B/212